HISTORY

OF THE

SCANDINAVIANS

AND

SUCCESSFUL SCANDINAVIANS

IN THE

UNITED STATES

VOLUME II

HISTORY

OF THE

SCANDINAVIANS

AND

SUCCESSFUL SCANDINAVIANS

IN THE

UNITED STATES.

COMPILED AND EDITED

BY

O. N. NELSON.

VOLUME II.

University Press of the Pacific
Honolulu, Hawaii

History of the Scandinavians and Successful
Scandinavians in the United States:
(Volume Two)

Compiled and Edited by
O. N. Nelson

ISBN: 1-4102-1681-0

Reprinted from the 1904 edition

University Press of the Pacific
Honolulu, Hawaii
http://www.universitypressofthepacific.com

In order to make original editions of historical works
available to scholars at an economical price, this
facsimile of the original edition of 1904 is
reproduced from the best available copy and has
been digitally enhanced to improve legibility, but the
text remains unaltered to retain historical
authenticity.

The Nationality of Criminal and Insane Persons

in the United States.

— BY —

O. N. NELSON.

I. CRIMINALS.

A high authority on mental and moral depravity has
said that there are three classes of criminals: "First, those
who are driven to crime by want or adversity; secondly,
those who have in their natures a taint of crime which may
be corrected by favorable circumstances; and, thirdly, those
of radically bad organization." But as the present article is
intended to deal principally with culprits as represented by
the various nationalities in this country, it would be out of
place to extensively discuss whether men become criminals
by predestination or by their own choice. Yet, since each
nationality and race has certain characteristics of virtue and
vice—due, perhaps, mainly to climate, heredity, religious
belief, and educational training—a careful examination of
the proportionate number of convicts by nationalities, may
serve as a key to arrive at the causes which lead people to
commit offenses against the law. Such a test can more
properly be made in this country because our population, as
a whole, is undoubtedly more cosmopolitan than that of any

other part of the world. Each of the many and numerous foreign elements is, at least in the census reports, placed on an equal footing, and may justly be compared with each other as to their respective virtues and vices. But the different governments of Europe pursue so many different methods in collecting and computing statistics, that a reliable comparison can not be made in regard to the amount of crimes committed by the people of each country. Deeds which one nation considers and punishes as a crime are no offense whatsoever in another country.

But while a comparison of the foreigners in our land is perfectly proper, a comparison of them with the native-born Americans is not exactly fair. In the first place, the latter have become fully assimilated with the climate and other physical, as well as intellectual and spiritual, conditions; and as a consequence they have had a much better chance to improve their moral and mental capacity than the foreign-born population. Secondly, nearly all the foreign-born are adults, while the native-born include, besides their own children, also the children of the foreign-born parents. This fact becomes very important when it is remembered that most crimes are committed by grown persons. As a consequence, the comparison between the proportionate number of foreign-born and of native-born criminals, as given in most of the following statistical figures, does not give the real relation, because the bases of computation are not alike. But it has been impossible to remedy the defect. Yet H. H. Hart, secretary of the state board of corrections and charities of Minnesota, has proved conclusively that the foreign-born people, as a whole, have, proportionately, less prisoners than the native-born; and those native persons having foreign-born parents have the worst record of all classes of people. His able article dealing with this subject was published in the *American Journal of Sociology* in November, 1896.

In 1880 there were, according to the United States census, 58,609 "prisoners" in the country. In other words, one person in every 856 of the total population was a criminal; one in 1,309, of the native white; one in 949, of the native-born; one in 523, of the foreign-born; and one in 396, of the colored. Ten years later the total number of culprits had increased to 82,329; but the proportion of the various elements mentioned above was about the same as in 1880, although a slight deterioration of all of them was noticeable.

In 1880 the Chinese-born had one prisoner for every 190 inhabitants; the Irish, one for 350; the Scotch, one for 411; the French, one for 433; the English, one for 456; the Canadians, one for 590; the Germans, one for 949; and the Scandinavians, one for 1,539.

The census for 1890, dealing with "prisoners," is peculiar, specifying only the nativity of the parents of the culprits, without stating, for example, how many of our criminals were born in Ireland, Germany, and other foreign countries. While this method offers a comparison of the descendants of the various nationalities in the second generation, it is impossible to compare the immigrants themselves with their offspring. If this omission had not occurred, it would undoubtedly have been possible somewhat to estimate the effect which our conditions have exerted upon our moral

development; then an approximation could have been
secured, with more exactness than now, whether the present
conditions here are less favorable to moral elevation than,
for example, in Germany and the Scandinavian countries.
At the same time it is surely not accidental that the Scandinavians have, in nearly every instance, the best record in
regard to crimes of any nationalities, and that the Germans
make such a fine showing; but must be largely due to the
excellent compulsory educational and religious training
which is prevalent in their countries.

In 1890 there were 8,085,019 white persons born in the
United States of foreign-born parents. Of this number,
12,601 were prisoners, giving a proportion of one prisoner
to every 641 persons. This is a very bad showing as compared with the standing of the native whites of native
parentage, who had a proportion of one to 1,638. But the
record of those natives whose parents were born in Ireland
is still worse, the number of prisoners of this class being
7,935 out of a total population of 2,164,397, giving the
shockingly large proportion of one criminal to every 273
persons. There are reasons for believing that the second
generation of the Irish in this country has a worse record
than the first. Nearly two-thirds of all the native-born
prisoners having white foreign parents were of Irish descent.
In the case of the natives of Scotch and English parentage,
the proportion was one to 559, and one to 816, respectively.
Natives of Canadian parentage had a proportion of one to
999, and the natives of German parentage had a slightly
better record than the natives of native white parentage.
Of the eight classes treated of in this paragraph, the second

generation of Scandinavian-Americans stands very far above all the rest, the proportion being one to 7,566. As a matter of fairness, however, it must be observed that the majority of the latter—as well as some of the other classes—are too young to commit crimes, because the Northern emigration is of comparatively recent date. It is another illustration of the great defectiveness of this department of the census for 1890, which was in charge of Rev. F. H. Wines.

In the United States census reports for 1880 and 1890, all grades of prisoners were enumerated, whether confined in the penitentiaries, county jails, or any other places; but in this article only those nationalities which had a population of over 100,000 have been referred to. In treating of the four following states, however, only the penitentiary culprits have been dealt with, except in the case of Iowa; and all nationalities having a population of about 25,000 in 1890 have been compared. In 1890 the total Scandinavian-born population in Illinois, Iowa, Minnesota, and Wisconsin was 516,723, or more than one-half of the whole number in the United States. The Irish in these states numbered 223,168, and the Germans, 842,402. A thorough test of the criminal standing of the foreign representatives in the four states mentioned will undoubtedly reduce the element of mere chance to a minimum, especially when the investigation covers a period of ten or fifteen years.

ILLINOIS. In the fall of 1880 there was, according to the penitentiary reports, one convict in the two penitentiaries of Illinois for every 1,774 inhabitants in the state. The record of the native-born population was a little better, and that of the foreign-born a little worse than the total.

Those born in Canada have by far the worst showing, the proportion of convicts to the whole number being one to 479. The standing of the Irish-born is slightly inferior to that of the total foreign-born. The German-born stand above the rest, the proportion being one to 3,368; and the Scandinavian-born come close to them, the proportion being one to 3,115.

A calculation based on the number of convicts "on hand" in the fall of 1892, shows great changes in the course of twelve years. In most cases a decided improvement is noticeable in regard to the foreigners. The showing of the total foreign-born is now three and a half per cent. better than that of the native-born. The proportion of total and native criminals are about the same as in 1880. The German-born, however, show a striking deterioration, the proportion being one to 2,333, while the Scandinavian-born now stand far above all the rest, with a proportion of one to 4,158. The showing of the Canadian-born is five times, and that of the Irish and English-born, three times as bad as the standing of the Scandinavians..

IOWA. Every person convicted of a crime of some kind figures in the official records of the state. Hence, the criminal statistics of Iowa, unlike the insanity records, are tolerably complete; and they put the Scandinavian-born inhabitants of the state in an exceedingly favorable light. The reports of the two penitentiaries in Iowa do not, however, like the Illinois reports, mention the nativity of prisoners " on hand" at a certain time; but only refer to the number of culprits "admitted" during biennial periods. The following result was obtained by dividing the population of 1885 and 1895

by the annual average of the number of convicts received
during the biennial periods of 1884-5 and 1894-5. By this
method any accidentally large or small proportion of prisoners "sent up" for one specific year is practically avoided.

There was one convict sent to one of the state penitentiaries for every 5,106 inhabitants in the state in 1885, and
one for every 3,000 in 1895. The Irish-born population has
the most unenviable record, the proportion of the number of
Irish-born convicted to the whole number of Irish-born
inhabitants being one to 4,050 in 1885, and one to 541 in
1895. The Germans make a fair showing, the proportion
for 1885 and 1895 being one to 8,304, and one to 1,883
respectively. The Scandinavian-born population had by far
the most splendid record at the latter date, the proportion
of the number of convictions to the whole number of inhabitants of Scandinavian birth being one to 7,720 in 1885,
and one to 4,200 in 1895. These figures, however, being
only based on the reports of the penitentiaries, can be sup-
plemented by the reports of the secretary of state relating
to convictions of criminals, which reports are absolutely
complete inasmuch as they give the whole number of convictions of all offenses against the law in every county of the
state for each year. In Illinois, Minnesota, and Wisconsin
no such reports are published. Those of Iowa have one
fault, namely, that although the nativity of the culprits is
recorded, no general summing up of the various nationalities has been made, consequently it is almost impossible
to compare them with each other. According to these
reports of the secretary of state the following result has
been obtained: In 1880 one out of every 743 foreign-born

persons was convicted of some crime; in 1885, one out of
every 709; and in 1890, one out of every 1,223. As to the
American-born inhabitants, the record was not half so ugly,
the proportion being one to 2,015, one to 2,224, and one to
2,500, for the years 1880, 1885, and 1890, respectively.
But the proportion of the whole number of Scandinavian-
born persons convicted of crimes to the total Scandinavian-
born population for the same years was only one to 5,756,
2,807, and 3,312.

MINNESOTA. The numerical strength of the Scandinavian element is greater in Minnesota than in any other
state in the Union. Thus, the United States census of 1890
shows that the whole number of Scandinavian-born persons
in Minnesota that year was 215,215. This fact alone gives
great weight to the statistical data bearing on them in
said state, the factor of mere chance being reduced to a minimum. Moreover, the reports of the penitentiary of Minnesota are more complete and thorough than those of similar
institutions in the neighboring states. Hence, the following
criminal statistics, as well as the deductions made therefrom,
ought to be of exceptional significance. In 1882 the Canadian-born had one convict in "confinement" in the penitentiary to every 1,743 inhabitants in the state. The Germans
and Irish had a proportion of one to 2,148, and one to
2,358, in the order given. In the case of the foreign-
born population, the native, and the total of all, the
proportion was one to 2,731, one to 2,835, and one to
2,798, respectively. But the Scandinavian-born had a proportion of one to 4,145. In other words, the standing of
the latter was more than 46 per cent. better than that

of their closest rival, namely, the native population. A computation made on the number of convicts in "confinement" in 1894 and on the state census of 1895 shows some very marked changes during a period of about fourteen years. In the case of the Irish-born, there was a deterioration of 64 per cent. The Canadian-born, the foreign-born, and the grand total had a far brighter record than before. The native population had a proportion of one to 3,146, and the Germans one to 4,054. The latter is the best record, excepting that of the Scandinavian-born, which had a proportion of one to 6,075.

WISCONSIN. The criminal statistics of Wisconsin afford a double basis for computing the proportionate representation of the different nationalities in the state penitentiary. For fourteen years past, from 1882-96, the nativity of all convicts "received" has been specified, and in 1882 the nativity of the whole number of convicts confined was recorded. By proceeding in the same manner and by the same method in regard to Wisconsin as was done in regard to Iowa, using the penitentiary biennial report for 1881-2 of the former state as the basis for computation, the result obtained is as follows: One out of every 3,021 inhabitants of the Canadian-born was annually convicted of some penitentiary offense; one of 5,539, of the English; one of 5,986, of the Irish; one of 7,584, of the native Americans; one of 9,453, of the Germans; and one of 9,469, of the Scandinavians. The native born Americans, the total foreign-born, and the whole population have nearly the same standing. Exactly ten years later, one in 1,442 of the Canadian-born received a sentence for some crime; one in 5,551, of the Irish; one in

6,346, of the native Americans; one in 7,876, of the English; one in 10,499, of the Scandinavians; and one in 10,605, of the Germans. Canada, it should be noticed, not only retains her position, but her standing is more than twice as ugly as ten years before, and Ireland shows only one-fourth as large a proportion of convicts as Canada. The native-born Americans, the foreign-born, and the total population show a general deterioration of nearly 13 per cent. in the course of ten years. The Scandinavian and the German-born, which were far ahead of all the rest in 1880-82, have made a further advance of over 11 per cent., and the mutual position of the two is changed in favor of the latter.

It must be observed, however, that the figures just given do not afford a key to the actual representation of the different nationalities at the penitentiary, because the mere conviction of a person does not show the gravity of the crime, nor the length of the term. Hence, other facts are submitted, showing the proportion of convicts confined at the penitentiary at a certain time to the total number of inhabitants. In 1882 there was confined in the Wisconsin penitentiary one convict to every 3,780 persons. One out of 3,296 of the total foreign-born population was a prisoner, and one out of 4,045 of the native Americans. Canada had one culprit for every 1,284 inhabitants in the state; Ireland, one for 2,328; England, one for 2,492; the German Empire, one for 4,388; and the Scandinavian countries, one for 6,026. These figures throw a new and most important light on the criminality of the different nationalities. The Canadians retain their position, clearly proving themselves to be the most vicious class of citizens in the state, the record of the second worst class, the Irish, being much brighter. There is one surprising difference between these and the other figures, namely, the distance between the Scandinavians and the Germans. In the former figures the two nationalities in question were far ahead of all the rest. They still retain their former vantage ground. But while the Germans have one convict to every 4,388 inhabitants, the Scandinavian-born have one to 6,026. In other words, the record of the latter is over 37 per cent. better than that of the former. If this signifies anything at all it proves that the average length of term served by Scandinavian-born convicts is between 30 and 40 per cent. shorter than that served by the German-born, which, again, points to a corresponding difference in the gravity of the crimes committed, in favor of the former.

II. INSANE PERSONS.

Several causes conspire to produce the real, or apparent, frequency of mental aberration among the foreign-born element in this country. In the first place, there are undoubt- edly general causes which operate among all the foreigners, and give them, perhaps, a much higher percentage of insanity than the native-born Americans. Upon the whole, emigra- tion is, probably, impelled more by fear than by hope; more by fear of the evils of the Old World than by hope of happi- ness in the New World. So many tender associations must be sacrificed, so many ties of kinship and friendship must be severed. The average emigrant leaves the old sod with a heart more or less wounded. To emigrate to a foreign land is a good deal like tearing up a plant by the roots and transplanting it into another locality; but with this difference, plants are removed in accordance with certain scientific and systematic methods, while people exchange countries in the most irregular fashion. Taking into consideration the complete change of climate, the new social conditions, and the severe struggle for existence, which all new-comers have to submit to, together with the general causes which produce insanity, it is no wonder that a large number of the immigrants mentally succumb. At the same time it is doubtful whether the foreigners in this country have a much greater, if any, percentage of insanity than the natives. Nearly all the foreign-born are adults, while the native-born include, besides their own children, also the children of the foreign-born parents. This fact becomes very important when it is remembered that in most cases only mature persons become insane. As a consequence, the comparison between the proportionate number of lunatic foreigners and insane natives, as given in most of the following statistical figures, does not give the real relation, because the bases of computation are not alike. Besides, the native-born population, as a whole, has achieved material independence to a greater extent than the foreigners, and, as a consequence, the former are in a much better position than the latter to take care of their insane relatives, especially the less dangerous ones. In general, the only available figures on insanity are those obtained from the various state hospitals for insane; but the wealthy Americans do not send their lunatic kindred to a state institution, but to a private asylum, from which it is difficult to secure any reliable statistical reports relating to the nativity of the patients.

According to the United States census for 1860, the Irish-born had one insane and idiotic person to every 464 inhabitants in the country; the French, one to 600; the Americans, one to 700; the English, one to 715; the Germans, one to 859; the Scandinavians, one to 896; and the Canadians, one to 957. Ten years later all the nationalities above mentioned had deteriorated from 25 to 40 per cent., except the Canadians and Americans who had slightly improved. In 1870 the Scotch and English had virtually the same record.

The census reports of 1860 and 1870 enumerate the nativity of the insane and idiotic persons, and since no such enumeration has been available; but in this article only those nationalities which had a population of over 100,000 at the latter date have been referred to. In treating the four following states, however, all the nationalities having a population of about 25,000 in 1890 have been compared.

ILLINOIS. The insanity statistics of Illinois must necessarily be defective, because the yearly published *Proceedings of the Board of Commissioners of Cook County*, and the reports from the Cook county insane asylum in those volumes, present the appearance of having been prepared and edited by the idiots themselves. By a great amount of original research, however, some of the worst gaps were filled; and the following deductions are tolerably reliable, being based on the official reports of the four state institutions, and on personal investigation of the diary of Cook county insane asylum. The average number of German-born patients annually admitted to the insane asylums in Illinois for the two years ending in the summer of 1892 was nearly 285, while, according to the United States census for 1890, the total German population of the state was 338,382. Thus, out of every 1,189 German-born inhabitants, one was committed to an insane asylum during one year. As to the Scandinavian population, the proportion was one to 769. But the Irish-born present a still worse showing, the proportion in that case being one to 660. Using the same data as above, but leaving out entirely the returns from the insane asylum of Cook county, the following proportion was obtained: For the native-born Americans, one to 3,242; the whole population, one to 2,236; the British-Americans, one to 1,796; the Germans, one to 1,659; the English, one to 1,453; the total foreign population, one to 1,431; the Scandinavians, one to 1,102; and the Irish, one to 965.

IOWA. Insanity evidently is on the increase in Iowa. In 1880-81 there was one patient annually admitted to the hospitals for every 3,056 inhabitants in the state; and in 1892-93, one for every 2,012. The record of the foreign-born population is much worse than that of the state, as a whole. Thus, in 1880-81 there was one German patient annually committed for every 1,358 Germans in the state; and in 1892-93, one for every 1,552. The proportion of British-born patients to the British population for the same years was one to 1,216 and 1,084, respectively. The record of the Scandinavians for 1880-81 was one patient annually received at the state hospitals for insane for every 2,092 inhabitants born in Denmark, Norway, and Sweden; but the number of patients increased so fast that the proportion was one to 1,048 in 1892-93. Thus the proportionate

number of Scandinavian patients was exactly doubled in
twelve years, while the proportionate increase for the whole
state was only a little over one-third. As a matter of fact,
the insanity records of Iowa are very incomplete, and the
above statistics by no means give the whole truth as to the
proportionate prevalence of insanity among the different
nationalities.   In 1885, for instance, there were 1,238
patients in the hospitals. But, according to the state census
of that year, there were 1,720 insane and idiotic persons
outside of the hospitals. Since the nativity of the latter is
not given, the reports of the hospitals may even convey a
wrong impression as to the proportionate representation of
the different nationalities, and this undoubtedly is the case
in regard to the Scandinavians. In 1885 the combined population of the five counties containing the largest number of
Scandinavians of all the counties in the state was about
98,000; but the number of insane and idiotic persons kept
in those counties was only sixty-one, or one for every 1,606
inhabitants. On the other hand, the combined population
of five other counties containing altogether only a few hundred Scandinavians was about 82,000, while the number of
insane and idiotic persons kept in these counties was eighty-
five, or one for every 965 inhabitants. This indicates that
the Scandinavian-born inhabitants of Iowa send a larger
proportion of their insane to the state hospitals than some
other nationalities do.

MINNESOTA. The insane asylum reports of Minnesota for
the years 1880-82 and 1892-94 seem to prove that insanity
is increasing in that state. So general is the downward
movement that every nationality represented by at least

25,000 persons in the state was carried along with it during that period. Thus, in the case of the natives, which have by far the best record, the proportion of the number of persons annually admitted to the insane asylums in the state for the years 1880-82 was one to every 4,008 inhabitants; but in the course of the next twelve years the proportion was one to 3,016, or an increase of nearly 25 per cent. Making similar computations for the different groups of foreigners, using the United States census for 1880 and the state census for 1895 as the bases in estimating the population, it appears that the Canadians have deteriorated about 44 per cent. during twelve years, having in 1892-94 one insane annually committed to the state institutions for every 1,188 persons. At the latter date the Germans sent, on a yearly average, one lunatic to the insane asylums for every 1,262 German-born inhabitants; the Scandinavians, one for every 953; the total foreign-born, one for every 937; and the Irish, one for every 544. In other words, the Germans, Scandinavians, total foreign-born, and Irish, made, during twelve years, a slide downwards of ten, twenty-four, thirty, and forty per cent., respectively.

WISCONSIN. The Irish-born in Wisconsin have the worst record as to insanity, an average of one person out of every 1,061 inhabitants of that nationality having been annually admitted to the insane asylums of the state during the years 1881 and 1882. The Scandinavians, however, have the second poorest showing, or one to 1,411; England and Germany follow at no great distance, with one to 1,555 and one to 1,624, respectively, and Canada has one lunatic to every 2,233 inhabitants. The total foreign-born population in the state had one insane patient to every 1,615 sane persons, and the native Americans, one to 4,233. Ten years later the Irish, the Canadians, and the native-born had deteriorated about thirty-five per cent.; the Scandinavians and Germans had a five or ten per cent. worse showing in 1892 than in 1882, but a better record than the total foreign element. The English were the only people who improved during the decade.

III. Conclusions.

The final result of all the investigations may, with more or less accuracy, be summed up in the following table. The number of prisoners, as enumerated in the United States census reports for 1880 and 1890, together with the number of convicts in confinement in the penitentiaries of Illinois, Minnesota, and Wisconsin at the end of a certain year, in the neighborhood of the time when the census was compiled, have been taken as the basis of the computation—it being impossible to reduce the reports of Iowa to harmonize with the statistics of the other three states. The reports of the insane asylums of Iowa, Minnesota, and Wisconsin mention only the nationalities of those received each year, without referring to the number of lunatics on hand at a specific time; consequently, it is the annual admittance to the insane hospitals of these states that has been tabulated.

In 1880 or '82, 1 out of 2,302 Persons was a criminal; in 1890 or '94, 1 out of 1,999.

In 1880 or '82, 1 out of 2,413 Americans was a criminal; in 1890 or '94, 1 out of 2,013.

In 1880 or '82, 1 out of 2,035 Foreigners was a criminal; in 1890 or '94, 1 out of 1,887.

In 1880 or '82, 1 out of 1,024 Canadians was a criminal; in 1890 or '94, 1 out of 1,080.

In 1880 or '82, 1 out of 1,338 English was a criminal; in 1890 or '94, 1 out of 1,103.

In 1880 or '82, 1 out of 1,600 Irish was a criminal; in 1890 or '94, 1 out of 860.

In 1880 or '82, 1 out of 2,713 Germans was a criminal; in 1890 or '94, 1 out of 2,715.

In 1880 or '82, 1 out of 3,706 Scandinavians was a criminal; in 1890 or '94, 1 out of 5,933.

In 1881 or '82, 1 out of 2,718 Persons became insane; in 1892 or '94, 1 out of 1,719.

In 1881 or '82, 1 out of 4,120 Americans became insane; in 1892 or '94, 1 out of 3,009.

In 1881 or '82, 1 out of 1,480 Foreigners became insane; in 1892 or '94, 1 out of 1,744.

In 1881 or '82, 1 out of 2,174 Canadians became insane; in 1892 or '94, 1 out of 1,325.

In 1881 or '82, 1 out of 1,278 English became insane; in 1892 or '94, 1 out of 1,378.

In 1881 or '82, 1 out of 1,061 Irish became insane; in 1892 or '94, 1 out of 769.

In 1881 or '82, 1 out of 1,161 Germans became insane; in 1892 or '94, 1 out of 1,439.

In 1381 or '82, 1 out of 1,588 Scandinavians became insane; in 1892 or '94, 1 out of 819.

It will be observed that in regard to crimes the Scandinavians had not only the best record in 1880, but that they improved nearly fifty per cent. in ten or fifteen years, while, virtually, all the other nationalities deteriorated. It is commendable in the Northmen, to say the least, that they can morally become better in this country, where, according to such high authority as Andrew D. White, more crimes, proportionately, are committed every year than in any other Christian land. As has already been pointed out, the excellent compulsory educational system of the Scandinavian countries, and the conservative and systematic religious training which every child receives there, have, probably, been the main forces that have moulded and assisted in developing stronger moral characters than can, perhaps, be done in this country under the present conditions. It must also be admitted, however, that the Northern emigrants, on the average, are mentally and morally superior to those who remain at home. In the United States there is free trade in religion; school children sometimes flog the teacher, and in a school in Michigan it was once discovered that thirteen youngsters carried pistols in their pockets; the family relations are loose, the husband often being the willing slave of his wife, who, in turn, obeys her offspring and permits the baby to assume the dictatorship of the household; and the frequency of cyclones and floods seem to indicate that even nature itself is more out of joint than in any other portion of the civilized world. In such a land, it is to be expected that the morality, as well as the general characteristics of the people, will be different from the results obtained in other countries where conditions are almost the reverse. The constant lack of order and system in many of the essential affairs of the family, church, and state must have a greatly demoralizing effect, especially upon the growing generation. The large proportion of criminals in this country is probably one of the prices that has to be paid for the blessings of freedom; and, applied in a different sense from that in which it was originally uttered, the exclamation of the French heroine might with justice be repeated: "Oh liberty! what crimes are committed in thy name!" That the Scandinavians in the Western continent have been able to rise above all other nationalities in regard to crimes, not only points toward the superiority of the religious and educational training of their native lands as the main cause, but it is a high endorsement of the work of those men who, through parochial schools, colleges, and churches, have endeavored to perpetuate the virtues, the characteristics, and the religious beliefs of their ancestors. The apparently great moral improvement of the Scandinavians during the past decade may be due, partly, to the betterment in recent years of the common schools in their own countries, and the more intense Christian earnestness which has penetrated the state churches, and consequently a moral improvement of recent immigrants; partly, to the fact that the character-making elements on this side of the water have been better able to take care of new-comers than formerly; and, partly, to poor criminal statistics, which, however, are quite reliable, and far superior to those dealing with insanity.

From 1860 to 1880 the Scandinavians, in regard to insanity, had almost the best record of any foreigners in the United States. Since, with the exception of the Irish, they, apparently, have had the worst; and their downward march towards lunacy has even been a little more rapid than their upward march towards moral perfection, being in the former case a deterioration of nearly fifty per cent. in about ten years. Science has not yet been able to decide whether it is the most brilliant or the most stupid who become insane. But it is often asserted that the gulf between the lunatic and the genius is not great. Maudsley, however, says, "Most instances lie between these extremes of strong and weak mental organizations." Yet, Lombroso maintains that the brilliant Jewish people pay a heavy penalty for their brilliancy by becoming insane in greater proportion than any other race upon the face of the earth, although, it is claimed, they have an excellent record in regard to crimes. It is difficult to assign any predominating cause, or causes, for the appalling increase, real or apparent, of mental derangement among the Scandinavians in America, and more difficult still to discover a check, or remedy, for the evil, which may be their "fate or fault." Probably the earnestness and depth of their character, coupled with a strong imaginative and poetical nature, unfits many of the immigrants for enduring the intense pressure of constantly recurring and often fanatical religious controversies, social upheavals and political excitement, disappointment in love and financial failures. A hypocrite or a mentally strong character can, for example, study the various religious systems of the world without danger and with some profit to himself. But a very earnest, uneducated person of average mental capacities is likely to become a lunatic before the process is over. Perhaps a majority of Scandinavians in America take a more serious interest in spiritual matters than the majority of other people; and some persons have, out of ignorance, taken advantage of this earnestness, and incited them beyond their strength. This assumption is strengthened, at least to a certain extent, by an appeal to statistics; for it appears that the Danish-Americans, who seldom become excited about religious affairs, are less subject to insanity than the Swedes and the Norwegians. No doubt, the indulgence in strong drinks or sexual abuses, either of the victim himself or of his ancestors, has been the means of landing many Scandinavians in the insane asylums. Yet, it cannot be proved, nor disproved, that they are worse in these respects than other nationalities. But the real point at issue, however, is not the great prevalence of madness among the Northmen; for, as has been observed, until recent years they were better off in this respect than other people. But the question of the questions is, what are the reasons for their alarming downward rush, real or apparent, in the last decade? They practice the virtue of temperance in all things just as much today as they did ten years ago, if not more. Have the religious contentions become more intense than formerly? As has already been pointed out, however, the insane statistics are very unsatisfactory. There is no law to compel persons to send their lunatic relatives to an asylum, as in the case of criminals. It cannot be determined whether the Scandinavians formerly kept a larger proportion of their insane at home than what is done today; and many lunatics born in this country of Scandinavian parents may be reported as belonging to the first generation. Probably the recent immigrants have been of such high nervous temperament that their fine fibers have been unable to properly endure the strain of the new conditions in America, and, in their eager desire to become wealthy and wise, they, like the Jews, have had to pay the price.

The United States census reports of 1890 on insanity and feeble-mindedness did not appear until this article had been electrotyped, in 1897. In regard to the different nationalities in this country, only the birthplaces of the mothers of the lunatics were recorded, and from these meager data the following deductions were made: 1 person in 208 of Irish birth or extraction was insane or feeble-minded, 1 in 222 of Hungarian, 1 in 352 of French, 1 in 381 of Scandinavian, 1 in 396 of German, 1 in 420 of Bohemian, 1 in 450 of English-Welsh, 1 in 465 of Scotch, 1 in 625 of Italian, and 1 in 666 of Canadian. One out of every 701 of the native-born white was insane in 1890, and one out of every 256 of the foreign born; but the former had one feeble-minded to every 602 sound-minded, and the latter one to every 1,004. As has been said elsewhere in this article, a reliable comparison cannot be made between the natives and the foreigners; yet some of the ablest American statisticians and educators maintain that the native born have, proportionately, more criminals than the foreign-born; and according to deductions made from the United States census of 1890, the native born white had one insane or feeble-minded to every 326 sane persons, which seems to indicate that the Americans have at least as large a proportion of idiots as any other class of people.

Historical Review of Luther College.

—BY—

PROF. ANDREW ESTREM.

Like the Puritans of New England, the early Norwegian immigrants made it one of their first cares to establish schools for the education of their children. Placed amid new influences in a new country, they felt the importance of clinging to those of their heritages which they held most dear—to their Lutheran faith always, to their language as long as might be. The Norwegians did not then, and do not now, deny the great usefulness, within their province, of the public schools; but they have always felt that there is an important educational work which these schools, because of their necessary limitations, cannot perform. This is the education of the religious element in man. To supply a higher education based on Christian principles, especially with a view to fitting young men for the study of theology, was the object for which Luther College was founded and for which it exists to-day.

It was in 1861 that the Synod of the Norwegian Evangelical Lutheran Church of America—commonly called the Norwegian Synod—resolved to build a college. Since 1858 the theological students of the synod had attended the col-

lege and seminary of the Missouri Synod in St. Louis, Mo.;
but when the Civil War broke out, the Norwegian Lutherans,
whose number was steadily growing, thought it wiser to
erect a college in their own midst. The new school was to
be located at Decorah, Iowa, but for the first year accommodations were secured in the Halfway Creek parsonage, a
short distance from La Crosse, Wis. The beginnings of the
school were necessarily small. Unpretentious as they are,
such beginnings have at least the advantage of revealing
better the stages of growth, and these it is always interesting
to witness. Two teachers and a total enrolment of sixteen
are matters of record for the school year 1861-62. Yet the
work went forward, and that local attachment and that
devotion to a common object which are sources of strength
to any institution were born. After a year's narrow-spaced
but open-hearted family life in this country parsonage, the
school was removed to Decorah. But as work on the college
building had not yet begun, the school was under the necessity of taking up temporary quarters in the business portion
of the city. On June 30, 1864, the corner stone of the new
building was laid, and on October 14, 1865, it was dedicated,
amid rejoicing and thanksgiving shared in by several thousand people. This day has been celebrated by the students
as dedication day ever since.*

The building was erected on an elevation on the left bank

---

*The building cost $75,000; the addition made in 1874, $23,000; the rebuilding,
after the fire, $56,000; and various other structures, for example, residences for some of
the professors, and the gymnasium, not far from $16,000, making a total expenditure for
building purposes of about $170,000. The yearly expenses for operating the institution
may be roughly estimated at $20,000, which would amount to $600,000 in the thirty odd
years of its existence. Nearly all these sums have been raised by voluntary contributions, only four legacies having been received, which altogether do not amount to
$10,000. The value of all the college property is about $120,000.—EDITOR.

of the picturesque Upper Iowa river, so as to command an unusually pleasant view of hill and dale, of city and country. Though architecturally plain, the structure presented a noble appearance, was quite large, and, for those times, well equipped. As the number of students increased, it was found necessary to build an addition to it, which had been provided for in the original plans. This addition, usually called the south wing, was completed in 1874, making the entire building 170 x 52, with accommodations for about one hundred and fifty students. In addition to the main building, several smaller ones have, from time to time, been built or adapted for college purposes. Among these is the gymnasium, a spacious frame structure built in 1885-86, the money for the purpose having been collected mostly by the students.

On May 19, 1889, the main building was destroyed by fire. The library and most of the other movable objects of value were saved; yet the loss was a heavy one. The pecuniary loss was, however, more than made up for by the active sympathy and love for the institution which the misfortune called forth or made manifest. Those who in the trying pioneer days had helped to raise the building again united their efforts, seconded by the younger generation of men who had experienced the benefits conferred by the school, and the result was the completion, in 1890, of a new edifice, reared indeed on the old foundation, but far more convenient, commodious, and handsome. The friends of the college had again occasion to rejoice and feel thankful. Amid a large concourse of people from far and near, the reconstructed college building was dedicated on the twenty-fifth anniversary of the first dedication.

Before the work of rebuilding at Decorah was entered upon, there had been some discussion as to the advisability of moving the college to some larger city and one located more centrally with reference to the school's constituency; but after various locations had been considered, particularly one in the vicinity of St. Paul, Minn., it was decided to raise the walls where they fell and where fond memories clustered about the ruins.

Luther College owes its origin mainly to a strong religious conviction. The existence of this conviction explains how it was possible for a comparatively small body of pioneers, during years burdened with the hardships of war, to erect a building that, according to the then prevailing values, cost $75,000. It should also be noted that the early Norwegian settlers were unaccustomed to the making of voluntary contributions for church purposes, and that their means as a rule were small. Even now, much as they have at heart the welfare of schools and churches, they are somewhat chary of making bequests or gifts of a larger nature. But under wise leadership their collective yearly contributions have been by no means inconsiderable. As leaders in the work of founding and supporting Luther College are to be mentioned Rev. Laur. Larsen, Rev. V. Koren, Rev. H. A. Preus, Rev. J. A. Ottesen. Others might be added to the number, but it is fitting that the names of these older men should stand out in relief. Of those who have given legacies to the school the late Mr. Halvor Gjerjord, of Stoughton, Wis., deserves special mention inasmuch as his was the first and, so far, the largest bequest the college has received. The name of a woman must also be recorded here —one who sought always to promote the comfort and the happiness of the students and who freely bestowed, especially upon the needy and deserving among them, her love and labor with such a tact and in such ways as are characteristic of a noble woman. This was Mrs. Diderikke Brandt. She died in 1885.

Being modelled after the Latin schools or gymnasia of northern Europe, Luther College has from the outset been essentially a classical institution. Through all changes made in the course of years this characteristic has been preserved inviolate. Yet mathematics and the sciences have perhaps received as much recognition as could have been expected in a college having, in the wider sense of the term, only one course of study. During the last ten years these subjects have gradually come to fill a larger place in the curriculum, especially in the preparatory department. Prior to 1881 the regular course covered six years, with no sharp line of division between collegiate and preparatory work. Since then the preparatory course has embraced three years, and has come to be treated more as a course of study by itself. The tendency in recent years has been toward a reduction of the number of recitations per week and toward the concentration of the student's energies on fewer studies at a time. Such economy will no doubt, if the student is directed aright, be found to be wise. One way of directing him that is now more employed than formerly is that of pointing out supplementary reading. In olden times a college library was but too commonly a storehouse for a limited number of poorly arranged books, to which references were rarely made. Now as a rule the school library is coming to be less of a mere repository and more of a students' workshop. At present the Luther College library contains between 7000 and 8000 volumes besides pamphlets and periodicals. Its growth has been most rapid during the last ten years. In the matter of museum the college has been poorly equipped; but promising efforts to build up one are now being made.

The work done at the school now has naturally a wider range than formerly. It is curious to notice, for instance, how restricted was the reading done in Greek and in English literature some twenty years ago. In Greek were read portions of Xenophon, of Homer, and of the New Testament; in English a series of readers were used, followed by Shakespeare. In some other subjects there was a corresponding lack of comprehensiveness and variety, a result of the then existing conditions. If one were to compare the quality of the work done now with that of the past, he would also notice progress. Methods have changed somewhat, but the pervading spirit remains the same, for faithfulness and thoroughness have ever been insisted upon. Superfine polish and glittering commonplaces have not been held in much esteem. Matter has been placed above manner. If finish and form have at any time been insufficiently attended to, the fault lay, no doubt, often in the clay that came to the potter's hand.

In keeping with its primary purpose, Luther College devotes considerable attention to Norwegian language and literature. For the church work within the synod has so far been conducted mostly in that language. But there are also good literary reasons for emphasizing this subject. In consequence of its doing so, the college has always had two mediums of instruction, and the student, so far as possible,

two mother tongues. This state of things may have made
his acquisition of each language somewhat slower than
otherwise, but it has also, without doubt, broadened his
knowledge of language and extended his acquaintance with
literature. In the early days of the school the Norwegian
language occupied the more important place both in the
class-room and outside. But as the Americanizing tendency
grew stronger among our people, the college endeavored to
adapt itself to this changing condition. English is now
used more than Norwegian as a medium of instruction; it is
also the predominant language of the literary societies, and
shares equal honors with Norwegian in the students' peri-
odical. The following figures give some indication of the
change that has taken place during fifteen years: In 1879,
123 of the weekly hours of instruction were given in Norwegian and 61 in English; in the fall term of 1894, 90 in
Norwegian and 106 in English—the relation having changed
in favor of the latter from one-third to somewhat more than
one-half. Besides an extended course in Norwegian language
and literature Luther College offers, or requires, short
courses in certain other subjects that are seldom found on
the programmes of American colleges. These subjects are
Hebrew, Old Norse, and Scandinavian History.

During the thirty odd years of its activity the college
has, in all, had twenty-three professors, besides a number of
instructors. Most of its early teachers had received their
education in Norway; in later years the college has obtained
its teachers largely from its own graduates or from those of
other schools of this country. Four of those who have been
professors at the college are now dead. The name of each

of these is intimately associated with some phase of the
school's history. Knut E. Bergh is fondly remembered by
the early graduates for his ability as a teacher and his
geniality as a man. Jacob D. Jacobsen was a man of broad
and exact scholarship. Conscientious, judicial-minded, modest, weak in body but strong in faith, he endeared himself to
all with whom he came in contact, and left a memory that
the college will not let die. Cornelius Narvesen and Ole
Ramstad, the latter the successor of the former, devoted
themselves to the task of giving the sciences a larger place in
the course of study. Both faithful workers, the one was
known more for his retiring modesty, the other for his energy.

The faculty of Luther College consists now of eight
regular members, with sometimes one or two teachers serving temporarily. The president is Rev. Laur. Larsen, who
has been connected with the school in this capacity since its
foundation. He is yet a vigorous man, of threescore and
odd years, and has in his day performed a great amount of
work, educational, administrative, pastoral, and editorial.
His administrative duties may have been somewhat light-
ened by the establishment, some years ago, of the principalship of the preparatory department; but the general
supervision continues, of his own choice, to rest with him.
In his relations with the students he has always emphasized
the duty of punctuality and of Christian conduct, and has
in an eminent degree won their respect. In him the college
has had a faithful and competent administrator of its affairs.
While conservative, he has yet been ready to introduce such
changes as seemed not inconsistent with the original aim of
the school, and as seemed to have the approval of time.

An important element of strength in the president's policy has been the confidence reposed in him by the clergy and the laity of the Norwegian Synod. It is this confidence in the school's administration, combined with the people's love for an institution which they themselves have built and whose character they have learnt to appreciate, that has made Luther College what it is, and that has ever constituted its chief endowment. Other than this it has a fund of only some eight thousand dollars, the income of most of which is distributed to deserving students who are fitting themselves for the ministry. The college is, therefore, supported mainly by voluntary contributions. This direct dependence of the college on the sympathy and support of the people within the synod, who also control its larger policy through the votes of their church delegates, gives it a strongly representative character. While the school would not on any consideration willingly lose this friendly support, it recognizes the importance of larger permanent funds for certain purposes.

As a tree is judged by its fruit, so the character of an institution of learning is, after all, best tested by inquiring into the quality of the men whom it sends forth. And first a word or two about the youths whom it seeks to develop into men. The large majority of Luther College students have come from farm homes of the Northwest, from which they have brought with them habits of industry, of straightforwardness, of economy. All have, previous to their coming, been instructed in the principles of Christianity in the parochial schools, and nearly all have had the benefit of some common school instruction. In recent years some have come from the academies organized within the synod. On entering, they had usually made up their minds to work, or if there were those who had not, most of these soon felt constrained to do so. Time was when some of the classes had as many as thirty-four recitations per week. Yet the class-room work, especially in the languages, has been fully on a par with that done in other colleges of the same grade. The class-room attitude of the student seems, however, to have differed from that of his American fellow in being less demonstrative, less inquisitive, less easy and self-assertive. That the greater reserve of the former is not due to a lack of interest is proved by general results. The difference, so far as there is one, may in part be due to early training. Moreover, the Norwegian student, like the people from which he springs, has an even tenor, and is but little given to mere intellectual display. While not often conspicuously brilliant, he has large capacity for work, is energetic and thorough-going, and impresses one by his reserve power and his pronounced sanity. These qualities have gained him a fair reputation wherever he has become known.

Student life at Luther College has, in the main, differed but little from that of other institutions where a healthy moral sentiment is inculcated and where the hardship of work is seasonably relieved by the tonic of recreation. Although a large number of the students enter the school with the idea of becoming ministers of the Gospel, they have quite generally been free from the fault of taking themselves too seriously. Their religious nature, while broadening and deepening, has flowed on more as an under-current. Their fresh contact with life in its serener aspects has contributed to make them good-natured and happy, and has tended to prevent a lop-sided development. While there have been few, if any, of such noisy demonstrations as might disturb the outside world, other forms of diversion and waywardness have not been wanting. There have been musical entertainments and un-musical rattlings down the stairs, city parties and smokers' feasts, carping at teachers and persecution of "preps," publication of pointless jokes and immolation of tedious text-books. Some of these practices have been of rare occurrence, and now several of them are no longer in vogue. None of the so-called fraternities have existed at this college, nor is the atmosphere favorable to them. In sport, especially in baseball, the students have won a fair name among neighboring colleges. But sports have not been a hobby with them. They yet practice, to a limited extent, the old-fashioned method of unbending their minds by bending their backs in the doing of minor services. †

In perhaps no enterprise outside the routine work have the students made so much progress as in music, and that often without a regular teacher. The college brass band and the orchestra have each above a score of members, and in addition to these there is generally a choir or a glee club. For the pecuniary support of these organizations, as well as for certain other objects, the students have contributed from time to time. Friends in the city of Decorah and elsewhere have sometimes lent a helping hand.

---

†For an entertaining and vivid description of Luther College life—at least, the less serious side of it—see Prof. P. O. Stromme's book, *Hvorledes Halvor blev Prest*.--
EDITOR.

The number of students enrolled has recently been about one hundred and eighty a year. In a few cases the number has exceeded two hundred, notably in years immediately following upon large building improvements. In the eighties the attendance, owing chiefly to a doctrinal controversy within the synod, dwindled down until, in 1887, it was only 118—the smallest number in nineteen years. Since then an opposite tendency has generally prevailed. For a better understanding of the figures respecting attendance, it should be noted that the school is not co-educational.

The territory from which the college has drawn its students naturally corresponds somewhat to the distribution of the Norwegian population. As might be expected, the newer states, though sending a number of students, have as yet furnished but few graduates. The states or countries in which the students of the last thirteen years had their homes during their senior year are as follows: Iowa, 50; Minnesota, 49; Wisconsin, 24; Illinois, 7; North Dakota, 3; Nebraska, 3; Michigan, 1; Natal, South Africa, 3.

It had once been the intention to add a theological department to the college, but this idea was for various reasons abandoned. A normal department, however, was early organized. After the normal course had been extended to three years and a professor had been added specially for its benefit, this department continued to form a part of the college until 1886. As it had never flourished in the measure hoped for, it was discontinued, with a view to the establishment of a separate normal school. Such a school was founded in Sioux Falls, S. D., in 1889. Nevertheless, the normal department in Decorah had sent out a fair number of teachers, some of them competent to take charge both of parochial and of common schools.

Luther College has, almost since its foundation, offered the same terms to its students no matter what vocation they finally had in view. That some students, on certain conditions, have received pecuniary aid is a matter apart. Nor has the college exacted from its graduates any promise —though it has always given them the advice—to study theology, holding it wiser to leave them free to decide according to the self-knowledge and the sense of duty which their studies, it is hoped, have helped them to attain. But whatever occupations they have chosen, the Luther College graduates bear with them, in mind and manner, the impress of the institution that sheltered them so long. Their number is now not far from three hundred. More than one-half of these have entered or are preparing to enter the Lutheran ministry, a considerable proportion are engaged as professors and instructors, some are practicing medicine or law, others are devoted to journalism, a few have entered the field of state or local politics, and two have been appointed to government service abroad. Some of the graduates have continued their studies at Eastern universities, eight of whom have at this writing (1896) received the degree of doctor of philosophy.

From a small preparatory school Luther College has grown to be, and gained the reputation of being, a high grade college. A large institution with many parallel courses of study it has not become, nor is it necessary that it should. The school has its limitations; within these, however, it might reach out yet farther. As it is, the college takes rank as the oldest and most influential institution of higher learning among the Norwegians of America. At this writing Luther College graduates are teaching in more than twenty advanced schools, including five colleges and two universities. In some of these schools the majority of the teachers consists of its graduates, and in the case of ten academies or normal schools the principalship is held by a Decorah alumnus. The influence of the college in educational matters has widened with the years.

As for the future, the college will, no doubt, adapt itself to its requirements as it has sought to conform to those of the past. If people of Norwegian descent remain true to the faith and the traditions of their fathers, this college will have a place to fill even when the language of the fathers shall have ceased to be a practical study in this country. As long as race distinctions exist here, one of its duties will be to stand as an exponent of what is best in Norse life and literature. In this way the school, while serving the cause of the church, will also contribute its mite towards the forming of a worthy national character.

TABLE I.

SHOWING THE NUMBER OF STUDENTS AND GRADUATES OF LUTHER
COLLEGE FROM 1861 TO 1896, AND ENUMERATING THE REGULAR
TEACHERS AND INDICATING THEIR LENGTH OF SERVICE.

YEAR.	STUDENTS.	GRADUATES.	PROFESSORS AND INSTRUCTORS.	LENGTH OF SERVICE.
1861	16	....	Laur. Larsen.................	1861-
1862	32	....	F. A. Schmidt.................	1861-72
1863	50	....	L. Siewers.................	1863-77
1864	58	....	N. Brandt.................	1865-78
1865	81	....	G. Landmark.................	1867-76
1866	83	8	Knut E. Bergh.................	1869-74
1867	73	....	L. S. Reque	1875-95
1868	106	3	J. D. Jacobsen.................	1872-81
1869	122	4	A. Seippel.................	1873-74
1870	147	5	C. Narvesen.................	1873-84
1871	147	6	John Bjarnason.................	1874-75
1872	159	3	A. K. Teisberg	1874-75
1873	190	7	Th. Bothne.................	1875-82
1874	229	6	A. Bredesen	1876-78
1875	217	6	A. A. Veblen.................	1877-81
1876	181	7	A. A. Sander.................	1878-79
1877	189	9	H. G. Roalkvam.................	1878-86
1878	173	14	O. J. Breda	1879-82
1879	159	19	Gisle Bothne.................	1881-83, 1884-
1880	165	13	G. A. Evenson.	1881-82
1881	145	18	T. O. Homme.................	1881-82
1882	137	11	E. Petersen.................	1882-87
1883	166	15	Chr. Naeseth...	1882-
1884	143	11	Rudolph Olsen.................	1883-85
1885	131	12	R. Monrad.................	1883-88
1886	133	17	O. Ramstad.................	1884-86,1887-89
1887	118	....	J. Tingelstad	1886-87
1888	136	12	J. G. Halland.................	1887-89
1889	145	9	Haldor Hanson.................	1888-90, 1895-
1890	206	9	Wm. Koren.................	1889-92
1891	213	9	H. W. Sheel.................	1889-
1892	188	11	Andrew Estrem	1889-90
1893	183	12	H. I. G. Krog.................	1890-96
1894	187	11	W. Sihler.................	1890-
1895	200	12	George Markhus.................	1892-
1896	191	13	J. A. Ness.................	1893-94
			J. E. Granrud.................	1894-
			K. Kvamme.................	1896-
Total	....	292		

Social Characteristics of the Danes

AND

A History of Their Societies.

—BY—

O. N. NELSON.

———

(REVISED BY C. NEUMANN.)

If reliable conclusions concerning the intellectual activity and moral condition of a people can be deduced from the quantity of their literary productions, the number of their church organizations, and the standard of their educational institutions, then the Danes in America present a marked contrast to their more numerous kinsmen, the Swedes and Norwegians. The two latter nationalities in this country can with truthful pride point to a respectable, although not a very critical, literature, both in prose and poetry, both in their own languages and in English. Not far from two hundred persons of Swedish or Norwegian extraction have written some original theological, historical, poetical, scientifical, or literary work, some of which possess considerable merit, and a few of which are recognized authorities on their

specialty. On the other hand, only a limited number of
Danish-Americans have brought any new learning into the
world; and a full collection of all their books and pamphlets
could, undoubtedly, easily be placed on a single shelf of an
ordinary book-case, while the literary achievements of each
of the other two classes of people would be from eight to
ten times as bulky. In other words, the Danish-Americans,
in proportion to their numbers, have produced only one-
third as much literary matter as their kindred folks. But
the difference is mainly in quantity, not in quality. In the
latter respect all the three Scandinavian-American nationalities are about on an equal footing.

But the difference between the Danes and the other two
nations of the North, manifested in the religious and educational aspects, is even greater than in the result of literary
achievements. Over one-third of all the Scandinavians in
the United States are members of some church, and about
three-fourths are regular church-goers. But only in the
neighborhood of 20,000 Danes were members of purely
Danish Protestant congregations in 1897, and even adding
10,000 more who may reasonably be supposed to have
religiously associated themselves with some other nationalities, yet scarcely more than one Dane out of twelve would
be a church member, estimating the total number of Danes
and their descendants in America at 350,000. In 1895 the
educational institutions of the Swedish Augustana Synod
alone were valued at nearly half a million dollars, and the
yearly "current expenses" for operating them amounted to
over two hundred thousand dollars; and it is claimed that
the contributions of the Norwegian Synod people for school

purposes have often exceeded three dollars per communicant in one year. But John H. Bille, in *A History of the Danes in America*, says: "During no consecutive five years up to 1894 had the Danes succeeded in raising as much as fifty cents per communicant for educational purposes." With probably one exception, none of their few schools rank with a first class American academy; while the Swedes and Norwegians own half a dozen colleges of recognized standing, where the majority of their cultured people have been trained.

The short-comings of the Danish-Americans in literature, and the two inseparable institutions, church and school, are not, however, due to any mental or moral inferiority, but to circumstances and to the fact that they have turned their energies in other directions, especially towards organizing and maintaining secular societies. They have, proportionately, just as many men as the Swedes and Norwegians who are capable of producing a novel, an epic poem, a historical compilation, a thesis on predestination, or an essay on the reformation of the universe. But there are not enough Danes in the country willing to patronize, financially, such undertakings; consequently, few of them are attempted and less realized. The small number of immigrants, however, is no sufficient reason for the diminutive church organizations and institutions of learning, because other nationalities have been more successful in these respects under less favorable conditions. Considering the smallness of their country, the Danes have excelled most nations in the grandeur and richness of their literature and art. But they seldom seem to have distinguished themselves as leaders of men, either military or otherwise. Nor have they been specially noted for a pietistic bent of mind; yet, they are far from being professed infidels, and are not extremists, either in their virtues or in their vices. It is also to a great extent the absence of enthusiastic and aggressive religious leaders, and the moderate as well as modern views concerning celestial existence, which have prevented the building up of great or numerous Danish churches and schools on the Western continent.

One of the leading characteristics of the Swedish-American people appears to be their quiet but whole-souled application to the building-up of the noblest institutions in society, while the Norwegians are probably in their true element when engaged in excited debates concerning the welfare of church or state. But the majority of the Danes in America seem to enjoy most the cheerful social intercourse and the good fellowship of each other's company, especially when they can revive the grand memories of their native land. Their conviviality and patriotism, coupled with the pecuniary advantages which organized union brings in case of need, have been the mainspring in successfully founding, promoting, and maintaining Danish societies in every part of the Union, from the Atlantic to the Pacific, from the Great Lakes to the Gulf of Mexico, wherever Danes are to be found. Even the unification of the different Scandinavian singing societies a few years ago was effected by a Dane, and shattered to pieces by the jealousies of the Swedes and Norwegians. This pronounced social aptitude may be due, partly, to the density of population in their native land, which draws the people into close relation with each other, both socially and financially; partly, to their dispersion in small numbers in a foreign country among a numerous population of various nationalities; and, partly, to other causes. Besides, a large proportion of the Danes born in Slesvig left the old sod on account of the oppression of the Germans, while nearly all of the Swedish and Norwegian emigrants have departed because they desired a wider and freer scope for action or adventure. At any rate the two latter peoples have failed to effect any kind of patriotic secular organization for the purpose of studying their native languages and perpetuating the memories of their ancestors, except of a local nature. On the other hand, the success of the Danes in this respect has been almost phenomenal, and in spite of the fact that no particular individual seems to have taken any special lead in the matter. It is true that not all the Danes are enthusiasts in regard to their nationality, for the writer of this article has met exceptional Danes who denied having been born in that kingdom, and yet were unable to construct and pronounce the denial in clear English. But the rank and file persist in using their own language, notwithstanding that they may be able to speak English better than the listener, who at times is unable to perfectly comprehend all the Danish idioms. And no one can become a member of a Danish secular society who does not, at least, "feel as though he were a Dane." It must not be assumed, however, that the Danes, on account of their ardent desire to cherish the memories of their native land, are hostile or dangerous to the free institutions of America. No nation upon the face of the earth, possessing such high degree of intelligence, has been so submissive to the powers that be,

so adverse to revolutions, so opposed to anarchy, as they
have been during their whole history from the fable-mixed
antiquity down to the present time. While they, like the
Germans, have fearlessly combated against the establishment of a Puritanic Sabbath and Prohibition, and sneered
at the idea that it is wicked to see a great drama, yet in the
course of time this defiance of American extremes will have
a conservative and steadying influence upon our changeable
institutions.

I. THE DANISH BROTHERHOOD IN AMERICA.

In 1881 the Danish societies at Omaha, Neb.; Davenport,
Iowa; and Neenah and Racine, Wis., united. Some of these
societies had been organized a few years before, and all were
exclusively composed of veterans who had participated in
the two Danish wars of 1848 and 1864. But in 1882 the
constitution of the organization was radically changed, and
henceforth a man's military experience played no part in his
eligibility as a member; the present name of the society, the
Danish Brotherhood in America, being also adopted at that
time. At the beginning of the year 1897 about one hundred lodges, scattered through the different parts of the
Union, belonged to the brotherhood, having a total membership of nearly five thousand. Besides, there are also some
forty sisterhood societies, which may be considered as annex
lodges. The latter are organized on a plan similar to that
of some American secret organizations. According to the
constitution, the object of the brotherhood is to unite the
Danes in America in one great fraternal association, to cherish the memories of Denmark, and to aid each other. In

order to accomplish these purposes, the members of the various lodges meet regularly, generally once a week, and most lodges maintain a reading room and a library; some even possess a hall or a building of their own, which frequently is open for the use of the members both on week-days and Sundays. The organization holds a general meeting every third year. From 1882 to 1897 the brotherhood has paid out, as life insurance to the relatives of deceased members, about $150,000, in sums of five hundred or one thousand dollars in each case, and during that time not far from $175,000 has been distributed as sick benefit contributions. All Danes or persons of Danish descent who can speak the Danish language, and are not under twenty-one or above fifty years of age, are eligible to membership; provided they are upright men and have never been convicted of any felonious offense. All proceedings at the meetings must be conducted in the Danish language, and no political or religious discussion is permitted. Like most similar organizations, the brotherhood has its president, secretary, treasurer, etc., who manage the different departments assigned to them. This is by far the strongest and most influential secular organization among the Danes in America, and its growth has been remarkable, especially during the last six years

II. THE UNITED DANISH SOCIETIES IN AMERICA.

In 1876 a society called Dania was organized at Racine, Wis., with a membership of about fifteen. Today this organization numbers in the neighborhood of five hundred; owns a building valued at $10,000; and has a library of nearly a thousand volumes. Persons of Danish birth or

descent who are conversant with the language are eligible.
After the organization of the Racine society, a number of
similar societies sprang up in different parts of the country,
often having the same name, and nearly always working for
the same ends; and one society in Chicago with that name
had been organized as early as 1862. In 1883 or 1884 an
effort was made to unite them, which resulted in the union
of four societies in Wisconsin. Since then about twenty-five
more have joined, and altogether they have not far from
3,500 members, being represented in several states. Each
society is incorporated, but not the organization as a whole
Nearly all the societies own a hall or a building, possess a
library, and meet once a week for business transactions and
social enjoyment. Dances and parties are also held now and
then. The representatives of the different societies assemble
every third year, and through a system of traveling-cards
members are afforded the same privileges in all the different
societies. The societies are not secret, and religious and
political discussions are prohibited. The life insurance in
connection with the general organization is optional with
the members, each policy drawing about $1,000. Consid-
erable sums have also been paid out to sick and disabled
members. There are also about sixteen Danish societies
on the Pacific Coast united into one organization, similar
to the United Societies.

III. ASSOCIATION OF DANISH PEOPLE OF AMERICA.

This organization dates its birth from the year 1887,
and is chiefly the result of the efforts of Rev. F. L. Grundtvig.
Its principal aims are to perpetuate the spiritual inheritance

of Denmark, and to preserve the language of that kingdom, without neglecting the duties of American citizens. Their rules read: "Men and women, who feel as if they were Danes, and are not hostile to the Christian chuich, can become members on equal terms." At the very beginning they actively commenced to organize local societies, to found libraries, to establish settlements, and to embark in various other enterprises. Bille, in his history, rightly or wrongly, says: "There has also been a general attempt on the part of this society to support the high schools, parochial schools, and churches; but the efforts along these lines have not produced any noticeable results, except in the case of the churches; and here it was far from accomplishing what was intended, for this society and its methods of working immediately aroused a storm of opposition from the ministers of Inner Mission proclivities. They claimed it was merely a scheme on the part of the Grundtvigians to create a party in every congregation in favor of their ideas, and thus to drive out all the ministers who did not agree with them." At several annual meetings of the Danish Lutheran Church the discussion of the subject was earnest, in some cases even bitter; and in 1891, for the sake of peace, it was agreed that the founder should use his influence in disbanding the society. But neither peace nor disbandment was obtained.

Besides those four large organizations enumerated above, there are several other independent Danish societies which are not connected with those different groups mentioned. Consequently, it is, perhaps, a fair estimate to assume that some fifteen or twenty thousand Danes in America belong to some society whose chief aim, apparently, is to perpetuate and cherish the language and memories of the fatherland. Taking into consideration that most of the members are men over twenty-one years of age, and that many of these men have families who are more or less interested in and influenced by the social atmoshphere of their husbands and fathers, it becomes clear to every unbiased observer that the Danish societies in America are powerful and influential institutions.

Historical Review of the United Danish Evangelical Lutheran Church in America.

—BY—

O. N. NELSON.

As has been pointed out elsewhere in this volume in an article on the Danish societies, the Danes are not, as a whole, ardent devotionalists. Not far from one person out of three of the total population of this country belongs to some religious concern, but only one out of twelve of the Danish-Americans is a church member. Taking the United States census of 1890 as the basis of population, including both the immigrants themselves and their children, and the different parochial reports for the same year, the result arrived at is as follows: About one person out of fifteen of all the Danes in America is a member of some Lutheran congregation; while this applies to one out of five of the Swedes; and to one out of three and a half of the Norwegians. The powerful Swedish Augustana Synod controlled, in 1892, about $4,000,000 worth of property, averaging in the neighborhood of forty dollars per communicant; all the Norwegian Lutherans, $5,000,000, averaging thirty dollars per communicant; and all the Danish Lutherans, $200,000, averaging twenty dollars per communicant. The deficiency of the Danes in this respect is, without question, chiefly due to the indifference of the people in regard to the supernatural, and the lack of aggressive pastors to direct them. Excepting Rev. C. L. Clausen, whose life-work was almost wholly devoted to the Norwegians, there have not been any successful leaders among the Danish-American Lutheran clergy. They have had both learned and devout pastors. But none has combined those rare qualities of piety and adroitness, of conservatism and firmness, which distinguished a Hasselquist and a Preus, and enabled them to manage wisely, and to act boldly. It is to be hoped that the right man, or men, will soon be found who can join all the Danish Lutherans into a close and true Christian alliance, under whose wings a large number of the Danish-American people can feel at home.

The Danish Evangelical Lutheran Church Association in America was originally a very small part of the Norwegian-Danish Evangelical Lutheran Conference, at whose theological seminary, Augsburg, about ten young Danes had been trained and ordained for the ministry. The annual report of the association for 1891, from which most of the facts contained in this paragraph were collected, says: "In a labor where 'Jew and Greek' are of our Lord placed on an equal footing, it certainly could not be His intention that there should be any high wall between Norwegians and Danes." This seems to be a very reasonable assumption, especially when both nationalities used the same language. And yet, probably for equally good reasons, the conference in 1875 appointed a committee to communicate with the leading church-men in Denmark concerning the missionary work among the Danes in America, which movement culminated in the withdrawal, with the consent of the conference, of six Danish pastors in 1884. At first the idea of joining the Danish Evangelical Lutheran Church in America was discussed. But nothing was accomplished, owing to the prevailing tendency of Grundtvigianism in the latter body. Consequently a new organization was effected 11–14 September, 1884; and three more clergymen united with the other six, each one serving about two hundred souls, making the whole organization at its beginning about fifteen hundred in number. But the Danes seem to have retained their share of that pietism, real or apparent, and that active aggressiveness which always distinguished the conference; but kept little or nothing of that combativeness for which the conference was noted from and including the day of its birth, even haunting as a ghost the United Norwegian Church. When the association was merged into the United Danish Church in 1896, there were forty clergymen who served nearly sixty congregations, the whole body numbering over 6,000 souls. Not much more than two-thirds of the above mentioned congregations, however, had formally joined the organization. They owned Trinity Seminary, at Blair, Neb. The building had cost $7,000, and the seminary was in operation from the fall of 1886 to the time of the union. The last year about fifty students of both sexes attended, and several of the pastors have received their theological training there. At the same place a publishing house was maintained, and *Kirkebladet* and a couple of other papers, issued. Contributions for various mission purposes were quite liberal, considering the smallness of the association.

The first volume of this work contains an historical article on the Danish Evangelical Lutheran Church in America, written by Rev. Adam Dan, which article is generally considered to be a fair and impartial account of that body. On page 170 he says: "Today there are two factions among us, the followers of Bishop Grundtvig, and the so-called *Mission People;* both are recognized by the Church of Denmark as belonging to the Lutheran church, and they are about equal in strength." Ever since the pioneers of the Scandinavian church-work set their feet upon American soil, this important religious controversy among the Danish-Norwegian Lutherans, known as Grundtvigianism, has been going on. It was, however, crushed in its infancy in the Norwegian Synod. But nearly ever since the organization of the Danish Lutheran Church in this country, in 1872, the subject has called forth many vigorous articles in the newspapers, and animated discussion at the annual meetings; and, finally, in 1894, it rent that organization in twain, and the same year one party organized the Danish Evangelical Lutheran Church in North America. But this schism probably does not end the era of strife and agitation, of patched-up peace and renewed bitterness, which the influence of the famous Danish bishop and poet, N. F. S. Grundtvig, has exerted upon the Scandinavian-American Lutherans. Perhaps, after all, history is only biographies of great men? As far as the Danes in this country are concerned, however, the culmination point appears to have been reached in 1893, when about one-half of the clergymen joined themselves together into a missionary association, within the Danish Lutheran Church, for the purpose of purging the latter body of its Grundtvigianism. The struggle has, apparently, been carried on chiefly on account of conflicting views regarding theological dogmas. But the manner and method of conducting their schools, the aim and practices of the Association of the Danish People, as well as other matters of more or less importance, have also been dragged into the contest; thus supplying the clergymen with excellent themes for discussion, as well as furnishing some spiritual food for the languid laymen, who have been rather lookers-on than participants in the controversy. As the parties in these disputes have been partly right and partly wrong, so the result will probably be both good and bad.

It is difficult to say in a few words what Grundtvigianism really is. Bishop Grundtvig himself insisted upon a more liberal interpretation of the Bible and greater freedom in regard to religious worship, than was generally permitted in the Lutheran state church of Denmark. He fought against rationalism and the vices of the age, yet he could hardly be called a pietist as that term is generally understood. He considered a good Christian life, baptism, communion, and the Apostolic Creed to be the very life and marrow of Christianity, rather than the Bible. There is, probably, some difference between Bishop Grundtvig's teachings and practices, and the tendency of Grundtvigianism, with its consequences, in this country. Besides, the conditions in Denmark and America are very different, so that no comparison can properly be drawn. That which may promote the moral and religious development in a certain country and a certain age,

may be a hindrance to this very blessing under other conditions; and this is exactly the standpoint which the opponents
of the Grundtvigians take. The Anti-Grundtvigians in
America charge the followers of Grundtvig in this country
with teaching the possibility of conversion of the soul after
death, and with rejecting the infallibility of the Bible; and
these views were virtually endorsed by the Grundtvigian
majority of the clergymen of the Danish Lutheran Church
at two of their annual meetings, one of which was held at
Cedar Falls, Iowa, in 1886, and the other at Manistee, Mich.,
in 1890. The practical tendencies of the two parties in this
country may be briefly summed up as follows : Most of the
Grundtvigian pastors have honestly believed, if they do not
all believe it now, that the only means by which the virtues
and characteristics of their people could be instilled into the
souls and minds of the coming generations, was the retention,
with little or no modification, of the religion, language,
social customs, and educational institutions of Denmark
upon American soil. To carry out this principle, some of
them have made great sacrifices, socially as well as financially.
It is a principle for which a large proportion of the very
best element of all the foreigners in the United States
have at some time or other fought, and lost. Besides,
they considered it their duty to direct the thoughts and
actions of the people in the widest sense, and endeavor
to guide their flocks, not only in spiritual matters,
but in regard to literature, drama, art, business, and
social intercourse. Most of the Anti-Grundtvigian clergymen, on the other hand, have been equally earnest in
retaining whatever was noble in the Danish character,

especially the religious feelings.   But, according to their opinion, piety was the chief aim in life; and, for the purpose of gaining and retaining the largest possible number of devout Christians, they have been advocating the gradual Americanization of all their institutions and been unwilling to identify themselves with anything outside of their professional duties.   According to Bille's history of the Danes in America, Prof. P.S.Vig—who, together with Rev.P.L.C.Hansen, has been the principal exponent and leader of the Anti-Grundtvigian sentiments—wrote a few years ago: "Even if the Danish language is lost to our posterity, they might still retain all that is good and true in the Danish character; for just as a man can take his material inheritance into a foreign country, so he can take his spiritual inheritance into a foreign tongue.   We older people must remember that we can hardly imagine ourselves in our children's places.   They have a fatherland which is not ours.   In a measure it is impossible for them to be Danes; for they lack the Danish environments, and in a measure the Danish tongue must always be a foreign tongue to them.   To keep the children born in this country from coming in contact with its language and life is a violation of nature which will at last revenge itself."

The first of October, 1896, the representatives of the Danish Evangelical Lutheran Church Association in America, and the Danish Evangelical Lutheran Church in North America, met in Minneapolis, Minn., and formed the United Danish Evangelical Lutheran Church in America.   According to their report of that year, the new organization comprised over seventy pastors and missionaries, seventy-five congregations in actual union, and in addition about fifty not formally united with the new body, but served by its clergy-men. Assuming that the 125 congregations had on an average 100 souls each, which was the exact proportion of the Danish Association at the time of the union, then the whole United Church would number 12,500 members; and all the persons in direct or indirect connection with that body would certainly not exceed 15,000. But as yet the organization is rather loose, several of the congregations served by Anti-Grundtvigian pastors having taken no formal step to separate themselves from the old alliance.

It was agreed at the first meeting that Trinity Seminary, Blair, Neb., should be the theological school of the church; the two papers, *Kirkebladet* and *Missionsbladet*, were con-solidated into *Dansk Luthersk Kirkeblad*; and a temporary arrangement was made for the management of Elk Horn College. The church sustains an Indian mission in Indian Territory, and a seamen's mission in New York.

Historical Review of the Moravian Church

AND

Its Scandinavian-American Work.

— BY —

REV. JOHN GREENFIELD.

The Unitas Fratrum was founded in Bohemia, in 1457, by followers of the Bohemian reformer and martyr, John Hus. It spread to Moravia, Prussia, and Poland, and flourished greatly in spite of frequent persecutions. In the first quarter of the seventeenth century it was overthrown, in its original seats, by the so-called Bohemian anti-reformation. Only a "hidden seed" remained. In Poland and Prussia, and eventually in Hungary, it continued to exist until the first quarter of the eighteenth century, when the few parishes that still bore its name were gradually absorbed by other churches. About the same time the secret remnant in Moravia was revived, and descendants of the ancient brethren began to emigrate to Saxony where they found an asylum on the estate of Count Zinzendorf, and built a town known as Herrnhut. They introduced the discipline of their fathers and the ancient episcopate, which had been carefully preserved in the Polish branch. As these refugees came from

Moravia the church at the present time is commonly known as the Moravian Church, but its real name is the Unity of the Brethren.

The church endorses the Augsburg Confession, and has a total membership in Europe and America of about 36,000, while in heathen lands no less than 96,000 souls are being ministered to by Moravian missionaries.

The first American colony of the brethren was founded at Savannah, Ga., in 1735, whence a remnant of it was transferred, in 1740, to Bethlehem and Nazareth in Pennsylvania.

The Moravian Church, since the renewal in 1722, has devoted its main energies to the evangelization of heathen nations. It was while the noble Count Zinzendorf attended the coronation of Christian the sixth of Denmark, in 1731, that he heard from the lips of a negro servant in Copenhagen the pitiful tale of his nation's wretched and degraded condition as slaves in the Danish West India Islands. On the same occasion the pious count also learned of the self-denying but hitherto unsuccessful labors of Rev. Hans Egede in Greenland. Within two years the Moravian Church at Herrnhut, consisting of only six hundred members, had sent forth missionaries both to St. Thomas, W. I., and to Greenland. These were the two first foreign missionary enterprises of the Moravian Church. Since that time, more than a century and a half ago, it has sent hundreds of missionaries into heathen lands. Not a few of its faithful and successful laborers have been Scandinavians. First and foremost must be mentioned Jens Haven, a Dane, who first served as a Moravian missionary in Greenland, and then

labored for many years in a similar capacity in Labrador.
The first attempt to evangelize Labrador had, humanly
speaking, failed. The devoted missionary, John Christian
Ehrhardt, was murdered by the native Eskimoes. The
second attempt was made by Jens Haven in 1764. Upon
his first landing the natives desired him to follow them to an
island half an hour distant. Considering the fate of Ehrhardt, Haven might well have refused to accompany them.
He says, however: "I confidently turned to the Lord in
prayer, and as soon as we arrived there, all set up a shout,
'Our friend is come!'" For a nnmber of years Jens Haven
labored in Labrador with great self-denial and success.
When nearly blind, and sixty-six years of age, he was
brought back to Europe where he spent the last six years of
his life. Another faithful and devoted Scandinavian missionary was Hans Torgersen, a Norwegian, who emigrated with
his parents to the United States in 1854, settling in Door
county, Wis., a few years later. He served a number of
years on the Indian mission in Moraviantown, Canada.
Thence he was called as one of the pioneer Moravian missionaries to Alaska. Only a few weeks was he permitted to
do service here. One day while sailing in the little mission-
boat, he fell overboard and was drowned.

The first Scandinavian Moravian church in America was
organized in the year 1849, in Milwaukee, Wis., and numbered fifteen communicant members. These persons had
become acquainted with the Moravian brethren in Norway
and Denmark through what is known as the *Diaspora*. It
has, namely, for upwards of a century been customary for
the Moravian Church to send forth evangelists for the pur-

pose of calling to repentance and living faith some of the
many who are nominal members of the state churches in
Denmark, Norway, and Sweden. The converts were not
received into the membership of the Moravian Church, but
remained in their respective state churches, and were called
the Diaspora brethren. A few of these formed the nucleus
of the first Scandinavian Moravian church in America. In
1850 the little congregation, under the leadership of Rev.
A. M. Iversen, of the mission-school in Stavanger, Norway,
and Otto Tank,* also a Norwegian, and formerly a missionary, left Milwaukee, and eventually established colonies
and congregations in Fort Howard, Sturgeon Bay, and
Ephraim, Wis., which places are still the principal strongholds of the Scandinavian Moravians in the United States.
A new edition of the Scandinavian Moravian hymn-book
was prepared in 1894, and for some years past a monthly
paper called *Det Glade Budskab* has been published. There
are at present in the United States one Swedish, one Norwegian, and four Danish Moravian ministers in active
service, who have in their pastoral care upwards of 1,500
souls of whom about 700 are communicant members.

*According to the fanatical *Autobiography* of A. Cederholm, later a Swedish
Methodist clergyman, this Tank was an old nobleman from Fredrikshald, who started
to build a town, on the Herrnhut plan, at Green Bay, and to erect a theological seminary
there. Cederholm, one Dane, and three other young men attended the school which,
however, in a short time was discontinued.—EDITOR.

According to "Appleton's Cyclopedia of American Biography," O. C. Krogstrupp, a
Danish Lutheran clergyman, became a Moravian in 1748; emigrated to America in 1753;
served Moravian congregations at Philadelphia and other places in the East until his
death in 1785; and was a powerful and eloquent preacher.—EDITOR.

Historical Review of the Scandinavians in Iowa.

— BY —

O. N. NELSON.

'The traveler, in wending his way across the fair state of Iowa, with its evidences of civilization upon every hand ; its magnificent churches, with spires pointing heavenward ; its school houses upon almost every hill ; its palatial residences, evincing wealth and refinement, can scarcely realize that half a century ago this "beautiful land" was the home only of the red man, who roamed over the fertile prairies, hunting in the woods and fishing in the streams. The change seems too great to be real. Yet these magnificent churches, numerous school houses, palatial residences, extensive railroads, and countless telegraph and telephone wires, have nearly all been located or placed on Iowa soil within the space of the last fifty years.' Numerous agencies of human activity have been employed to bring about this great, almost miraculous change. The mind of man has been taxed to its utmost by bold speculation, undreamt-of inventions, and daring achievements. The industry, energy, and perseverance of the hands of men have almost made a garden out of the wilderness. To accomplish these wonderful results in such a short space of time, the Scandinavians have, during the whole history of Iowa, been powerful agents, not only in assisting in developing the natural resources of the state, but also in promoting its intellectual and religious welfare. The numerous well cultivated farms, owned and tilled by Northmen, largely contribute to the material wealth of the state. About forty Danish, two hundred and fifty Norwegian, and one hundred and fifty Swedish churches of various denominations testify to their spiritual and moral activity. A large number of these churches maintain parochial schools, and all of them employ Sunday-school teachers. Besides, there are half a dozen Scandinavian schools of a higher grade in the state of Iowa.

I. PIONEERS AND SETTLEMENTS.

The first permanent settlement of whites in Iowa was established at Dubuque as early as 1788. But emigration westward must not have been very rapid in those days, and there were scarcely 25,000 persons, within what is now the boundary lines of the state, fifty years later. There were in all probability some scattering Scandinavians in Iowa at the very beginning of this century, although no person can be mentioned with certainty until the year 1837, and no permanent settlement of Northmen occurred until eight years later. But as the increase, for the last forty years, of the population of each of the Scandinavian nationalities in every county in the state can be found in the tables published at the end of this article, it has been deemed unnecessary to endeavor to describe all the settlements separately, as a general result can be obtained by examining said tables. Besides, it would have been impossible to give the correct data concerning the origin even of half the Scandinavian colonies; therefore, only a few of those settlements which were established before 1856 will be mentioned.

DANISH. In 1837 N. C. Boye arrived and settled in Muscatine county—his biography is in this volume. But as there were, according to the United States census, only nineteen Danes in Iowa in 1850, no important Danish settlement could have been made until after that year. In 1852 the well-known Rev. C. L. Clausen became the leader of several Norwegians, who settled in Mitchell county—Clausen's biography can be found in the first volume. According to the state census of 1856, there were only one hundred and seventy-two Danes in the whole state at that time, and fourteen years later about three thousand. Since, however, a large number have arrived, and in 1857 there were in the neighborhood of 40,000 Danish-born or having Danish parents within the state. There were also several thousand Danes, especially in the counties along the Mississippi river, who were born in Slesvig, and as a consequence some of them were probably classified as Germans in the census reports.

NORWEGIAN. There were undoubtedly Norwegians in the southeastern part of the state, near Keokuk, probably as early as 1840; but the various authorities do not agree regarding the particulars, except that the settlement was not permanent. Reiersen, in his *Veiviser for Norske Emigranter*, published in 1844, claims that the colony consisted of thirty or forty families, several of whom were Mormons;

that the land was rich, but covered with dense woods; and that the settlers would, perhaps, be unable to pay for their claims. The probability is that the whole colony was simply a gathering of adventurers of the Kleng Peerson type, and he is said to have been the founder of the settlement. But there were Norwegians in the northeastern counties as early as 1848, at least, but no permanent settlement was established until 1850, when two caravans of Norwegian imigrants, consisting of about a dozen persons, came from Racine and Dane counties, Wis., and founded a colony in Winneshiek county. Other pioneers soon followed, and Winneshiek county has always been, and is, one of the most important Norwegian strongholds in the United States, where about half of the total population are of Norwegian birth or extraction. A small settlement was founded in 1851, near McGregor, Clayton county; and, of course, the counties farther west were not settled until a few years later; for example, the first Norwegians in Story county did not arrive there until 1855, although today that nationality is very numerous in that part of the state. The most interesting account of the establishment of a settlement is that given in regard to Rev. Clausen's colony. Clausen had visited Iowa in 1851, and the next year, in the spring, he and about twenty families, besides several unmarried men, left Rock county, Wis. In order to avoid confusion in marching such a large number in one body, the crowd was divided into two sections. Clausen himself and family, being the only persons who rode in a carriage, led in advance. The caravan consisted of numerous children and women in wagons, men on foot, and two or three hundred cattle—all obeying the

command of the leader. Most of these immigrants settled at
St. Ansgar, Mitchell county, and later some of them in turn
became leaders in establishing settlements in counties farther
west. According to the United States census of 1850, there
were only 361 Norwegians in the whole state at that time;
six years later they numbered nearly 3,000. In 1870 about
17,500 Norwegian-born persons resided in Iowa, and twenty
years later 10,000 more had settled within its boundary
lines. There were about 75,000 Norwegians of the first and
second generations in 1897.

SWEDISH. Iowa has the honor and distinction of being
the first state in the Union where a permanent Swedish settlement of any importance was founded in the nineteenth
century.   This occurred at New Sweden, Jefferson county,
in 1845.   This is also the first prominent Scandinavian
colony established in the state—but for full particulars concerning the foundation of this interesting settlement, see
Peter Cassel's biography in this volume. Burlington seems
to have been the place through which nearly all the first
Swedish pioneers of Iowa passed, and, as a consequence,
several resided here at an early date. Norelius claims that
about two hundred Swedes lived in and around Burlington
in 1850, and Col. F. Brydolf located there in 1846—his
biography is in this volume. At Swede Point, Boone county,
a settlement was effected in 1846, and the next year some
pioneers located at Munterville, Wapello county, while Rev.
John Linn has the honor of being the father of the first
white child that was born in Webster county, which happened Jan. 8, 1851—an interesting account of pioneer life
can be obtained by reading John Linn's biography in this

volume. Some Swedes settled in the northeastern part
of the state, near McGregor and Lansing, in the early fifties.
According to the United States census there were 231
Swedish-born persons in Iowa in 1850, twenty years later
they numbered nearly 11,000, and in 1897 about 75,000 of
the first and second generations resided in the state.

CAUSES OF IMMIGRATION TO IOWA. It is impossible to
determine the causes which have been operative in directing
the northern immigration to Iowa. But the chief reason has
been, undoubtedly, the same as that which directed the movement toward the northwest. Such well-known pioneers as
Peter Cassel, Rev. C. L. Clausen, Prof. L. P. Esbjörn, Rev. V.
U. Koren, and Dr. T. N. Hasselquist have done a great deal
in directing the Scandinavian immigration towards the
state. But the honor and credit of settling the state with a
good class of people, does not belong exclusively to one, or
a few but to hundreds and thousands of Scandinavian immigrants who induced their relatives and friends to join
them. It might also be noticed in this connection that a
large portion of the early Norwegian settlers in Iowa had
previously resided in Wisconsin, while many of the Swedish
pioneers had arrived from Illinois.

II. THE CIVIL WAR.

During the Civil War over seventy-five thousand men
from Iowa served as soldiers in the Union army, some outside of the state regiments, and about two-thirds of that
number entered the service before the year 1862 ended, all
being volunteers up to the last of 1864, when a few were
drafted into the army. According to the reports of the

adjutant-general of Iowa for the years 1861-66, not less than twenty Danes, one hundred seventy-eight Swedes, and four hundred twenty-five Norwegians—in all 623 Scandinavians—fought against the Confederates. But as many names of all nationalities are omitted in these reports, not to mention the difficulty of correctly counting all the names in such publications, it is fair to estimate that 1,000 Scandinavians from Iowa enlisted under the Stars and Stripes. In 1860 Iowa had a population of 675,000. One-ninth of the total population of the state enlisted under the Union flag, and the same proportion, at least, of the Scandinavians in Iowa fought for their adopted country; while every sixth Northman in Minnesota and Wisconsin served in the army during the war, although only about one-eighth of the total number of persons in the latter states participated in the struggle. Unlike their kinsmen in Wisconsin, Illinois, and Minnesota, the Scandinavians in Iowa seem to have had no leader to organize them or spur them to action. Not one of the many Norwegians became widely known as an officer; a few were promoted to minor commands of but little importance. The Swedes, on the other hand, had such men as Lieut. C. E. Landstrum, of Des Moines, who after the fierce battle of Shiloh and other engagements received special mention of his superiors for excellent conduct. Col. F. Brydolf also distinguished himself—his biography is in this volume. But these two men had, during their service, little or nothing to do with their countrymen. About fifty Norwegians, mostly from Winneshiek county, enlisted in the Twelfth Iowa Infantry the latter part of 1861, constituting half of Company G; twenty-five of them fell in the battle of Shiloh the 6th

and 7th of April, 1862, and most of the remaining enlisted
afterwards in other regiments. Not less than sixty-five Norwegians from the northeastern counties of Iowa joined the
famous Fifteenth Wisconsin, or Scandinavian, Regiment, in
1861-62; and about half of Company K of that regiment
were from Iowa; while a Dane from that state, Rev. Clausen,
was chaplain of the regiment. Perhaps half of the Norwegian soldiers in Iowa came from Winneshiek county, and
nearly all from the northeastern part of the state; but the
Swedes seem to have hailed from different localities. In this
connection it might not be amiss to mention that only four
Scandinavian-born—all Swedes—have ever, up to 1893, graduated from the United States military academy at West
Point, and two of these were appointed from Iowa.

III. POLITICAL INFLUENCE.

The present state of Iowa is a small portion of that
immense stretch of land which was ceded by France to the
United States in 1803, for a consideration of $11,250,000,
and out of which a large number of states have since been
carved. In 1838 the territory of Iowa was organized, and
the state organization dates from 1846. At the latter date
there were perhaps one hundred persons of Scandinavian
birth in the state, mostly Swedes. In the course of fifty
years this handful has increased, until at present nearly one-
tenth of the population of Iowa is of Scandinavian birth or
parentage. But, unlike their kinsmen in some other states,
they have never held their proportion of the higher offices in
the gift of the voters of the state. It would be rash to
assume any one particular reason for this defective represen-

tation in politics among a race which unquestionably has an inborn knack for practical politics. It seems, however, that the political apathy of the Northmen of Iowa is largely due to a peculiar lack of able and aggressive leaders. But, on the other hand, the office holders have generally been above the average in point of character and ability, and therefore have been a credit to their countrymen. The first Scandinavian who occupied a seat in the legislature was Rev. C. L. Clausen, a Dane, who represented his district in 1856-57. For the next four years no Scandinavian was elected to the legislature. Since 1876 there has always been one or more Scandinavian-Americans in the legislature. In other words, the Scandinavian-born inhabitants of Iowa have been represented by one or more of their own country-men in 15 out of the 20 general assemblies which have been elected since the election of Clausen in 1855. During 1892-96 four of the members were of Scandinavian birth or parent-age, this being the largest number of that category occupy-ing seats simultaneously. Of the whole number of Scandi-navians elected members of the legislature, two were Danes, five Swedes, and about a dozen either Norwegians or the sons of Norwegians. Only four Northmen were senators, viz: M. N. Johnson, Ole N. Oleson, G. S. Gilbertson, and C. J. A. Erickson. The first mentioned has since for years represented North Dakota in the United States Congress. No Scandinavian has ever been elected to any state office by a popular vote. But in 1888 the legislature elected Otto Nelson as state binder. Lars S. Reque was appointed United States consul to Hol-land by President Cleveland in 1893. Ole O. Roe has served as deputy state auditor since 1892. A glance at the names

of the county officers will soon convince any one that the
Scandinavians have been very poorly represented, Worth and
Winneshiek being the only counties where the number of
Scandinavian office-holders has somewhat corresponded to
the Scandinavian population.

IV. OCCUPATION.

Of course, most of Iowa's Scandinavians have been, and
are, common laborers, servants, and farmers. Yet today
there is not a single learned profession in which they cannot
be found, and in some they have distinguished themselves
and become famous. Three of the best and most widely circulated Scandinavian newspapers in the country are published in Iowa, and at least half a dozen well-known authors
and literary men of Northern extraction reside in the state.

V. STATISTICS.

In 1850 one out of every 310 persons in Iowa was a
Scandinavian by birth; twenty years later, one out of 38;
and in 1890, one out of 26. This, however, includes only
those people born in the North, while a much larger per cent.
have Scandinavian parents, and as a consequence can not
only speak the language of their ancestors, but can feel as
Northmen. For example, according to the United States
census for 1890, there were 25,240 persons in Iowa born in
Denmark, or having Danish parents, this being the largest
number of Danes in any one state; 59,822 Norwegians; and
52,171 Swedes—in all 137,233 Scandinavians. But the
census reports are far from being correct; they omit many
persons of all nationalities, and frequently confound foreign-

ers with native-born; but, as a general thing, the reports fall below and not above the real number. And, without doubt, the nearest approach to the truth in regard to the number of Danes, Norwegians, Swedes, and their children in this country, can be had by multiplying the Scandinavian-born by 2½. The number of Scandinavian-born persons in each state and territory, from 1850 to 1890, can be found on pages 256-60 in the first volume; and in each county in the state of Iowa from 1856 to 1895, in the following statistical tables: Therefore, by multiplying the numbers found in these tables by 2½, a fair estimate can be obtained of the total Scandinavian population of the first and second generations of any state, territory, or county. According to this calculation, there were about 190,000 Scandinavians in Iowa in 1897; that is, nearly one out of every ten persons in the state was a Northman by birth or parentage. It might, in this connection, not be out of place to remark, that although the Norwegian-born in Iowa in 1890 numbered over 3,000 less than the Swedes; yet the former nationality, the same year, exceeded the latter by 7,500, when both the first and second generations are taken into consideration.

TABLE II.

SHOWING THE NUMBER OF SCANDINAVIANS BORN IN THE SCANDINAVIAN COUNTRIES, AND THE TOTAL POPULATION IN EACH COUNTY OF IOWA.

COUNTIES.	STATE CENSUS OF 1856.				U. S. CENSUS OF 1870.			STATE CENSUS OF 1895.			
	DENMARK.	NORWAY.	SWEDEN.	TOTAL POPULATION.	DENMARK.	SWEDEN AND NORWAY.	TOTAL POPULATION.	DENMARK.	NORWAY	SWEDEN.	TOTAL POPULATION.
Adair				663	1	14	3,982	58	25	53	15,564
Adams				1,019		9	4,614	24	83	34	12,934
Allamakee	6	505	84	7,709	7	2,180	17,868	14	1,094	146	17,981
Appanoose				9,075	2	4	16,456	36	4	398	25,383
Audubon				283		4	1,212	1,252	18	44	12,836
Benton	1	10		6,247	340	396	22,454	57	323	73	24,244
Black Hawk		3	9	5,538	247	37	21,706	805	31	40	26,941
Boone		19	70	3,518	16	1,230	14,584	94	101	2,461	27,039
Bremer		2	4	3,188	4	15	12,528	18	4	23	15,403
Buchanan			15	5,125	1	14	17,034	174	12	43	20,539
Buena Vista					2	194	1,585	541	606	1,019	15,029
Butler		2	2	2,141	20	15	9,951	143	12	23	16,966
Calhoun				119	6	51	1,602	130	76	434	15,788
Carroll				251	1	189	2,451	31	10	57	19,493
Cass				815	77	142	5,464	334	72	126	20,926
Cedar				9,481	7	14	19,731	167	35	26	19,008
Cerro Gordo			1	632	16	197	4,722	201	399	172	18,302
Cherokee					4	99	1,967	89	88	543	15,664
Chickasaw		24		2,651	19	333	10,180	34	227	14	15,696
Clarke				3,978	5	9	8,735	5	5	8	11,515
Clay					19	32	1,523	399	137	236	11,277
Clayton		274	13	664	39	1,327	27,771	6	580	143	26,570
Clinton	21	14	24	13,441	195	564	35,357	1,015	260	509	43,398
Crawford				235	5	187	2,530	102	25	511	20,069
Dallas				3,991	4	177	12,019	14	22	118	21,023
Davis		1		11,528		11	15,565	7	1	14	15,015
Decatur	1	3		6,269	1	5	12,018	11	17	20	16,639
Delaware		1	14	8,099	3	23	17,432	4	8	126	18,103
Des Moines	39	2	227	20,198	65	1,039	27,256	204	12	2,019	37,629
Dickinson					1	60	1,389	63	184	34	6,023
Dubuque	1	8	26	25,871	2	61	38,969	56	25	97	60,177
Emmet						285	1,392	287	610	119	7,619
Fayette			1	8,357	5	512	16,973	44	470	19	24,794
Floyd				2,441	6	80	10,768	8	68	43	17,114
Franklin				780	2	172	4,738	420	167	92	13,679
Fremont			1	3,368	5	14	11,174	37	4	92	17,176
Greene				1,089	3	21	4,627	30	3	52	16,299
Grundy				435	82	7	6,399	327	16	20	13,418
Guthrie				2,149	64	26	7,061	30	3	52	17,958
Hamilton					28	596	6,055	293	1,643	594	18,514
Hancock					17	30	999	368	257	272	11,141
Hardin	1	1	1	4,033	11	83	13,684	100	406	59	20,576
Harrison			9	1,900	17	39	8,931	213	32	118	23,091
Henry	1	10	38	15,395	7	429	21,463	10	3	469	18,278
Howard				444	33	140	6,282	56	254	23	13,221
Humboldt					1	114	2,596	305	1,149	36	11,431
Ida					3		226	44	90	363	11,425
Iowa		10		4,873	30	88	16,644	19	85	15	18,964

TABLE II.—CONTINUED

COUNTIES.	STATE CENSUS OF 1856. DENMARK.	NORWAY.	SWEDEN.	TOTAL POPULATION.	U. S. CENSUS OF 1870. DENMARK.	SWEDEN AND NORWAY.	TOTAL POPULATION.	STATE CENSUS OF 1895. DENMARK.	NORWAY.	SWEDEN.	TOTAL POPULATION.
Jackson.............	17	....	7	14,077	19	24	22,619	166	3	26	23,471
Jasper..............	....	1	....	7,490	34	53	22,116	57	19	220	25,891
Jefferson...........	....	....	294	13,305	8	872	17,839	12	1	598	16,405
Johnson............	7	....	4	14,457	16	22	24,898	16	4	30	23,563
Jones..............	....	....	1	9,835	3	11	19,731	21	37	51	20,088
Keokuk............	....	....	2	10,646	3	6	19,434	2	3	29	23,732
Kossuth............	....	....	....	397	1	75	3,351	230	246	757	18,345
Lee................	10	68	19	27,273	41	1,226	37,210	46	50	520	39,528
Linn...............	1	6	2	14,702	13	23	31,080	193	88	229	49,905
Louisa.............	....	....	9	9,568	10	43	12,877	3	2	54	12,786
Lucas..............	....	....	3	4,408	10	164	10,388	7	....	401	13,545
Lyon...............	....	....	....	......	2	85	221	40	449	96	11,684
Madison............	....	....	1	5,508	4	19	13,884	14	1	37	16,597
Mahaska............	....	....	1	13,050	4	135	22,508	5	80	411	32,496
Marion.............	44	....	....	14,160	7	8	24,436	1	....	47	23,191
Marshall...........	....	....	....	4,460	57	279	17,576	172	501	386	27,320
Mills..............	1	15	1	3,102	11	58	8,718	19	10	155	15,187
Mitchell...........	4	188	9	1,901	52	956	9,582	136	845	131	14,431
Monona.............	....	....	....	459	8	253	3,654	384	546	250	16,005
Monroe.............	....	....	18	6,860	14	92	12,724	3	3	448	15,790
Montgomery.........	....	....	....	872	3	275	5,934	16	38	1,653	17,119
Muscatine..........	3	1	3	12,569	11	27	21,688	48	5	27	25,339
O'Brien............	....	....	....	......	....	13	715	69	216	183	15,609
Osceola............	....	....	....	......	....	....	......	39	35	43	7,377
Page...............	....	1	....	1,964	....	156	9,975	8	16	1,182	22,026
Palo Alto..........	....	....	....	......	15	51	1,336	358	475	127	12,109
Plymouth...........	....	....	....	......	....	47	2,199	146	37	212	21,991
Pocahontas.........	....	....	....	......	20	70	1,446	189	202	581	12,442
Polk...............	....	10	9	9,417	44	759	27,857	260	547	2,170	72,888
Pottawattamie......	....	1	2	3,495	328	276	16,893	1,959	92	463	46,012
Poweshiek..........	....	....	....	4,460	9	163	15,581	13	87	93	18,524
Ringgold...........	....	....	....	1,472	....	4	5,691	2	2	14	14,065
Sac................	....	....	....	251	....	3	1,411	121	51	640	18,868
Scott..............	7	2	17	21,521	154	129	38,599	157	25	342	45,869
Shelby.............	5	....	....	456	192	16	2,540	1,499	182	48	17,798
Sioux..............	....	....	....	......	....	1	676	54	106	102	21,406
Story..............	....	107	....	2,868	194	1,160	11,651	330	1,989	117	19,930
Tama...............	....	2	1	3,520	24	57	16,131	73	87	24	22,966
Taylor.............	....	3	....	2,079	....	7	6,989	1	9	48	17,347
Union..............	....	....	....	806	9	123	5,986	6	8	321	17,043
Van Buren..........	1	....	20	15,921	....	41	17,672	1	....	48	16,829
Wapello............	....	....	70	13,216	1	498	22,346	10	9	1,050	33,293
Warren.............	....	....	....	7,500	1	18	17,980	5	6	22	18,506
Washington.........	....	....	1	11,113	2	14	18,952	1	....	11	18,845
Wayne..............	....	....	....	4,183	4	11	11,287	22	....	38	16,155
Webster............	....	2	70	3,088	9	1,353	10,481	203	1,055	2,253	26,945
Winnebago..........	....	....	....	......	1	624	1,562	110	2,317	276	10,707
Winneshiek.........	1	1,451	11	7,506	13	5,511	23,570	29	3,094	67	22,748
Woodbury...........	....	....	....	950	20	352	6,172	646	1,333	1,766	46,202
Worth..............	....	....	....	......	8	886	2,892	111	1,943	134	10,285
Wright.............	....	....	....	427	25	35	2,392	178	797	101	16,024
Total..............	172	2,782	1,116	517,875	2,827	28,350	1,194,020	17,043	27,428	31,085	2,058,069

Historical Review of the Scandinavian

Schools in Iowa.

—BY—

J. J. SKORDALSVOLD.

In proportion to its numerical strength, the Scandinavian element of Iowa has established a large number of institutions of learning. The most of these institutions have been started by devout Lutheran church members, not for the sake of making money, but in order to lead the rising generation to better and nobler lives. As a consequence, the schools are pervaded by a Christian spirit. The Scandinavian languages are gradually yielding to the English. This process, indeed, is so rapid, that the first catalogue of Jewell Lutheran College, for instance, does not indicate by a single sentence whether a single Scandinavian word is ever to be used in the classes. The same catalogue does say, however, that the college will be "fully America 1 in all its spirit and in all its methods," and this statement, somewhat modified, may be applied to the most of them. The good men and women who built those schools intended to do what little they could towards educating their sons and

75

daughters to become better citizens than the average native American of our day. That is the main reason why they paid out their hard-earned dollars and cents for the establishment of colleges and academies in a country which already is fairly dotted with similar institutions. It takes time before the results of the work carried on at these schools can be fully realized; but even now it may be stated without fear of contradiction that the fair state of Iowa can boast of no better class of citizens or Christians than those who have attended the colleges established by the Northmen and their descendants.

DANISH. Elk Horn College, at Elk Horn, is the oldest and largest Danish institution of learning in America. It was established in 1878 by Rev. O. S. Kirkeberg, who transferred the property to the Danish Evangelical Lutheran Church in America in 1880. At first the school was a pattern of the Danish high schools, one characteristic of which is that the boys attend in winter, and the girls in summer. In 1887 the building was destroyed by fire, but was immediately rebuilt on a much larger scale. At this time the whole plan of the school was made much more practical, which change at once doubled the attendance. In 1890 Rev. K. Anker bought the institution and extended the change commenced three years before, and the attendance now reached one hundred. In 1894 the Danish Lutheran Church in North America bought it, and in 1896 it came under the control of the United Danish Evangelical Lutheran Church in America. The school offers six distinct courses of study. There are nine professors and instructors, and the total annual enrollment is about one hundred and fifty. The value of the property connected with the school is about $6,000. The catalogue for 1895 says: "This is a sectarian school, and it maintains a strict moral discipline among its students. It is our proud boast that a code of stringent rules is found unnecessary in governing the student body. A high moral culture is secured by a proper management. A pleasing unanimity of action pervades the entire atmosphere, and Christian love and obedience do for the school what severe rules never accomplish."

The University of the Danish Evangelical Lutheran Church, at Des Moines, was opened in 1896. The building is furnished with up-to-date improvements, and the property is worth $20,000. Three professors have charge of the work, and the attendance is between 30 and 40.

NORWEGIAN. St. Ansgar Seminary and Institute, at St. Ansgar, was established in 1878 by a number of people belonging to the Norwegian-Danish Lutheran Conference, the moving spirit of the enterprise being Rev. Johan Olsen. H. S. Houg was the first principal of the seminary, and is still one of its professors. The school has had its ups and downs; but at present the work carried on there is not only more thorough, but also more extensive and systematic than before. It offers five distinct courses of study, and employs half a dozen instructors. The annual enrollment is from 75 to 90, and the number of students graduated during the history of the school is about 60. The aim of the school is "to pay particular attention to the training of teachers. To young people, therefore, who have not made up their mind as to their future vocation, but desire a general education, this school offers greater advantages than a common high school or an academy, as it gives the student an opportunity of learning all the studies taught in such schools, and, in addition to this, prepares him, if he chooses, for the teacher's profession." The property is valued at $13,000.

The theological seminary of the defunct Norwegian Lutheran Augustana Synod was opened at the parsonage of the Springfield congregation, in Winneshiek county, in the fall of 1874, the attendance for the first year being seven. In 1876 the seminary was removed to Marshall, Wis.; but in 1881 was again removed, this time to Beloit, Iowa, where it remained until 1890. At the latter date it was discontinued, as a result of the Norwegian Augustana Synod being merged into the United Church. David Lysnes was the president of the seminary during its whole existence, and as such he educated about a score of young men for the ministry.

Bode Lutheran Academy, at Bode, dates from the fall of the year 1886, when a class was started in a small common school house. It was "an outgrowth of the recognition of the importance of preserving the rising generation for the Lutheran church, and of giving the young men and women a sound, solid, and liberal education," Rev. O. A. Sauer, Capt. T. A. Rossing, and other members of the Norwegian Synod congregation of the place being the principal promoters of the undertaking. In 1887 the school secured a building of its own, valued at $4,000.

Valder Business and Normal School, at Decorah, was founded by C. H. Valder in 1888. In spite of a brisk competition on the part of older rivals, this school has enjoyed a most healthy and vigorous growth, its enrollment being about 500. This is practically an American school in every sense of the term, but its founder and forty per cent. of its students are Norwegians. In 1896 G. A. Oliver bought a one-half interest of the school. The work of the institution is carried on in rented quarters.

Jewell Lutheran College, at Jewell, was opened in the fall of 1894 in a splendidly appointed building, erected at a cost of about $25,000 by Norwegian Lutheran church members who live in the neighborhood. This college at once entered upon its career with half a dozen instructors and an equal number of courses, boldly asserting in its first catalogue that it will "present such studies and devote to them such amount of time and attention as are required for admission to such institutions as Harvard or Yale Universities." The enrollment is about 125.

Humboldt College, at Humboldt, became the property of J. P. Peterson and A. L. Ronell in the summer of 1895, and since the fall of that year it has been in operation as a "practical school for practical people." Over a dozen distinct courses are taught, and a large number of instructors are employed. The attendance is about 300, and the value of the property of the college is $40,000.

The Scandinavian Quakers, or Friends, for several years past have been operating the Friends' Boarding School, near Dunbar, with an average attendance of 40 to 50 pupils. Two teachers and a matron are employed. The value of the school building is $3,500. There is also a boarding school near Centerdale, where children of Scandinavian-Quaker parentage attend.

SWEDISH. In the fall of 1873 C. Anderson, a Swedish

preacher, but a Dane by birth, opened up a theological seminary at Keokuk. The establishment of the school had previously been authorized by the Swedish Evangelical Lutheran Mission Synod; but a part of this body withdrew and organized the Swedish Evangelical Lutheran Ansgarii Synod in 1874, and henceforth said school belonged to the latter organization. The seminary was removed to Knoxville, Ill., in 1875. It was instrumental in preparing about half a dozen young men for the ministry while it remained at Keokuk.

The Iowa Conference of the Swedish Augustana Synod some fifteen years ago took steps to establish " a high school for girls" at Swede Point (now Madrid). In 1883 it was decided to open the school to both sexes; but as the necessary means were not forthcoming, the undertaking was abandoned in 1887.

At the close of the eighties, Rev. A. J. Östlin, of the Augustana Synod, started an academy at Stanton. The work performed was of a high grade, and at one time the attendance was large; but the school was in operation only two or three years.

OTHER INSTITUTIONS. Although the higher educational institutions sustained and operated by Scandinavian-Americans in Iowa at present have an aggregate enrollment of 1,400, the attendance of that class of students at the other institutions of the same grade does not seem to be materially affected thereby. Indeed, it has been observed that local Scandinavian schools have aroused such an active interest in educational matters as to positively increase the attendance at other schools. The attendance of students of Scandinavian birth or parentage, for instance, at the State University, is from 30 to 40, or three per cent. of the total attendance. Prof. A. A. Veblen deserves credit for the efforts he has made to induce his young countrymen to attend the state university, at Iowa City. In regard to the standing of this class of students, A. A. Veblen says: "Our Scandinavians have had many representatives here who have won high distinction, and they have so far carried away honors altogether out of proportion to their numbers. In fact, I can not now recall a single case of a Scandinavian doing very poorly."

Historical Review of the Scandinavian

Churches in Iowa.

—BY—

O. N. NELSON and J. J. SKORDALSVOLD.

The religious activity of the Scandinavian-born Iowans ever since they began to settle in the state about fifty years ago has been almost phenomenal. In the course of that period an even dozen of distinctly Scandinavian synods or associations have gained a foothold in the state, the number of local congregations representing each of these ranging from eight to more than one hundred. The Lutheran churches are by far the strongest; but there is also a respectable sprinkling of Baptists and Methodists. The total number of congregations is about 450, and the aggregate number of communicant members, 45,000. A little figuring will bring out the full meaning of these numbers. The total membership, including the children of the communicants, must be at least 75,000, while the whole number of inhabitants of Scandinavian birth or immediate descent may be put at nearly 200,000. Thus it will be seen that

83

practically forty out of every one hundred Northmen in
Iowa are church members. But several thousand Scandinavians belong to churches wholly outside of the twelve
organizations mentioned below, and all of these, combined
with people who are not church members, but nevertheless
attend this or that favorite church fully as regularly as many
actual members do, swell the number of church-going Scandinavians in Iowa to a grand total of about 150,000, or
three-fourths of the whole number of inhabitants.

THE UNITED CHURCH. Since the United Norwegian Lutheran Church of America does not by any kind of organization recognize the boundary lines of Iowa, there is no
sufficient reason for devoting a separate article to that
church. But its strength in that state entitles it to more
than passing consideration. Although its organization dates
only from 1890, the elements out of which it was formed
may easily be traced a long series of years back of that date.
The Norwegian Lutheran Synod was organized at Koshkonong, Wis., in 1853, seven ministers and forty congregations uniting in forming the new body. Northern Iowa
soon became the great stronghold of the synod, and the
rival organizations made but slight inroads into its ranks
until the Anti-Missourian Brotherhood withdrew during the
eighties. When the United Church was organized, twelve
Anti-Missourian ministers and forty churches served by them
in Iowa, were, with some exceptions, incorporated into this
body. The other organizations which were merged into the
United Church in 1890 were the Norwegian-Danish Augustana Synod, and the Norwegian-Danish Evangelical Lutheran Conference, both of which dated their organization

from the year 1870. During the first year of its existence, the former consisted of ten ministers and about twice that number of congregations in the whole United States. Originally, the conference was not much stronger, having only four ministers and ten congregations in the state; but it contained a number of energetic men who were bound to succeed, and twenty years later, when they joined the United Church, the conference had forty-one churches and twelve ministers, and the Augustana Synod had two churches and four ministers in Iowa. At the time of the union the Augustana Synod had a theological seminary at Beloit, and the St. Ansgar Seminary was owned and controlled by members of the conference. The United States census of 1890 puts the value of the church property held by those congregations in Iowa which participated in the formation of the United Church, at $220,100. During the years 1890-96 the contingent of the United Church in Iowa increased as follows: The number of congregations from seventy-two to eighty-two, and the number of ministers from twenty-seven to thirty-eight. According to the United States statistics, the number of "communicants or members" was 14,891 in 1890, which figures are too ambiguous to mean anything. But the parochial reports for 1896 seem to indicate that the total membership, including the baptized children, was a little over 15,000, and if the twenty-five congregations are added which do not belong to the organization, but are served by its pastors, the total number of persons in Iowa in sympathy with the United Church will be in the neighborhood of 20,000. This calculation includes the Friends of Augsburg, or Minority, who have not been deducted from the members given in the official reports, although they have practically left the church.

HAUGE'S SYNOD. Elling Eielsen visited Keokuk in the early forties. Thus the father of the present Hauge's Evangelical Lutheran Synod in America seems to have been the first Scandinavian clergyman who put his foot upon Iowa soil. Afterwards, however, the immediate followers of Eielsen did not effect any religious organization in the state until 1854, when a church was started at Stavanger, Fayette county. There are only four churches in Hauge's Synod which are older than this one. The statistics of the synod show that about twenty congregations in Iowa were connected with the organization in 1896, and nearly all of them have church buildings of their own. The total membership at that date, including the children, was 4,000; and the value of the property held by those congregations now totals $35,000. Hauge's Synod received its present name in 1875. Shortly afterwards Elling Eielsen and a few others withdrew, retaining the old constitution and the old name of the organization. This organization at present is represented in Iowa by two ministers who are serving congregations at Clear Lake and Forest City.

DANISH LUTHERANS. No Danish Lutheran church was organized in the United States in the nineteenth century before the year 1868. Three years later Rev. C. L. Clausen organized one at Cedar Falls, Iowa, and the next year a few ministers and laymen met at Neenah, Wis., and established the Church Mission Society, which in 1874 received the name of the Danish Evangelical Lutheran Church in America. This body in the course of time has become the strongest Danish

church organization in the country. In Iowa it was represented by some thirty congregations with about 2,500
members. They had about a score of church buildings, and
the value of the property belonging to them aggregates
$30,000. But this organization was rent in twain in 1894,
and one faction united with the Danish Lutheran Association in 1896, forming the United Danish Evangelical Lutheran Church in America.

In 1884 lay delegates from six churches, and six Danish
ministers belonging to the Norwegian-Danish Evangelical
Lutheran Conference, withdrew from this body, and organized the Danish Evangelical Lutheran Church Association in
America, this step also being favorably looked upon by the
former body. The latter organization did not grow very
fast, its representation in Iowa at the time of the formation
of the United Danish Church being nine congregations,
which had an aggregate membership of almost 1,000. The
value of the property held by these churches was about
$5,000.

METHODISTS. A Swedish Methodist church was organized by Jonas Hedstrom at New Sweden, Jefferson county, in
1850—for a full account of the religious contention prevailing at that place in the middle of this century, see the
biography of M. F. Hokanson, in this volume. Since that
date the growth of Swedish Methodism in Iowa has been
steady. One of the most earnest workers for a period of
thirty-five years was John Linn, whose biography may be
found in this volume. In 1874 the Iowa district was established, and five years later the Burlington district. The latter
includes Iowa, Missouri, and a part of Illinois. There were

a score of congregations in Iowa in 1896. They had about
fifteen church buildings, and the total number of communicant members was 800. The church property was valued at
$36,000.

O. P. Petersen, the Nestor of the Norwegian Methodists
in America, preached in Winneshiek county as early as 1851,
and the next year three men and four women at Washington
Prairie, in the same county, united in forming the first
Norwegian Methodist congregation in the state—Petersen's
biography is given in the first volume of this work. The
following statistics show the strength of the Norwegian
Methodists in Iowa at the close of the year 1896: Fifteen
congregations with 500 communicant members; 10 church
buildings and several parsonages, valued at $17,000.

BAPTISTS. A Swedish Baptist church was started at
Village Creek, Allamakee county, in 1853, by F. O. Nilson,
whose biography is given in the first volume of this work.
Three years later another church was organized at Swede
Bend, Webster county, and in 1896 the number of churches
had increased to about 20, which constitute the Iowa conference. The number of communicant members was about
1,000. The property held by the conference was valued at
$30,000. In 1896 there were a dozen of Norwegian-Danish
Baptist congregations in Iowa, which had 800 communicant members.

SWEDISH MISSION. Previous to 1868 no Swedish Mission
church was organized in this country. That year one was
started at Swede Bend, Webster county. The first pastor
of this church was C. A. Björk, who for years has been the
president of the Swedish Evangelical Mission Covenant

which was organized in 1885. The Swedish Covenant is represented in Iowa by 20 congregations. About one-half of the congregations submitted reports at the annual meeting of the covenant in 1895. The following statistics were obtained by doubling the figures given by the ten congregations which sent in reports: Members of all ages, 1,800; number of church buildings, 16; value of property held by the churches, $41,500. As will be seen from the way these figures were obtained, they are only approximately correct. The Swedish Free Mission is the name generally given to a large number of congregations which originally co-operated with those churches which formed the Swedish Evangelical Mission Covenant in 1885. The Swedish Free Mission is represented in Iowa by a dozen of congregations whose membership is about 800,

QUAKERS. There are some six or seven hundred Scandinavian Friends, or Quakers, mostly Norwegians, in Iowa. They have no congregations of their own, but are connected with purely American churches in the different localities. In some cases, however, they have been in the habit of using their mother tongue at religious gatherings.

Historical Review of the Iowa Conference

of the Augustana Synod.

— BY —

REV. JOS. A. ANDERSON.

As the name indicates, this conference is a part of the Evangelical Lutheran Augustana Synod of North America, better known as the Swedish Augustana Synod. Originally it embraced only the state of Iowa, but in 1891 the state of Missouri, with the exception of Kansas City, was added.

The conference was at first a part of the Mississippi Conference, and this body met, for the first time in Iowa,* at New Sweden, in 1853, when Dr. T. N. Hasselquist presided. In 1868 the Mississippi Conference was divided into the Eastern and Western Mississippi conferences. The former later assumed the name Illinois, and the latter adopted the name of Iowa in 1870.

The first meeting was held at Swede Bend, now Stratford, February 18-21, 1869. At the organization the conference consisted of eleven congregations and six pastors. Of these six, the Revs. H. Olson, B. M. Halland, and C. J. Malm-

*For a more complete discussion of the first Swedish Lutheran organization in Iowa, see Rev. M. F. Hokanson's biography in this volume.—EDITOR.

berg were present. A Norwegian pastor, O. Sheldahl, was also in attendance. The lay delegates were three. Olson was elected president, and Halland, secretary and treasurer. At first the officers were elected at every semi-annual meeting, but since 1870 the term of office has been one year.

At all the meetings from the first the home mission work has been the most important subject under consideration. But it was not only discussed at the meetings, for during the first years almost every pastor of necessity became an itinerant preacher. The ministers were few, while the field was large and growing. That our veteran clergy did not have an easy time of it, we learn from the reports delivered at the meetings. The means of communication were very poor, and often a minister had to walk many miles in order to keep his appointments. He was not always treated with courtesy when he did arrive. This is not to be wondered at. Many of the settlers were from the rural districts of Sweden and, therefore, not very refined. The freedom enjoyed in this country for many meant only a license to display their course and selfish tastes. Other denominations proselyted among our countrymen, and encouraged the suspicion and the rude manners displayed toward our ministers. The so-called Mission Friends, the followers of Waldenström, were also at that time springing into existence, so that many members of our congregations and former sympathizers with our work wavered in their allegiance, if they did not wholly side with the new movement.†

†This movement, which began in the state in 1868, does not, however, appear to have been very popular among the Swedes in Iowa in later years; because in 1897 the Swedish Mission Covenant and the Swedish Free Mission, together, did not have more than 2,400 members, including the children, in the whole state; while, on the other hand, the Swedish Lutherans amounted to nearly seven times that number.—EDITOR.

Under such circumstances the most indispensable qualities of a minister were patience and perseverance. But the work had its bright sides. Many were hungering for the word of God, preached in accordance with the faith of their fathers. Such received the visiting pastor with open arms, and let him freely share all that their hospitality could provide. Surely many survivors of the earliest settlers recall with joy to this very day the first time they had the opportunity of hearing a Swedish Lutheran sermon in their new home.

Though none of our ministers at this time can be said to be over-paid, yet there has been a marked increase of salary since the early days of the conference. At least one pastor, a man with a family, had only $150.00 a year; not because he did not need more, nor that the congregation did not wish to pay more, but because the members were too poor to raise a larger salary. The example given may have been an extreme case, yet the salary of the better paid pastors were in proportion. But as the material prosperity increased the ministers were made sharers thereof.

Our pioneer ministers were strict confessional Lutherans, and therefore laid a solid foundation for succeeding generations to build upon. The first theological question under discussion at any meeting of the conference was this: In what respect does the Lutheran Church differ from other denominations? Afterwards at several meetings the articles of the Unaltered Augsburg Confession were discussed; and, as a general introduction, the importance of having a confession of faith was considered.

One thing that cannot escape notice, when studying the minutes of the first meetings, is the brotherly spirit that prevailed. The conference was a family. At the annual meetings every pastor gave an oral report of his work and of the spiritual condition of his flock. When the congregation was vacant, the lay delegation reported upon its condition and needs. As the conference grew in size, the work at the meetings of necessity became more systematized; for example, since 1873 the president annually delivers a written report to the conference, and the pastoral reports to the same body have been written. Five years later it was decided that the pastoral reports should be sent to the president and consulted by him in preparing his report.

At first, besides the regular annual business gatherings of the conference, mission meetings were held once a year, which were solely for the spiritual edification of the ministers and the congregations. In 1870 it was decided that such meetings were to be held quarterly. On account of the great distance and the cost of traveling, as well as the desire to give every congregation an opportunity to hold such a meeting each year, the conference decided in 1871 to divide itself into two mission districts, the Northern and the Southern. The Southern district comprised, "the congregations and settlements along the B. & M. R. R."; and the Northern district, "the congregations and settlements situated north and northwest of Des Moines as far as Sioux City." These districts were to assemble once every month in the different congregations. In 1874 the Southern district was divided into two, and nine years later the Northern district was also divided. The difference of time between these divisions would tend to show that the conference grew more rapidly in southern Iowa.

This fact was undoubtedly owing to the large Swedish settlement at and south of Stanton. Besides, the northern
counties of the state have, in general, been settled later than
the southern. In 1887 the districts received their present
names—Burlington, Stanton, Des Moines, and Sioux City.
The last mentioned was in 1896 divided into two, Sioux
City and Algona. The regulations for the districts are very
simple. Their officers are a president, a secretary, and a
treasurer.

The conference had no constitution until 1877 when one,
modeled after that of the Minnesota Conference, was adopted.
The previous constitutional committee reported inability
to perform their duty, because the question of the division
of the Augustana Synod into district synods was then agitated. The constitution of 1877 was in force ten years,
when a new one, prepared by Rev. Forsander, was adopted.
This was in turn superseded by the constitution adopted in
1895, of which Rev. M. P. Oden is the chief author. The
seal of the conference was adopted in 1880. The following
year articles of incorporation for the separate congregations
were accepted, and each congregation must be incorporated
before it can be admitted into the conference. The conference
was incorporated in 1896.

The conference owns and controls one charitable institution, The Orphans' Home, located a little south of Stanton.
The erection of such a home was first proposed at Des
Moines in 1870. Rev. Halland made the motion, and he,
with Rev. H. Olson, was made a committee to locate the
home. They reported the following year that 160 acres of
land had been purchased near Stanton. Since, 80 acres have

been added, and in 1894 the farm was valued at $13,200. In 1880 the conference chose the site for the Orphans' Home building, and a house was erected there, which was dedicated Oct. 31st, 1881. This house has since been considerably enlarged. In January, 1882, five children were received, and in 1897 there were thirty-seven. Children of any nationality and any creed are received, but preference is given to Swedish children who are residents within the conference. The children receive a good school education in English and Swedish, and also receive religious instruction. When a child reaches the age of 18 it is dismissed from the home.

In 1888 Rev. J. Jesperson and A. P. Soderquist were appointed to prepare a constitution and by-laws for a proposed insurance association to be formed under the auspices of the conference. As a result the Swedish Lutheran Mutual Fire Insurance Association of Burlington, Iowa, was organized, which is now doing business in almost every state in the Union. In February, 1895, 467 policies were in force, representing a value of $657,050. Only the property of churches and of pastors of the Augustana Synod is insured.

During the four years ending 1885, the conference either owned or controlled the *Bethania*, a religious journal published monthly.

The statistics for 1880, about ten years after the organization of the conference, show the following: 44 congregations; 28 churches; 15 parsonages; 17 pastors; 4,849 communicants; 9,032 members; 34 Sunday schools; 17 parochial schools; contributions to purposes outside of congregations, $4,633; regular expenses for local congregations, $25,283. The value of the church property was not given until 1885, when it amounted to $166,375, excluding the Orphans' Home. Statistics for 1896 are: Congregations, 71; churches, 64; parsonages, 38; commun'cants, 9,850; members, 15,985; Sunday schools, 63; parochial schools, 43; value of church property, $356,155; debts, $47,785; contributions for other than local congregational purposes, $10,522; regular expenses of local congregations, $57,500.

The following clergymen have been presidents of the conference in the order mentioned: H. Olson, C. P. Rydholm, M. C. Ranseen, B. M. Halland, O. J. Siljestrom, C. A. Hemborg, J. E. Erlander, and M. P. Oden.

Historical Review of the Iowa District of the

Norwegian Synod.

—BY—

REV. ADOLPH BREDESEN.

The Synod of the Norwegian Evangelical Lutheran Church of America, commonly called the Norwegian Synod, though not formally organized before February, 1853, may be said to have begun its work in Iowa in 1851. In the summer of that year Rev. C. L. Clausen, one of the original founders of the Norwegian Synod, visited some of the Norwegian settlements in northeastern Iowa and preached there, being the first Lutheran minister to preach a sermon in the Norse language on Iowa soil.* The following year he organized a church at St. Ansgar, which joined the synod later. In the fall of 1851 Rev. Nils Brandt visited the settlements in northeastern Iowa, and again in 1852 and 1853. But the real pioneer minister of the Norwegian Synod in Iowa, and the father of the Iowa District, is Rev. Vilhelm Koren, now the venerable president of the synod. In March, 1853, Koren, then a young man of twenty-six, accepted a call from "set-

---

* As stated in the article Historical Review of the Scandinavian Churches in Iowa, Elling Eielsen visited Iowa in the early forties.—EDITOR.

tlers in Winnesheik, Allamakee, Fayette, and Clayton counties," and entered upon his duties in the autumn of that year.
For four years he was the only regularly educated Norwegian
Lutheran minister west of the Mississippi, and for twelve or
fifteen years he was a traveling missionary rather than a
settled pastor. Koren's pioneer work in Iowa and Minnesota deserves far more than the passing mention that can
be given here. It is a heart-stirring story, not only of heroic
endeavor and endurance and cheerful sacrifices, but also of
unswerving fidelity to truth and principle. It is one of the
brightest pages of the long history of the Norwegian Synod.

In 1857 F. C. Claussen, the second resident minister of
the synod west of the Mississippi, was installed over the
churches in Houston and Fillmore counties, Minnesota, and
relieved Koren of his missionary duties in southeastern Minnesota and the northeastern part of Winnesheik county in
Iowa. The ensuing year Rev. B. J. Muus took charge of the
churches in Goodhue and Rice counties and the adjacent
mission field in Minnesota. Rev. O. J. Hjort came to Iowa
in 1862, and Rev. T. A. Torgerson in 1865, and at the
organization of the Iowa District, in 1876, the number of
clergymen within its limits was no less than forty.

As related in Vol. I. of this work, page 187, it was found
expedient in 1876—the Norwegian Synod having by this
time spread over ten or twelve different states and territories—to divide the synod into three districts. The districts
formed were named the Eastern, the Iowa, and the Minnesota. By the synodical act of 1876 the Iowa District was
made to comprise all the churches and pastors in the state of
Iowa, the southern tier of counties in Minnesota, and the

southern part of Dakota; and in addition the few scattering
churches in Nebraska, Kansas, and Texas. It was also
agreed that the Iowa District should attend to the mission
work to be done on the Pacific Coast. The Iowa District
was organized at Decorah, June 22, 1876. The first officers
elected were Rev. V. Koren, president; Rev. T. A. Torgerson,
secretary; and Rev. O. H. Smeby, treasurer. Koren served
as president until 1894, when he was succeeded by Torgerson.

The statistics of the district at the time of organization
were as follows: Churches, 155; pastoral charges, 35; pastors, 40; communicants, 19,420; number of souls, 36,659.
In 1896, twenty years later, the statistics were as follows:
Churches, 141; pastoral charges, 47; pastors, 60; communicants, 16,157; number of souls, 27,854. The small
increase in the number of pastors and pastorates, and the
material decrease in the number of churches and total membership, may seem surprising. It is not, however, owing
to any lack of aggressive spirit and activity on the part
of pastors and people. It is partly due to the formation
of a fourth district, but principally to the withdrawal from
the synod of the Anti-Missourians some years ago. In 1893
all the churches on the Pacific Coast were detached from the
Iowa and Minnesota districts and organized into the Pacific
District, which now numbers sixteen pastors with their
charges. In 1887 Prof. F. A. Schmidt, the leader of the
Anti-Missourian faction, carried his followers out of the Norwegian Synod and subsequently into the United Norwegian
Lutheran Church. About one-fifth of the pastors and
churches of the Iowa District were among the seceders.

Since its formation the Iowa District has held annual
meetings in connection with the meetings of the joint synod
every third year, and separately the intervening years. At
all meetings, both of the joint synod and of the various districts, it is customary to devote all the morning sessions to
the consideration of some important scriptural truth or
principle tc be held and confessed; some christian duty to be
discharged; or some sin or evil to be avoided and combated.
Among the matters thus discussed at the annual meetings
of the Iowa District are the following: Sanctification;
Schisms in the Church; Christian Liberty; Election; the New
Birth; the Spiritual Impotency of the Natural Man; the
Scriptures our only safe Rule of Faith and Life; the Right Use
of the Law; Modern Assaults upon the Bible; Parochial
Schools; Overcoming the World by Faith; the Second Advent
of Christ.

In accordance with the settled policy of the Norwegian
Synod, the Iowa District as such has no institutions of
education or charity. In the Swedish Augustana Synod it
is the custom to incorporate separately the many conferences into which the synod is divided, and the conferences as
such acquire property, establish and maintain colleges,
academies, orphans' homes, hospitals, etc. Such is not the
policy of the Norwegian Synod. The districts are not incorporated, and all institutions of learning and charity, except
such as may be established by merely local associations, are
owned, controlled, and supported by the whole synod. The
result of adopting and following this policy is that sectional
interests and feelings are not created to the detriment of the
synod as a whole, and its institutions and interests. The

only work which, under the synodical constitution, is entrusted to the districts as such, is the home mission work. Each district has its own board of home missions and home mission fund, and attends to the work to be done within its own bounds. For the work carried on under the supervision of its board of home missions, the Iowa District has collected and expended, from 1877 to 1895, the sum of $34,399. The district now supports missions at Waco and Dallas, Texas; St. Louis, Mo.; Omaha, Lincoln, and Hemingford, Neb.; Council Bluffs, Iowa; Lead City, S. D.; Denver, Col.; and other places too numerous to mention.

Within the limits of the Iowa District are located Luther College and the Lutheran Publishing House, both at Decorah, Iowa; the Lutheran Normal School and the Sioux Falls Hospital, both at Sioux Falls, S. D.; and Luther Academy, at Albert Lea, Minn. The hospital and the academy are owned and controlled by local corporations composed of members of the Norwegian Synod. The college, the publishing house, and the normal school are the property of the synod. Elsewhere in this volume is found a history of Luther College. The Lutheran Publishing House is well equipped, and its last annual report was as follows: Assets, $56,530; liabilities, $237; net profit, $6,072. Luther Academy is provided with a fine and commodious building, beautifully located, and enjoys excellent patronage. The Normal School, which educates common-school and parochial school teachers, has two substantial and well appointed buildings, and is well patronized. At Bode, Iowa, an association of pastors and people of the Norwegian Synod conducted for a number of years an academy.

To the various funds of the Norwegian Synod the Iowa District has contributed, from 1877 to 1895, the sum of $213,882. If to this sum be added the $34,399 given for home mission work, and also large amounts given by the people of the Iowa District to different educational institutions, and the Church Extension Fund, the sum total must be in the vicinity of $300,000—surely a large sum considering the size of the district, and also the fact that nearly the whole amount has come out of the hard earnings of farmers, mechanics, and day laborers. In 1890 the district contributed for home missions and synodical purposes the sum of $30,024, or about two dollars per communicant.

Historical Review of the Scandinavians

in Wisconsin.

—BY—

O. N. NELSON.

It is claimed that Jean Nicolet was sent in 1634 by the governor of New France to explore the northwest, and he landed on Wisconsin soil near the mouth of Fox river. "Clothed in silken robes he advanced into the village of the Winnebagoes, discharging pistols held in each hand. He was received with welcome. A great feast was then held, 120 beavers being eaten." He undoubtedly was the first white man who visited the state of Wisconsin. For the next two hundred years various explorers, traders, trappers, hunters, and missionaries traversed the state; and towards the close of this period the lead-miners were probably the most numerous of all classes. But few permanent settlements could have been made during that time, because in 1836, when the census was taken, there were not quite 12,000 persons within the boundary lines. Since, however, the material, intellectual, and spiritual development has been very rapid, in all of which the Scandinavians, espeically the Norwegians, have taken an active and honored part.

I. PIONEERS AND SETTLEMENTS.

There were, perhaps, some Scandinavians scattered through portions of Wisconsin at the very beginning of this century, although no person can be mentioned with certainty until about 1819, and no settlement of Northmen was founded until twenty-four years later. It is to be regretted that no state census has enumerated the various nationalities in the different counties of Wisconsin, as some other states have done. If such enumeration had been made, the increase of the Scandinavians in each county would have furnished an excellent clue to the history of the settlements. It is no credit to the numerous public and literary men in Wisconsin of Norwegian and German extraction, who justly claim to have exercised a great influence upon the affairs of the state, that the state censuses are among the worst in the country, as far as the different nationalities are concerned. As it is utterly impossible to give the full facts concerning all the Scandinavian settlements, or even one-half of them, only a few of the earliest will be mentioned.   At the end of this article, however, the population of each county has been enumerated, which may be of some value in tracing the migratory movements. Up to 1890 Sweden-Norway was, in the United States census regarding this matter, considered as one country; but as there were not quite 3,000 Swedes in the whole state in 1870 against 40,000 Norwegians, it may safely be assumed that in most counties the great majority of the two nationalities belonged to the latter. Hardly any Swedes resided in the southern part of the state, the very stronghold of the Norwegians, and those few may be said to have become *Norwegianized*.

DANISH. C. W. W. Borup—his biography can be found in the first volume—undoubtedly was in Wisconsin before 1830, and some other Danes appear to have settled within the borders of the state, especially in the southeastern part, a few years later. But as there were only 146 Danes in Wisconsin in 1850, according to the United States census, not many Danish settlements could have existed at that time, and ten years later only 1,150 persons of that nationality resided in the state. Since 1870, however, their number has materially increased, and in 1897 there were in the neighborhood of 35,000 Danish-born or having Danish parents within the state. With the exception of Iowa, there were more Danes of the first and second generations in Wisconsin than in any other state in the Union.

NORWEGIAN. In 1838 Ole K. Nattestad—his biography is in this volume—bought land and settled at Clinton, Rock county, being, as far as is known, the first Norwegian who set his foot on Wisconsin soil, and for a whole year he saw none of his countrymen and few other people, as there were only about half a dozen in the vicinity. It is, however, reasonable to assume that some Norwegian adventurers, trappers, traders, hunters, or lead-miners had before that time visited the state; in fact, it is very strange if they did not, considering that the Swedes and Danes had done so years before, and the names of many pioneers who were in the state before 1838 indicate a Scandinavian origin. In

1839 Nattestad's brother, **Ansten, returned from a trip to**
Norway, and brought with him several persons from Numedal, most of whom settled near Clinton.   Since, many other
Norwegians from Telemarken and Hardanger have joined
them.

One of the most interesting and humorous stories of the
whole Scandinavian emigration is connected with the first
Norwegians who came directly from their native land to
Wisconsin.   In 1837 three peasants with their families emigrated from Tinn, Telemarken, and settled at Fox River,
La Salle county, Ill.   At that time the attachment to birthplace must have been very great among some of the common people in Norway, because the three poor farmers were
considered, on account of their emigrating, to be confirmed
idiots.   But a couple of years later about forty more persons
from that vicinity had been smitten with the same disease,
and were anxious to leave their own country, which act had
been considered a crime before that time.   This is a forcible
illustration of the great reflex influence which the thoughts
of the New World have exercised upon the thoughts of the
Old World, being the main blessing which America has
bestowed upon Europe as a small return for the untold
wealth, both material and intellectual, which the former has
received from the latter.   The movement from Telemarken
in 1839 was effected, partly, through the influence of private
letters written by immigrants in this country, partly, by
Ansten Nattestad's return to Numedal; but mostly, perhaps, on account of the appearance of Ole Rynning's book,
Sandfärdig Beretning om Amerika, published in 1838, which
work was extensively read, and greatly influenced the

whole Norwegian emigration, especially as the author gave a glowing and vivid description of the advantages of America. To improve their economic conditions was undoubtedly the mainspring which induced the majority of the peasants to leave their native land in 1839; yet, there was considerable of romance in the affair. Nattestad was looked upon with as much curiosity as if he had returned from a trip to the moon, and persons traveled over 150 English miles in order to get a chance to speak to him about America. Nattestad and his party sailed from Drammen directly to New York, while the people from Telemarken embarked at Skien the 17th of May,* 1839, and proceeded to Gothenburg, Sweden, where they met another group of about twenty emigrants from the vicinity of Stavanger. Both parties joined and took passage on an American vessel loaded with iron, paying about $50.00 a person as fare between Gothenburg and Boston, reaching the latter place after a nine weeks' voyage. After having gone to New York, they went by canal boats, drawn by horses, to Buffalo, and from thence to Milwaukee on a vessel loaded with gunpowder, and so poor that the passengers were in much greater danger of going down to the bottom of one of the lakes than of being blown up into the air by the explosion of the cargo. They reached Milwaukee seventeen weeks after having left Norway, and some excitement was created,

---

*Most authorities assert that the first Norwegian-American emigrants, the Sloop-folks, sailed from Stavanger on the 4th of July, 1825. It seems rather strange that the departure of these two noted emigration parties should have occurred on the two great national holidays of the United States and Norway. The incident might, accidentally or purposely, have happened; but probably the apparent agreement of dates is to be found in the human desire to try to harmonize their past actions, no matter how insignificant, with more important events.

on account of their strange speech and dress, at the former
place, which did not have a single beer-brewery until two
years later. As far as is known, they were the first Norwegians seen or heard in this part of the country, and the first
German immigrants arrived the same year. Their intention
was to proceed to Chicago, and from thence to the Fox
River settlement; but the good people in Milwaukee did not
relish the idea of permitting a neighboring state to receive
the benefit of the labor of such able-bodied men. But a few
years later the Know-Nothing element of the wealthy Americans secured the passage of a bill through the legislature by
which the locality where the Telemarken folks had settled
was organized into the town of Norway, in order that the
Norsemen should be compelled to take care of their own
paupers, as it was feared that a large portion of the people
would be a burden to any community. The future, however, proved that the mountaineers of the North could drain
marshes more satisfactorily and create better farms than
their American neighbors. The Norwegians were advised
to remain in Wisconsin by a venerable looking man—a person
found all over the United States, present on every occasion,
and always known by the name of An Old Settler. This
infallible light produced all the syllogisms of logic, and gave
the most minute description of the miserable climate in the
state of Illinois in contrast to the paradisiacal state of Wisconsin, in order to convince the descendants of the Vikings
of the advantages of the latter state. To clinch his argu-
ments he presented to the confiding Norwegian peasants
two persons, one strong, healthy, and robust; the other the
very shadow of death, a walking skeleton, a mere excuse for

a man. 'There,' said the old settler, pointing to the fat
man, 'you see a man from Wisconsin, the other is from
Illinois.' The Norwegians saw, believed, remained. The
story may not be true; but it is undoubtedly a fair illustration of the confiding simplicity of a large portion of the
Scandinavian immigrants, and the vulgar jocularity practiced in nearly every new American community. The mountaineers of Telemarken, having little knowledge of the world,
could not possibly dream that professional liars existed, who
practiced their craft, with pleasure, as one of the finer arts.
An interpreter, a Dane, had been with the emigrants from
Gothenburg, but he was drowned at Milwaukee, and afterwards the party had to make themselves understood the
best they could by signs. The city council, thinking that
the Norwegians were better fitted for fishing and hunting
than for anything else, secured a guide for them who took
them to Lake Muskego, Waukesha county, about fourteen
miles from Milwaukee. The summer heat having dried the
marshy land, it appeared beautiful, with plenty of grass
and timber. Excepting a couple of persons, all the sixty
Norwegians settled here. Government land was bought at
$1.25 per acre, each man securing forty acres. But the land
was unfit for farming, the very purpose for which it was
bought; besides, the swamps produced fever and ague, and
finally, in 1849-50, cholera swept off a large proportion of
the population. Most of the remaining people removed a
little farther south to the more prosperous settlements of
Norway, Waterford, Raymond, and Yorkville, all in Racine
county, which had a combined Norse population of about
600 in 1844.

The large Koshkonong settlement in Dane county may be said to have been founded by Norwegians who had tried their luck in other parts of the country, but failed, or at least desired to change location. Few, if any, of the first pioneers in Dane county came there directly from Norway. The settlement was not begun, perhaps, before 1840, although Norsemen had visited that part of the state the year before. It is undoubtedly the most widely known Norwegian colony in America. This is due, partly, to its large size and numerous population, partly, to the fact that a very large number of prominent Norwegian-Americans, both of the first and second generations, hail from that vicinity, and have made their names honored throughout the land, and even in Europe. Rev. Adolph Bredesen claims that there were about seven or eight hundred Norwegians in the colony in 1844; and about 3,000 Norsemen in the state at that time, bunched in twelve or fourteen settlements. According to the emigration reports of Norway, only about 1,300 Norwegians had exchanged their native hills for the American wilderness during the twenty years from 1820-40, and at the latter date there were, perhaps, not more than a couple of hundred Norsemen in the state of Wisconsin. But ten years later in the neighborhood of nine thousand, or about two-thirds of the total Norwegian population in the whole country, resided in the state. Out of the 44,000 Norwegians in the United States in 1860, nearly one-half lived in Wisconsin, and during the next ten years their number almost doubled. They were undoubtedly represented in every county in 1870, as the statistical tables at the end of this article seem to indicate. In 1897 not far from 175,000 persons of Norwegian birth or parentage resided in the state of Wisconsin, or about one-fourth of the total Norse population in the United States.

It should be stated that although over a dozen different authorities have been consulted in regard to the Norwegian settlements in Wisconsin, yet *Billed-Magazin*, edited by Prof. Svein Nilsson, has chiefly been relied on; and all later works which refer to that subject have failed to add any important historical matter. But, properly speaking, history should not merely register facts and chronicle dates, but, also describe the social life of the period dealt with. The editor of this work must admit, somewhat with a blush, that in most cases it has not been done; partly, on account of inability, and partly, because this series of volumes is an historical cyclopedia, intended for reference rather than for ordinary reading. But a vivid and brilliant narrative of the trials and triumphs of the Norse pioneers in this country can be had by reading the first part of Prof. P. O. Strömme's book, *Hvorledes Halvor blev Prest*. Rev. Adolph Bredesen, in a lecture delivered in 1894, gives a brief and excellent summary of the condition of the Wisconsin Norwegians half a century before that time. He says: "Wisconsin, now so populous and wealthy, was, in those early days, still a territory, and almost an unbroken wilderness, the happy hunting-ground of the red men. There was not a mile of railway within her borders, and even passable wagon roads were few and far between. Horses were scarce. I am told that the seven or eight hundred Norwegians on the Kosh-konong prairies had one horse between them, and that a poor one. 'Buck and Bright' and a *kubberulle*, or other

primitive wagon, were about the only means of transpor-
tation, and Milwaukee, or Chicago, was the nearest market.

"Our Norwegian pioneers were poor, but they were not
paupers. They had not come here to beg and steal, nor to
sponge on their neighbors. It was not their ambition to be
organ-grinders, peanut-venders, or rag-pickers. They had
come to make, in the sweat of their brow, an honest living,
and they were amply able to do so. They possessed stout
hearts, willing hands, and robust health, and nearly all had
learned at least the rudiments of some useful trade. And
the women, our mothers and grand-mothers—God bless
them!—were worthy consorts of the men who laid low the
giants of the forest, and made the wilderness rejoice and
blossom as the rose. They girded their loins with strength.
They were able to stand almost any amount of privation
and toil. They were not afraid of a mouse. They were in
blissful ignorance of the fact that they had nerves. They
knew nothing of 'that tired feeling,' and did not need the
services of the dentist every other week. They did not have
soft, velvety hands, as some of us, who were bad boys, have
reason to know; but, for all that, they had tender, motherly
hearts. They could not paint on china, or pound out 'The
Mocking-bird' on the piano, but they could spin and knit and
weave. The dear souls could not drive a nail any better
than their grand-daughters can, but they could drive—a yoke
of oxen, and handle the pitchfork and the rake almost as
well as the broom and the mop. Our mothers and grand-
mothers did not ruin our digestion with mince-pie and
chicken-salad, but gave us wholesome and toothsome *flat-
bröd* and *mylsa* and *brim* and *prim* and *bresta*, the kind of

food on which a hundred generations of Norway seamen and mountaineers have been raised.

"Our Norwegian pioneers were ignorant of the language, the laws, and the institutions, of their adopted country, and in this respect were, indeed, heavily handicapped. The German immigrant found compatriots everywhere, and, at least in all the larger cities, German newspapers, German officials, German lawyers, doctors, and business-men. The Norwegian had not a single newspaper, and, outside of a few struggling frontier settlements, there was practically not a soul with whom he could communicate. But, though our pioneers were ignorant of the English language, they were not illiterates. They had books, and could read them, and by and by astonished natives were forced to confess, 'them 'ere Norwegians are *almost* as white as we are, and they kin read, too, they kin.' If in those early Norwegian settlements books were few, a family Bible and some of Luther's writings were rarely wanting, even in the humblest homes. If the people were not versed in some of the branches now taught in almost every common school, they were well grounded in the Catechism, the *Forklaring*, and the Bible History, as all their good and bright grand-children are to-day.

" The homes of our pioneers of fifty years ago were log cabins, shanties, and dug-outs. Men and women alike were dressed in blue drilling, or in coarse homespun, brought over from the old country in those large, bright-painted chests. In 1844, I am told, not a woman on the Koshkonong prairies was the proud possessor of a hat. Some of the good wives and daughters of those days sported home-made sun-bonnets, but the majority contented themselves with the old country kerchief. Carpets, kerosene-lamps, coal-stoves, or sewing-machines, reapers, threshing-machines, top-buggies, and Stoughton wagons, were things not dreamed of."

SWEDISH. Undoubtedly Jacob Falstrom—his biography is in the first volume—was in Wisconsin before 1819, being the first Scandinavian in the state. When Gustaf Unonius came to Milwaukee in 1841, he met Captain O. G. Lange there, who had been in America several years before, and who later became extensively known as the originator of the idea and the advocator of the celebration of the Swedish fore-fathers day. It is almost certain that there were Swedish settlers who tilled the soil of Wisconsin before Unonius arrived, and he mentions many of his countrymen who had traversed a large portion of the New World, before 1840, almost as thoroughly as the Wandering Jew is said to have done in the Old World. Unonius may be said to have given the first impetus to the regular Swedish emigration in the nineteenth century, and he believes that his party of about half a dozen people were the first who took advantage of the new law which granted the privilege of leaving the kingdom without special royal permission. Being young, energetic, and fearless, and having just graduated from the University of Upsala, he possessed many of the qualities, both physical and intellectual, which were necessary for the severe struggles in the American wilderness. He and his young wife and their companions embarked from Gefle, and reached New York in the early part of September, 1841, after having spent three months on a sailing vessel, and proceeded to Milwaukee on the slow boats on the Erie Canal and the Great Lakes, reaching their destination about six months after they had left Upsala. The party settled at Pine Lake, about thirty miles west of Milwaukee. This was, undoubtedly, the first Swedish colony in America in the nineteenth century. The founder had left his native land in order to improve his economic conditions, to test the sweet experience of adventure, and to satisfy a youthful desire for change. Excepting the first, his dreams were fully realized. His book, *Minnen*, contains an admirable description of the early pioneer life in the West; and his contributions to the newspapers in Sweden drew some educated adventurers, noblemen, ex-army officials, bankrupt merchants, and a large proportion of criminals to the colony—most of whom were totally unfit for the hard struggle on the western frontier. As a consequence the settlement at Pine Lake, named New Upsala, failed; but the attempt was not wholly without influence upon the Swedish-American history, because several of the participants were voluminous letter writers, and thus they became the mediums of calling the attention of the common people in different parts of Sweden to the advantages of America, which shortly after resulted in a heavy emigration and the founding of large Swedish settlements in various places in the United States. The large and well-known colony at New Sweden, Iowa, the first permanent Swedish settlement in the New World in the nineteenth century, was the direct result of letters sent from Pine Lake. Even the famous Fredrika Bremer visited the Wisconsin colony in the early fifties. In this connection it is proper to remark that the emigration from Sweden appears to have begun with the upper classes instead of with the common people. This might serve as another lesson to that school which looks to the lower strata of society for the originators of all great popular movements. Rev. E. Norelius claims that some of his countrymen resided in Sheboygan, Waupaca, Douglass, and Portage counties at a very early date. But as there were only eighty-eight Swedes in Wisconsin in 1850, according to the United States census, not much in the line of settlements could have been accomplished before that time; and twenty years later about 3,000 resided in the state. Since 1880, however, the Swedish immigration into Wisconsin has been quite heavy, and in 1897 there must have been in the neighborhood of 50,000 persons of the first and second generations.

II.   CAUSES OF IMMIGRATION TO WISCONSIN.

It is claimed that some of the greatest historical events are purely accidental. Pascal says, "Had the nose of Cleopatra been a little shorter, the whole face of the world might have been changed." It is also possible that the little incident at Milwaukee in 1839, when a fat man was presented to the Telemarken folks as an evidence of the excellent climate in Wisconsin, is the main cause why Wisconsin has up to late years been the very stronghold of the Norwegians in America. It is certain that where these pioneer emigrants settled, at Lake Muskego, some of the most influential Norwegian-Americans located shortly after, having undoubtedly been attracted to that place by the first settlers. It was here that many well-known pioneers lived and acted, for example, Knud Langeland, Col. Hans Heg, and Rev. O. J. Hatlestad—their biographies are in this volume—with their influential relatives, as well as other leading persons. It was here also that the first Norwegian-American newspaper, *Nordlyset*, was started in 1847. But while greater and less personages somewhat directed the Norwegian migratory movement towards and into Wisconsin, there were other, and perhaps greater, causes which operated in securing a highly desirable class of Norsemen to locate within the border of the state. Chance, climate, and the fact that the state was first opened up to settlers at the same time as the Norwegian emigration began, have been powerful factors in directing the movement. But as these are exactly the reasons which induced the majority of the Scandinavians to prefer the Northwest to any other part of the country, it will be unnecessary to restate here what has already been asserted in three or four other places in this work. What has been said, in the first volume, about the variety of the natural resources and the beautiful scenery of Minnesota, as an inducement to settlers, applies with equal or even greater truth to the state of Wisconsin. The climate, as a whole, of the latter state is undoubtedly more like the climate of the Scandinavian countries than that of the former. The moisture produced by Lake Michigan and Lake Superior, and the immense pine forests have a powerful effect in modifying the temperature and making the atmosphere somewhat similar to that of certain parts of Sweden and Norway.

III. THE CIVIL WAR.

During the four years of fierce and bloody struggle and civil anarchy, over 91,000 men from Wisconsin endeavored, on the battlefield, to preserve the Union. According to the original and unpublished records of the adjutant-general of Wisconsin, about 100 Swedes, 200 Danes, and 3,000 Norwegians assisted, during the whole war period, in making the cause of the South a *Lost Cause*. But to count correctly all the Scandivians as enumerated in over fifty large and unprinted volumes, is a task which few will undertake, and none can perform satisfactorily, especially as several companies and even whole regiments, do not mention the nativity of the men enrolled. Yet, since nearly three thousand names of Northmen were actually computed, it must be fair to assume that not far from 4,000 Scandinavians were enlisted in the various Wisconsin regiments, including one or two hundred Northmen from neighboring states who served in the Fifteenth, or Scandinavian, Regiment. Both in Wisconsin and Minnesota about one-eighth of the total population fought in the Union army, but one in every six of the Northmen in these two states served his adopted country on the bloody fields of the American rebellion. As the history of the Fifteenth Regiment has appeared in the first volume of this work, it will be out of place to discuss the same here; at the same time only a short space can be devoted to the Scandinavian soldiers in other regiments, on account of the lack of materials. At the very beginning of the war the Scandinavians flew to arms. At least a couple of Norwegians were in the troop which Wisconsin sent in answer to President Lincoln's call of 75,000 volunteers. Not less than 125 descendants of the Vikings evinced, by enlisting in the Third Wisconsin Volunteer Infantry, as much courage as their savage ancestors, and perhaps more sense.

Nearly all, both men and officers, of Company H of the Twenty-seventh Regiment were Norwegians, Chas. Corneliusen being captain of the company. There were, undoubtedly, Scandinavians in all the fifty-three Wisconsin regiments. But while the Norwegians supplied a large number of common soldiers, they do not appear to have distinguished themselves at all as officers. Outside of the Fifteenth Regiment, there was not a single Wisconsin Norwegian of all the 3,000 who participated in the Civil War that rose to a higher position in the army. A couple of Danes, Adolph Sorensen, of Waupaca county, and Chas. Hall, of Dane county, were captains of Company D of the Forty-seventh Regiment and Company A of the Forty-ninth Regiment, respectively.

IV. POLITICAL INFLUENCE.

The territory of Wisconsin was organized in 1836, but no Scandinavian served in any of the legislative branches during the twelve years of territorial government, nor did any Northmen hold any kind of public office during that period. If the constitution which was framed in 1846 had not been rejected when submitted to a vote of the people the following year, no descendants of the Vikings would have assisted to form the constitution of Wisconsin, under which so many sons and daughters of the North have toiled and prospered. As it was, James D. Reymert, then residing at Norway, Racine county, sat in the constitutional convention of 1847-8, being also a member of the assembly in 1849 and 1857, and represented his district in the state senate in 1854 and 1855. Reymert was of Norwegian-Scotch extraction, and had been educated in both those countries. Politically, he sympathized with the Free Soil party. He was editor of the first Norwegian-American newspaper, *Nordlyset*, which was established in 1847, and he was undoubtedly the first Norseman in the United States who exercised any influence upon public affairs, either state or national, or held any public trust in the gift of the people. P. C. Lutkin, of Whitesville, Racine county, was a member of the assembly in 1857, being, unquestionably, the first Dane in Wisconsin who was elected to fill any responsible public trust.   Since, about six other Danes have served in the lower branch of the legislature, but none in the upper. Before 1860 there had not been more than half a dozen Scandinavians in the legislature; but that year Knud Langeland and C. G. Hammerquist, both Republicans, served.   The latter, then residing at Fort Atkinson, was the first, and with a couple of exceptions, the only Swede who ever sat in any of the legisl_tive branches of the state of Wisconsin. During the last thirty-five years, there have been Northmen in the assembly at nearly every session, and some of them have been re-elected many times. But only three or four Norwegian state senators have been elected, among whom is the well-known J. A. Johnson—his biography is in this volume. Since the constitution was adopted in 1848 and up to 1896, there have been about fifty persons of Norwegian birth or descent in the two legislative branches. In other words, over twice as many Norsemen have exhibited their wisdom or ignorance in the arena of the capitol of Minnesota during the last forty years, as their compatriots in Wisconsin have done during the last fifty years.

Col. Hans C. Heg was elected state prison commissioner in 1859, and was, perhaps, the first Norwegian who was elected to any state office in America. Hans B. Warner was secretary of state from 1878–82, and Sewall A. Peterson was elected state treasurer in 1894. N. P. Haugen, Atley Peterson, and Thomas Thompson have all served as railroad commissioners. The latter is the only Swede ever elected to any state office in Wisconsin, and Halford Erickson, who was appointed commissioner of statistics in 1895, is the only person of that nationality ever appointed to any important state office. A few other Northmen might be mentioned in connection with the political review of the Scandinavians in Wisconsin, but as the biographical department of this volume deals with the various public men in the state, it would be too much of a repetition to enumerate many of them here. At the same time it should be stated that Prof. R. B. Anderson was appointed United States minister to Denmark in 1885 by President Cleveland, and that N. P. Haugen was in Congress for eight years, serving longer than any other congressman of Scandinavian extraction. A glance at the names of the county officials seems to indicate that in most counties Scandinavians have been office-holders, but seldom in proportion to their numbers.

Although all the blue books and several legislative journals have been carefully examined, yet it is very difficult to write a political history of the Scandinavians in Wisconsin, or even to ascertain the exact number who have been elected to the two branches of the legislature. The nativity of the members has not always been given. Most of the law-makers and officials born in the North have been

fully Americanized, or have pretended to be; as a consequence it is questionable whether the Scandinavian legisla-
tors in Wisconsin have ever succeeded in passing a single
measure, the substance of which had before been in vogue in
their own country, and perhaps they never tried. Nor have
they had much of a chance either, because purely American
topics have always been awaiting solution. In nearly all, if
not in all, the great questions agitated in the state, the house
(of Norway) has been divided against itself. They have, perhaps, never worked in solid concert for any great public
end, although most of them have been Republicans. While
some of the Norwegians in Wisconsin, as individuals, have
had a powerful influence upon the affairs of the state, yet in
their public career they have often been more American than
the natives themselves.

What has been said about the Scandinavians in Wisconsin is also true of them in other parts of the Union. In fact,
it is to be doubted whether there is any direct legislation in
the land that can be traced to a Scandinavian origin, and
which has been incorporated into the statutes as the result
of Scandinavian-American statesmanship, except the establishment of courts of conciliation in North Dakota, in 1893,
which was said to be "a striking instance of the influence
exerted by a body of adopted citizens upon American legislation." It is also remarkable that the Gothenburg system
of controlling the traffic in liquors, which for a long time has
been in successful operation both in Sweden and Norway,
has never been attempted to be introduced in the strong
Scandinavian states, but in South Carolina and Massachusetts. This fact becomes more curious when it is remem-

bered that temperance and prohibition agitation has been going on in the Northwest for several years, and that in these movements the Northmen have taken an active part.

V. OCCUPATION.

The Scandinavians have been a great factor in laying the material foundation of the state of Wisconsin. The Northern countries have furnished a large number of the sailors on the lakes, the laborers in the numerous lumber camps in the immense forests, the hands in factories, and the farmers on the prairies. While it is true that the majority of the Northmen in Wisconsin, as well as in other states, have been and are common laborers, servants, and farmers, yet there are undoubtedly more Scandinavian manufacturers, in proportion to the population, in this state than in any other part of the Union. The intellectual activity of the Wisconsin Scandinavians is about on the same level as in the neighboring states. Both the legal and the medical profession are well and ably represented. About two dozen Norwegian authors and literary men reside, or have died, in the state; some of whom have made their names honored and revered on both sides of the Atlantic. But, strange to say, seldom has any great Norwegian-American newspaper been published in the state.

VI. STATISTICS.

In 1850 one out of every 34 persons in Wisconsin was a Scandinavian by birth; twenty years later, one out of 22; and in 1890, one out of 17. But this only includes persons born in the North, while a much larger per cent. have Scan-

dinavian parents and grand-parents. The second generation of the Norwegians in the state is a powerful element,
not only in numerical strength, but in intellectual and spiritual advancement. According to the United States census
for 1890, there were 23,882 persons in Wisconsin born in
Denmark or having Danish parents; 130,737 Norwegians;
29,993 Swedes—or in all 184,556 Scandinavians of the first
and second generations. Many persons, however, of all
nationalities are omitted from the census reports; and undoubtedly the nearest approach to the truth in regard to
the number of Northmen and their children in any state, can
be had by multiplying the Scandinavian-born by 2½. The
number of Scandinavian-born persons in the different states
is given on pages 156-60 in the first volume of this work,
and the population in each county of Wisconsin is published
at the end of this article. By multiplying the numbers
found in these tables by 2½, a fair estimate of the Scandinavian-American population of the first and second generations may be obtained. The Northmen and their children in
Wisconsin numbered, in 1897, about 260,000; that is, one
out of every seven persons in the state was a Scandinavian.

TABLE III.

SHOWING THE NUMBER OF SCANDINAVIANS BORN IN THE SCANDINA-
VIAN COUNTRIES, AND THE TOTAL POPULATION IN EACH COUNTY
OF WISCONSIN.

COUNTIES.	U. S. CENSUS OF 1870.			U. S. CENSUS OF 1890.			
	DENMARK.	SWEDEN AND NORWAY.	TOTAL POPULATION.	DENMARK.	NORWAY.	SWEDEN.	TOTAL POPULATION.
Adams	32	537	6,601	142	384	4	8,889
Ashland		3	221	120	947	1,357	20,063
Barron		98	537	70	2,373	566	15,416
Bayfield		1	344	46	1,085	774	7,390
Brown	371	451	25,168	819	439	104	39,164
Buffalo		556	11,123	6	1,165	45	15,997
Burnett		551	706	5	497	1,541	1,393
Calumet	22	3	12,335	45	14	16	16,639
Chippewa	20	439	8,311	47	1,379	217	25,143
Clark	3	79	3,450	87	605	169	17,708
Columbia	49	1,515	28,802	74	862	34	28,350
Crawford	11	764	13,075	5	801	14	15,987
Dane	131	6,601	53,096	449	6,728	222	59,578
Dodge	37	383	47,035	39	180	14	44,984
Door	82	344	4,919	314	962	549	15,682
Douglas	3	93	1,122	80	1,058	1,572	13,468
Dunn	51	1,336	9,488	109	3,167	155	22,664
Eau Claire	21	871	10,769	131	3,897	546	30,673
Florence				28	55	500	2,604
Fond du Lac	98	156	46,273	45	55	25	44,088
Forest				9	22	10	1,012
Grant	13	543	37,979	7	400	15	36,651
Green	12	1,017	23,611	37	623	12	22,732
Green Lake	15	27	13,195	50	17	18	15,163
Iowa	3	1,647	24,544	13	901	8	22,117
Jackson		944	7,687	51	2,507	275	15,797
Jefferson	15	384	34,040	24	245	19	33,530
Juneau	55	379	12,372	302	518	69	17,125
Kenosha	71	29	13,147	554	53	170	15,581
Kewaunee	44	97	10,128	31	72	9	16,153
La Crosse	55	2,646	20,297	87	4,371	267	38,801
Lafayette	3	993	22,659	1	927	94	20,265

TABLE III.—CONTINUED.

	U. S. CENSUS OF 1870.			U. S. CENSUS OF 1890			
COUNTIES.	DENMARK.	SWEDEN AND NORWAY.	TOTAL POPULATION.	DENMARK.	NORWAY.	SWEDEN.	TOTAL POPULATION.
Langlade........................				69	39	55	9,465
Lincoln....				92	489	320	12,008
Manitowoc.....................	38	1,420	33,364	27	900	14	37,831
Marathon......................		73	5,885	90	348	308	30,369
Marinette....				304	867	1,407	20,304
Marquette.....................	5	31	8,056	70	14	......	9,676
Milwaukee.....................	130	636	89,930	381	1,904	386	236,101
Monroe....	2	573	16,550	186	837	30	23,211
Oconto	60	321	8,321	388	193	257	15,009
Oneida....				21	142	211	5,010
Outagamie........	56	37	18,430	217	70	80	38,690
Ozankee.......	16	98	15,564	3	51	18	14,943
Pepin.........................		484	4,659	3	67	739	6,932
Pierce.........................	19	1,052	9,958	210	1,835	1.281	20,385
Polk..........................	106	483	3,422	844	1,311	1,600	12,968
Portage.....	47	795	10,634	118	1,048	185	24,798
Price.........................				19	140	982	5,258
Racine........................	1,294	1,088	26,740	2,893	949	278	36,268
Richland......................	3	237	15,731	32	288	15	19,121
Rock..........................	52	1,428	39,030	128	1,632	150	43,220
St. Croix......	71	940	11,035	320	2,638	694	22,397
Sauk..........................	9	93	23,860	31	123	26	30,575
Sawyer........................				13	423	113	1,997
Shawano.......	23	146	3,166	200	709	103	19,236
Sheboygan.....................	8	234	31,749	37	199	32	42,489
Taylor........				50	143	168	6,731
Trempealeau....................	9	2,633	10,732	21	4,118	204	18,920
Vernon........................	39	3,138	18,645	34	3,387	45	25,111
Walworth......................	28	579	25,972	93	515	139	27,860
Washburn................... .		...		21	155	322	2,926
Washington...................	2	40	23,919	23	25	5	22,751
Waukesha......................	278	486	28,274	393	326	56	33,270
Waupaca..................... .	557	1,225	15,539	962	1,270	161	26,794
Waushara......................	369	220	11,279	342	291	20	13,507
Winnebago.....................	723	762	37,279	1,210	562	114	50,097
Wood......	51	106	3,912	213	466	249	18,127
Total	5,212	42,845	1,054,670	13,885	65,696	20,157	1,686,880

Historical Review of the Scandinavian

Schools in Wisconsin.

—BY—

.J. J. SKORDALSVOLD.

No less than nine different institutions of learning have
been started by Norwegian Lutherans, and two by Danish
Lutherans, within the borders of Wisconsin. Two of them
were removed to Iowa, and one to Minnesota; and four of
them have been discontinued, leaving only four, all of which
are in a prosperous condition. Of those which have been
either removed or discontinued, three were theological seminaries, two were colleges, and the rest were schools of lower
grades. It is a noteworthy fact that the three oldest Norwegian institutions of learning in America were started in
Wisconsin, the years of their establishment being 1861,
1865, and 1869. But it is equally noteworthy, by way of
commentary on the instability, or at least mobility, of the
early Norwegian-American schools, that the only institutions of this class existing in the state at this writing
were established as late as 1885, 1888, and 1893, respectively. During the sixties and seventies a large proportion of

the progressive element of the Norwegian population of Wisconsin removed farther west, and this movement was highly unfavorable to the growth of institutions of this kind. But during the past ten years a vigorous rally is clearly noticeable, due, no doubt, partly to the greater ability of later educators to meet the practical needs of the rising generation, but chiefly to the fact that a larger proportion of the young and progressive element remain at home. Three of the schools now in operation are academies, and one is an Ind an mission school. The three academies devote only a small amount of time to religious instruction, but the chief aim of the proprietors in establishing the schools was to build up Christian character in the youth, and save them from drifting away from the Lutheran church. Norwegian is catalogued as a regular study at the academies, and perhaps nine-tenths of their attendants are of Norwegian birth or extraction. The aggregate annual enrollment of the three academies is about 375, and that of the Indian mission school from 120 to 150, making a total of 500. The latter, as well as Stoughton Academy, have already proven themselves to rank among the best institutions of their kind in this part of our country, and they are an ornament to those good people who established them; while the academies at Mount Horeb and Scandinavia as yet have scarcely had time enough to demonstrate their efficiency, their establishment dating only from the fall of 1893.

NORWEGIAN. Luther College, Decorah, Iowa, was started at Halfway Creek, near La Crosse, on September 4, 1861; but after one year's work, which closed on June 5, 1862, the institution was removed to Decorah. A lengthy and able historical sketch of Luther College is found in this volume.

In 1865 an attempt was made by members of Hauge's Synod to establish a school in Dane county; but the undertaking failed for lack of support.

The Norwegian Augustana Synod, one of the organizations which were merged into the United Church in 1890, operated an academy at Marshall, Dane county, from 1869 to 1881, and also a theological department therewith during the same period, excepting the years 1871-75.

Luther Seminary, the theological seminary of the Norwegian Synod, was established in 1876 at Madison, where it remained until 1888. During this period Prof. F. A. Schmidt and Prof. H. G. Stub successively served as president of the institution. The work carried on here during the eighties was marred by doctrinal controversies, in which Prof. Schmidt was the central figure. Nevertheless, about fifty young men were graduated from the seminary while it was located at Madison.

Monona Academy was established by the Norwegian Synod people at Madison in 1876. The attendance was fairly good for a number of terms; but financially it proved a heavy burden, and the school was discontinued in 1881.

The Bethany Indian Mission and Industrial school at Wittenberg was the only Lutheran institution of its kind as long as it was controlled by its founders. It was established in 1884 by the Norwegian Synod. The school was originally held in a log house four miles west of the village of Wittenberg, and five boys, all belonging to the Winnebago tribe, were in attendance the first term. The next year the children were transferred to the orphans' home at Wittenberg; but in 1887 the school was removed into a fine building erected for that purpose near the northwest limits of said village. From this time on the attendance increased at a rapid rate, the tribes represented being the Oneidas, Winnebagoes, Chippewas, Stockbridges, and Mohawks. The work performed was eminently satisfactory, and the influence of the teachers upon their pupils may be inferred from the fact that many of the latter joined the Lutheran Church of their own choice. A few of them afterwards entered college, and the most of them are growing up into a useful and respectable set of people. No single man did more for the building-up of this institution than Rev. T. Larsen, who resigned his position as superintendent in 1893. For a number of years the school was liberally supported by the federal government, the amount annually received from this source being $108.00 per pupil. A law which was passed by congress for the purpose of gradually abolishing all appropriations for sectarian schools, applied to this school, too, and the United States government assumed control of the school in 1895, leasing the buildings for a period of five years, dating from July 1, 1895. The people of the Norwegian Synod had spent thousands of dollars in the interest of this school, and, in order to avoid serious disturbances in its good work, the government appointed one of their own men, Axel Jacobson, to the superintendency of the school, which position he still holds.

Stoughton Academy and Business Institute is one of the foremost institutions of its kind in the state. It was started in a rather tentative way in 1888, but enjoyed a vigorous growth almost from the start. It offers five complete courses, and as an index to its efficiency may be mentioned the fact that graduates from its university course can enter the State University without examination. This institution is owned by a stock company, the majority of which are members of the Norwegian Synod. The yearly enrollment is about 200, and the value of the property belonging to the academy is $8,000.

Mount Horeb Academy dates from the fall of 1893. It was started, and is still controlled, chiefly by members of the United Norwegian Church. The school offers four different courses. The total attendance is about 100, and the property is worth $20,000.

Scandinavia Academy, at Scandinavia, was started in 1893, and the most of those who contributed to its establishment, and who have controlled it since, are members of the United Norwegian Church. The enrollment is about 75, and the property owned by the institution is valued at $15,000.

DANISH. A Danish high school was started in West Denmark, Polk county, in the eighties; but the attendance was so small that the work had to be discontinued. Later attempts were no more successful. Th. Helveg for a number of years conducted the theological seminary of the Danish Evangelical Lutheran Church in America at the same place, and about a score of students in attendance afterwards entered the ministry of the gospel.

OTHER INSTITUTIONS. Albion Academy, Beloit College, and Galesville College at one time or another have been largely attended by Scandinavian students. For twenty-five years past, however, the State University has been drawing a larger part of the bright and ambitious Scandinavian youth than has any other school in the state. It must be recorded as an historical fact that R. B. Anderson, as instructor and professor in the university during a part of the sixties and the seventies, was instrumental in drawing a large number of Norwegian students to the university. Another drawing card is the library, which contains 1,500 volumes of choice Scandinavian literature. The fact that three of the professors, namely, Julius E. Olson, Storm Bull, and Fritz Wilhelm Woll, are Norwegians, also tends to make their countrymen feel at home in the university. Nor must it be forgotten that the university offers a complete Scandinavian course. This volume contains biographies of said professors. Of late, the attendance of students of Scandinavian extraction has been about 80, which is almost exactly five per cent. of the total attendance. This class of students are not only holding their own, but during the last few years many of the boys have distinguished themselves at oratorical contests.

Historical Review of the Scandinavian Churches in Wisconsin.

— BY —

O. N. NELSON AND J. J. SKORDALSVOLD.

The first attempts to perpetuate the tenets and practices of the Lutheran Church among the Norwegian-Americans were made in the Fox River settlement in Illinois at the close of the thirties. As yet, however, there was no ordained Norwegian minister in America, and church work under the guidance of ordained clergymen did not commence until 1843, at Muskego, Wis. This year marks a turning point in the history of the Norwegian-American churches. Thenceforth, very few of those religiously inclined left the Lutheran Church; so far the accomplished result is practical unity. But from that very year some division of the Norwegian-American Lutheran church has been the scene of internal controversies, the contending parties at times being represented by as many as half a dozen distinct associations; so far the accomplished result is, apparently, diversity. And southeastern Wisconsin is the scene of the inauguration of this era.

Here Eielsen and Clausen were estranged from each

135

other before the close of the year 1843, and this soon led to open hostility. Here Dietrichson laid the foundation of the most conservative and best organized of the Norwegian-American church associations, thereby incurring the natural odium of all who are impatient of restraint. Here the organization of the two oldest Norwegian church associations was perfected, and even the powerful Swedish Augustana Synod points to southern Wisconsin as its birthplace; Hauge's Synod and the Swedish Augustana Synod having been organized at Jefferson Prairie, and the Norwegian Synod at Koshkonong, which two places are only about forty miles apart. Here was the home of Rev. H. A. Preus, who for about a third of a century guided the Norwegian Synod with imperturbable firmness. And here Prof. F. A. Schmidt accomplished a part of that work by which his name was to be indelibly graven upon the pages of the history of the Norwegian-American Lutheran church.

The total number of Scandinavian congregations in Wisconsin is about 550; the aggregate number of communicant members, 55,000; and the total membership, including the children, not far from 90,000. That is, over one-third of the Scandinavian people in the state belong to some of the leading church organizations. But several thousand Northmen are associated with churches wholly outside of those enumerated below, and all of these, combined with people who are not church members, but nevertheless attend this or that favorite church fully as regularly as some actual members do, will undoubtedly swell the number of church-going Scandinavians in Wisconsin to a grand total of about 180,000, or over two-thirds of the whole number. But as

lengthy accounts of the different Scandinavian church associations have been given in the first volume of this work, the
present chapter will be made short in order to avoid too
many repetitions.

THE UNITED CHURCH. Since the United Norwegian
Lutheran Church does not by any kind of organization recognize the boundary lines of Wisconsin, no separate chapter
will be devoted to it here. But, having a large representation in the state, it nevertheless deserves special attention.
Rev. J. C. Jensson, the secretary of this body, says: "At
the time of the organization of the United Church it was
found that 121 congregations in Wisconsin had formally
adopted the articles of union and the prospective constitution, and thus became members of the new organization.
Of these congregations, 63 had belonged to the conference;
55, to the brotherhood; and 3, to the Norwegian Augustana
Synod. Two more joined the United Church immediately
after the organization of that body, making a total of 123
congregations in Wisconsin in the year 1890." According
to the same authority the total membership of those congregations at that time exceeded 25,000. But according to
the United Church parochial reports of 1890, published in
the annual report of 1891, only 103 congregations in Wisconsin were in actual union with the organization, and 32
more were served by its pastors, making a total of 135 congregations in the state, which were supposed to be more or
less in union or sympathy with the general body.

The United States census for 1890, on the other hand,
puts the number at 187. Thus, there is a difference of over
50 congregations. This discrepancy may be partly accounted

for. The United Church at that time was in the process of formation, and a large number of people who sympathized with the movement had as yet taken no steps whatsoever to attach themselves to the organization. Nevertheless, these sympathizers were counted as members of the United Church. The difference in the number of congregations as given by the official report of the church in 1890, and that of the United States census for the same year, affords an illustrious instance of reliability! For it appears that at least 10,000 Norwegian Lutherans in Wisconsin who, in the United States census of 1890, are reported to be in connection with the United Church, had taken no formal steps in that direction. Even six years later the number of congregations in Wisconsin in actual union with the United Church fell nearly 70 below what was reported in the United States census of 1890. Nor can it be denied that the annual reports of the organization itself appear to be "waste and void" on the point in question; and to extract any kind of statistical light from them takes much diligence and more patience. For during the years 1890-96 a number of congregations appear to have joined; but Jensson again says that in 1896 only 119 congregations were in actual connection with the organization, and that 65 others were served by United Church ministers. These statistical data include the Friends of Augsburg, or the minority, who had not as yet been excluded from the reports, although they have effected a seperate organization of their own. In other words, in spite of the addition of several new congregations, the whole number of congregations formally belonging in 1896 was four less then the number which was supposed to belong in 1890, according to the estimation of Jensson. Yet, as he points out, some of the smaller congregations have, since 1890, been joined together into one. But the average membership per congregation, in direct or indirect connection with the United Church, was a trifle more in 1890 than in 1895, averaging 184 in the former year and only 182 in the latter. It is true that in 1896 the average membership per congregation appears to be 205, and it is so asserted by the secretary of the United Church in his report for that year. But this statement as well as the statistical tables are misleading, because the average membership has not, as in the previous years, been based upon the total number of congregations of the organization, but upon those only which reported; and, of course, it is nearly always the small and vacant congregations that fail to send in reports. After a thorough and careful investigation of the statistics, it does not seem reasonable that the congregations in Wisconsin, served by United Church ministers, will average more than 185 souls each at the beginning of the year 1897, which would make a total membership in the state of nearly 35,000, of whom about 20,000 are communicants. About 25,000 souls in Wisconsin, including the Friends of Augsburg, are today actual members of the United Church.

In point of membership Minnesota by far exceeds Wisconsin, but during the whole history of the church most of its important offices have been held by residents of Wisconsin. It is difficult to give any statistics in regard to the value of church property, because no light is thrown on that subject by the official reports of the organization. But the total value of the property of the United Church in Wisconsin may be estimated at about half a million dollars. The orphans' home at Wittenberg—an account of this institution is given in the biography of E. I. Homme, in this volume—which provides food and shelter for many children and aged people, is partly under the influence and control of the United Church.

SWEDISH AUGUSTANA SYNOD. This great association dates from a meeting which was held at Jefferson Prairie, close to the Illinois boundary line, June 5, 1860. The oldest congregation in the state now belonging to said synod, namely, that of Stockholm, Pepin county, was, however, not organized until the following year. In 1880 the number of congregations was only fifteen; but since that year the growth has been rapid, the number of congregations having more than trebled in the course of the past seventeen years. The communicant membership is about 4,000, and the total number 7,000. There are forty church buildings, and the value of the church property is about $125,000. For administrative purposes, the state is divided between Minnesota and Illinois conferences.

DANISH LUTHERANS. The United Danish Evangelical Lutheran Church in America was organized at Minneapolis in 1896, being a union of the Danish Lutheran Church Association and several congregations and clergymen formerly connected with the Danish Lutheran Church in this country. The association at the time of the union was represented in the state by half a dozen congregations having a total membership of about 600. Thirteen congregations are reported as having joined the United Danish Church, and sixteen more in the state are served by its pastors. If each congregation averages 100 souls, then there should be in the neighborhood of 3,000 persons in Wisconsin who are connected, directly or indirectly, with the new movement.

The Danish Evangelical Lutheran Church in America had in 1890, according to the United States census, over 2,000 members in Wisconsin. But since many of the largest and oldest congregations—for example, those of Racine, Waupaca, and Neenah—have, virtually, become identified with the United Danish Church, the oldest Danish religious society in the country has been considerably diminished. As no regular annual reports, however, have ever been issued by this organization, it is impossible to give any reliable statistics. It is difficult even to determine when the Danish Lutherans began their religious work in Wisconsin, which certainly was not later than 1872; for by that time congregations were in existence at Racine and Waupaca.

HAUGE'S SYNOD. During the years 1843–46 Rev. Elling Eielsen gathered a number of devotionalists in southeastern Wisconsin into groups which may, perhaps, be called congregations, and which in turn were organized into the Evangelical Lutheran Church of America by Eielsen and a few others who met for that purpose at Jefferson Prairie, Wis., April 13 and 14, 1846. This society, therefore, enjoys the distinction of being the oldest Scandinavian organization of its kind in America. In 1875 a schism occurred, the majority re-organizing themselves into Hauge's Synod. Eielsen laid such a tremendous stress upon the importance of the salvation of the individual as to positively discourage and neglect organized effort. And for the past half century the growth of Hauge's Synod in Wisconsin has been very slow as compared with that of other Norwegian Lutheran organizations in the same field. Thus, the present contingent of Hauge's Synod in the state of its birth is only twenty-eight congregations with an aggregate communicant membership of a little over 2,000, and about 3,800 souls. In other words, only one-eighth of the members of the synod worship in the state, where nearly one-fourth of the total Norse population in the country reside. At Lodi, at least, there is still a charge which adheres to a small association which remained with Elling Eielsen and the old organization.

METHODISTS. Rev. C. B. Willerup, a native of Denmark, was sent by the Methodist Church to preach to the Norwegians in southern Wisconsin. He entered upon his work at Cambridge in 1850, and in the summer of 1851 the first Norwegian Methodist congregation in the state was organized at the same place. It may be stated as an interesting historical fact that the first Norwegian Methodist church building in the world was erected here in 1851. It is a stone structure which costs about $3,000, and is still in good condition. In 1856 there were seven Norwegian-Danish Methodist congregations in the state; this number has increased to forty, and the aggregate number of communicants is about 1,600. There are eight Swedish Methodist churches with an aggregate communicant membership of 300. The property held by these churches, including five church buildings, is $6,500

BAPTISTS. The first Swedish congregation in Wisconsin was organized at Wood River, Burnett county, in 1869. There are now twenty-five in the state, and their total communicant membership is 1,200.   They have fifteen church buildings, and the aggregate value of the property held by them is $25,000.   The Norwegian-Danish Baptist Church is represented by 1,000 communicant members, who are organized into twenty congregations.   There are fifteen church buildings, and the value of the property is $25,000.

SWEDISH EVANGELICAL MISSION COVENANT.   This association is represented by half a dozen congregations in Wisconsin.   Some of them have church buildings of their own. The total number of communicant members is not quite 400, but the value of their church property is reported to be worth nearly $20,000.   There are also a number of Free Mission Friends, and Swedish and Norwegian Congregationalists in the state.

Historical Review of the Eastern District

of the Norwegian Synod.

···BY··—

REV. ADOLPH BREDESEN.

The seven pastors and twenty-eight churches that, in
February, 1853, at East Koshkonong, Dane county, Wis.,
founded the Norwegian Synod, were nearly all located in
southern Wisconsin, and for a number of years this state
continued to hold the bulk of the pastors and churches of
this organization. For this reason the synod was sometimes called the Wisconsin Synod. By the year 1876, however, the synod had spread over ten or twelve different
states and territories, and a division of the synod into districts had for some time been felt to be a necessity. The
revised constitution adopted by the synod in June, 1876, at
Decorah, Iowa, made provision for such division into districts. The constitution also provided for triennial meetings
of the synod and for annual meetings of the districts. Three
districts were formed, namely, the Eastern, or Wisconsin;
the Western, or Iowa; and the Northern, or Minnesota.

The Eastern District was made to include all the pastors and churches of the synod located east of the Mississippi and St. Croix rivers. These pastors and the representatives of these churches attending the synod meeting at Decorah in 1876, convened, June 22, 1876, and organized the Eastern District, electing the following officers: President, Rev. P. A. Rasmussen, of Lisbon, Ill.; vice-president, Rev. J. B. Frich, of La Crosse, Wis.; secretary, Rev. C. M. Hvisten-dahl, of Stoughton, Wis.; treasurer, Halle Steensland, of Madison, Wis.; lay member of the church council, J. J. Naeset, of Stoughton, Wis.; auditors, T. J. Widwey and John Lienlokken, both of La Crosse, Wis. At the time of its organization the Eastern District numbered 49 pastors and 175 churches. Of the latter, 145 were in Wis-consin, 14 in Illinois, eight in Michigan, two in New York, two in New Jersey, one was in Indiana, one in Ohio, one in Maine, and one in Ontario. The following, compiled from the parochial reports, show the growth of the district during its first decade: Pastors, in 1876, 50, ten years later, 68; churches, 180, and 225; communicants, 25,862, and 32,313; number of souls, 46,788, and 57,118. It will be seen that the growth of the Eastern District during the decade, though steady, was comparatively slow. This was due chiefly to little immigration, and much emigration to states and territories farther west. During the next decade the numerical strength of the district was greatly reduced, through the withdrawal of the Anti-Missourian faction, at the close of the great controversy on election, or predesti-nation, and kindred questions. The story of the great con-troversy, which lasted for years, and resulted, in 1887, in the disruption of the Norwegian Synod, is told in Vol. I of this work. The Eastern District suffered most severely through this sad schism. In this district two of the founders and fathers of the Norwegian Synod were deposed by Anti-Missourian majorities in churches which they served. One of the two was Rev. H. A. Preus, for thirty-two years the president of the Norwegian Synod. The Eastern District at Ashippun, Wis., in 1886, and at Stoughton, Wis., in 1887, by a majority vote sustained all pastors thus deposed, and recognized the protesting minorities in the churches that deposed them. At the district meetings in 1884–85 the presidency of the district was a matter of contention and heated discussion, the Anti-Missourians attempting to oust President Frich and to seat Rev. P. A. Rasmussen. The matter was submitted to a committee of arbitration, consisting of Judge G. R. Willett, of Decorah, Iowa; Judge J. H. Carpenter, of Madison, Wis.; and Hon. Elihu Colman, of Fond du Lac, Wis. The decision of the arbitrators was in favor of President Frich. After the Synod meeting of 1887, held at Stoughton, Wis., the Anti-Missourians, or adherents of Professor F. A. Schmidt, gradually withdrew from the synod, and peace was restored. The statistics of 1889 bear witness to the severe losses suffered by the Eastern District through this secession. In that year the strength of the district was: Pastors, 48; churches, 163; communicant members, 19,682; number of souls, 34,707. In January, 1896, the figures were: Pastors, 68; churches, 196; communicants, 20,410; number of souls, 35,018. Of these 196 churches, 131 were in Wisconsin, 32 in Michigan, 18 in Illinois, three in Indiana, three in Ohio, three in Tennessee, seven in New York, four in New Jersey, two in Massachusetts, two in Ontario, and one was in Rhode Island. Rev. J. B. Frich, of La Crosse, Wis., Rev. O. Juul, of Chicago, Ill., and Rev. H. Halvorsen, of Westby, Wis., have held the office of president of the Eastern District. Rev. P. A. Rasmussen, of Lisbon, Ill., was elected president in 1876 and in 1883, but both times refused to accept office. He was again elected in 1885, but his election was declared illegal by the committee of arbitration mentioned above.

The annual meetings of the Eastern District have been held as follows: In 1877 at Winchester, Wis.; in 1878, pending synod meeting, at West Koshkonong, Wis.; in 1889 at Lee, Ill.; in 1880 at Wiota, Wis.; in 1881, during synod meeting, at Spring Grove, Minn.; in 1882 at Blair, Wis.; in 1883 at Perry, Wis.; in 1884, during synod meeting, at Minneapolis, Minn.; in 1885 at Roche-a-Cree, Adams county, Wis.; in 1886 at Ashippun, Wis.; in 1887. during synod meeting, at Stoughton, Wis.; in 1888 at Rush River, Wis.; in 1889 at Spring Prairie, Columbia county, Wis.; in 1890 at Minneapolis, Minn., pending synod meeting; in 1891 at Lee, Ill.; in 1892 at Menomonie, Wis.; in 1893 at Chicago, during synod meeting; in 1894 at West Koshkonong, Wis.; in 1895 at Halfway Creek, Wis.; and in 1896 at La Crosse, Wis., during synod meeting.

At these meetings of the district the rule has always been to devote the afternoon sessions to business matters and the morning sessions to the elucidation of doctrines and principles. This is an unwritten law in the Norwegian Synod, as has been explained in the article on the Iowa District in this volume. Among the topics thus discussed in the Eastern District were the following: The Divinity of the Scripture; Gratitude to God for Blessings Bestowed; Religious Awakening; the Scriptural Doctrine of Election; Conversion; Assurance of Salvation; the Nature of the Divine Call; Ways and Means of Building up True Lutheran Churches; Dangers that Threaten the Church in Our Day; True and False Lutheranism; Ephesians II. 8–10; the Nature and Object of Missions; the Missionary Spirit; Home Missions; Seamen's Missions; Mission Work Among the Mormons.

Under the constitution of the Norwegian Synod, each district has its own board of home missions, and attends to the home mission work to be done within its borders. Of late years the amount which the Eastern District has expended for home mission work has been about $4,500 annually. At present twenty missionary pastors, serving fifty-one churches, are receiving more or less aid from the home mission fund. Of these missionaries, five are stationed in northern Wisconsin, three in the state of New York, two in Chicago, three in northern Michigan, and the others in Tennessee, Canada, New Jersey, Rhode Island, and Massachusetts.

The Eastern District, as such, owns and controls no institutions of learning or charity. In the Norwegian Synod districts are not incorporated, and all such institutions are established, controlled, and supported either by the synod, or by merely local associations. The theological seminary of the Norwegian Synod, Luther Seminary, was located at Madison, Wis., from 1876 to 1888, when the institution was removed to Minneapolis. Monona Academy was established at Madison, Wis., in 1876, by the churches around Madison. The academy was discontinued in 1881. In 1882 Rev. E. J. Homme built an orphans' home at Wittenberg, Wis., the churches and pastors of the Norwegian Synod furnishing the necessary means. This home is now well housed and in a flourishing condition and doing good work, Rev. Homme still being the superintendent. The institution is not now connected with the Norwegian Synod. It was lost to the synod eight or nine years ago, as the result of the withdrawal from the synod of Rev. Homme and other Anti-Missourians.

The Bethany Indian Mission School, opened in the autumn of 1884, is owned by the Norwegian Synod. It is located on a farm of 120 acres, near Wittenberg, Wis., and has a neat church and two brick buildings, steam-heated, with accommodations for about 160 inmates. This Indian school was conducted by the synod, under the contract system, down to 1895, when the grounds and buildings were leased to the United States government. The institution was then changed into a government school, but the principal, the teachers, and the matrons were retained. The Tabitha Hospital, opened three years ago, at Humboldt Park in Chicago, is the property of the Tabitha Society, a local organization. The hospital has a commodious and well-appointed building, and a fine staff of physicians, surgeons, and trained nurses. The Stoughton Academy and Business Institute, at Stoughton, Wis., was opened in the fall of 1888, and is conducted by the Stoughton Academy Association. The academy building is of brick, three stories above basement, and beautifully located. The average annual attendance is nearly 200.

The Martin Luther Orphans' Home, near Stoughton, Wis., is the property of the Norwegian Synod. This institution was opened in 1889 at Madison, Wis., but was removed to Stoughton in the spring of 1894. The home is located on a farm of over 100 acres, two miles from the city of Stoughton, and has two fine frame buildings, steam heated, affording accommodations for about 100 children. The number of inmates at present is seventy-six.

From 1877 to 1896 the annual contributions of the Eastern District to the treasury of the Norwegian Synod have averaged about $11,000, ranging from about $5,000 to over $20,000, the total amounting to nearly $215.000. To the annual remittances to the synodical treasury and to the home mission fund of the district should be added large sums given to the orphans' homes at Wittenberg and Stoughton, to the church extension fund, to the Monona and the Stoughton academies, to the Pacific Lutheran University, to the Lutheran Ladies' Seminary at Red Wing, Minn., to the Tabitha Hospital, to various relief funds, etc.

The officers of the Eastern District at present (1897) are: President, Rev. H. Halvorsen, of Westby, Wis.; vice-president, Rev. A. K. Sagen, of La Crosse, Wis.; secretary, Rev. J. Nordby, of Lee, Ill.; treasurer, A. H. Dahl, of Westby, Wis.

BRYNILD ANUNDSEN, DECORAH

A. ANDERSON, SIOUX CITY.   REV. J. A. ANDERSON, CRESTON.

A. CARLSON, DES MOINES.   REV. A. NORRBOM, SWEDESBURG.

Biographies of Scandinavians in

Iowa.

Anderson, Andrew G., the hero of the flood of 1892—Sioux City—born 1854, in Lena, Vestergötland, Sweden; died 18 May, 1892. He emigrated in 1870, settling in Sioux City three years later; at first worked as a common laborer; was fireman and engineer on a ferry-boat at Sioux City, and in 1876 fireman on the steamboat Tiger, the boat that made the first trip up the Yellowstone river; and at the time of his death was employed as stationary engineer of the Sioux City brick and tile works at Springdale, a suburb of Sioux City. Anderson was a member of the Scandia Lodge of K. P., and of the Brotherhood of Stationary Engineers; was married in 1879; and at his death left a wife and three children. The deeds accomplished by Andrew G. Anderson during the last moments of his life perhaps have no counterpart in the history of the world, and entitle his name to be remembered to the end of time. In the disastrous flood which visited western Iowa, he, at the evident risk of his own life, 18 May, 1892, saved twenty-seven persons from drowning. Though almost exhausted, he swam out to save one more, a woman who was struggling for life; but his strength failed, and both were drowned. *Nordlyset*, a

Danish weekly, published in New York, said of Anderson's heroism: "Such a deed can be explained only in one way— 'I love my neighbors more than myself.'" Rev. D. L. Mackenzie, in his funeral sermon over the remains of Anderson, expressed himself thus: "Braver Knights never buckled on armor and went to the fray. An expert waterman, he was inspired by naught but unselfish desire to save human life, and he breasted waves that made the stoutest hearts grow faint. But after twenty-seven people had through his efforts been saved he was at last compelled to yield up his life to the remorseless waters. Our heroes of Gettysburg immortalized themselves, yet they fought for home and native land. This hero won greater honors, for he fought for no such selfish result." The funeral services took place at the Trinity Lutheran Church of Sioux City, 22 May, under the auspices of the Scandia Lodge of K. P., Rev. J. A. Christenson speaking in Swedish, and Rev. Mackenzie in English.

Anundsen, Brynild, publisher—Decorah—born 29 Dec., 1844, in Skien, Norway. He commenced to work in a cigar factory at the tender age of seven, and afterwards in a stone quarry and in small grist mills. At the age of fifteen he learned the printer's trade and then followed the sea for a couple of years. Anundsen was kept so busy during his boyhood that he could attend school only at irregular intervals and in the evenings. He left for America in 1864, and tried his hand at various occupations in Wisconsin. He soon settled at La Crosse, however, as type-setter in the office of *Faedrelar det og Emigranten*, where he remained until 1866. About this date he started a paper of his own,

Ved Arnen, a monthly magazine for "novels, stories, poems, etc., by the best authors." At the close of the first year of the existence of the paper, its financial condition was such that the publisher had to balance its accounts by working on the road for some time. In 1868 Anundsen removed to Decorah, Iowa, with his printing outfit, which, together with the rest of his earthly possessions, made up two wagon loads. Here he continued the publication of his magazine and also printed *Kirkelig Maanedstidende,* the official organ of the Norwegian Lutheran Synod; but in spite of his best efforts, the receipts of his magazine persisted in lagging behind the expenditures, and after a three years' struggle, *Ved Arnen* gave up the ghost. Anundsen continued the printing of the organ of the synod, besides occasional pamphlets for the same body, until the synod started a printing office of its own. In 1874 he began the publication of *Decorah-Posten,* at first only a highly unpretentious local weekly. This marks the turning-point in the life of Anundsen, and the paper through which this was accomplished deserves more than passing mention. *Decorah-Posten* differs from the average Scandinavian-American newspapers in that it does not meddle with opinions on any subject whatever. It is perfectly colorless as to religion and politics. In order to avoid all kinds of controversy it has no editorials. But on the other hand, its reading matter is exceedingly varied. The aim of the paper seems to be exclusively that of furnishing interesting reading matter. And to judge by the phenomenal success which the paper has made, Anundsen hit the nail squarely on the head when he conceived the idea of such a paper. In less than twenty years after its establishment, the circulation of it exceeded that of any other newspaper printed in the Norwegian language, and now it has over 35,000 regular subscribers. *Ved Arnen* was revived again a number of years ago, and is sent as a supplement to *Decorah-Posten*. The latter has been published twice a week since the fall of 1894. All this business is managed on a sound cash basis; consequently, Anundsen is looked upon as one of the most solid and substantial business men in that part of the state, and the people of Decorah take pardonable pride in his establishment which now employs thirty men the year round. A few years ago Anundsen bought a large brick building for his establishment. Anundsen is a member of the United Norwegian Lutheran Church. He was married in 1865 to Mathilda Hofström, of Östergötland, Sweden. They have grown children.

Bergh, Knut E., educator and state legislator—Decorah —born 27 May, 1838, in Voss, Bergen stift, Norway; died in Hardanger, Norway, in 1875. He emigrated to America in 1857; began to teach parochial school the same year at Liberty Prairie, Wis.; then attended English schools at Liberty Prairie, Madison, and Evansville, Wis., successively; attended Concordia College, in St. Louis, in 1860 and 1861; and entered the school of the Norwegian Synod at Halfway Creek, Wis., in the fall of 1861, but was forced to leave at the close of the first term on account of poor health. Bergh then spent three years in teaching, devoting his spare moments to study. In 1864 he entered Luther College at Decorah, but poor health again interrupted his studies. His health improving, he took up the study of law, and was

admitted to the bar in 1869. The same year he accepted a
chair at Luther College, and for several years was connected
with the institution. In 1870 he began the publication of
For Hjemmet; and a couple of years later was elected a
member of the state legislature by an overwhelming majority. In this capacity he served on several important committees. Bergh was a powerful speaker, mastering the
tongue of his adopted, as well as that of his native country,
and those who attended his classes at Luther College have
spoken of his work as a teacher in glowing terms.

Boye, Nils Christian, pioneer—Iowa City—born about
1786, in Laaland, Denmark; died of cholera in 1849, in St.
Louis, Mo., where he had gone for the purpose of buying
goods. He received a good education in his native land;
emigrated to this country in 1827, for the purpose of
attending to some inheritance which had been left by one of
his brothers who had come to this country a couple of years
before, and who had surveyed the state of Virginia. N. C.
Boye had also lost thousands of dollars in Denmark during
the anarchy of the Napoleon wars. He had been a merchant
and miller in Denmark, and for seven years had a small store
in Philadelphia, but went to Muscatine county, Iowa, in
1837. After having resided at the latter place for about one
year, he settled in Linn county, and moved to Iowa City in
1842, where he engaged in merchandise. Boye is the first
Scandinavian settler in Iowa, as far as could be ascertained
by all the researches made for the compilation of this
work. Of Boye's thirteen children, one son became quite
prominent as a merchant in New Orleans, and one son in
Denmark became a noted physician.

Brydolf, Fabian, pioneer and soldier—Burlington—born 28 Nov., 1819, in Hellestad, Östergötland, Sweden; died 25 Jan., 1897. His father was a minister in the state church of Sweden. Young Brydolf received a good general education, and at an early age developed a talent for landscape painting, which profession he followed with considerable success until 1841, when he emigrated to this country. At first he located in Cleveland, Ohio; worked at his profession in various cities until 1846, when he came with a party of Swedish immigrants to Burlington, Iowa, being their interpreter on the journey, as well as assisting them in securing land after their arrival at their destination. In 1847 Brydolf enlisted in the Fifteenth Regiment of the regular U. S. army, and participated in several battles during the Mexican War. From 1848 to the outbreak of the Civil War he worked quietly at his profession in Burlington; then organized a company, of which he became captain, and joined the Sixth Iowa Infantry. The 6th of April, 1862, while leading his company to action in the fierce battle at Shiloh, Tenn., he lost his right arm; but nothing daunted the brave descendant of the Goths, and shortly afterward Brydolf was promoted to lieutenant-colonel of the Twenty-fifth Iowa Infantry. He served in that regiment until the capture of Vicksburg, Miss., in 1863, when he resigned, and President Lincoln commissioned him lieutenant-colonel of the Second Regiment of the Veteran Reserve Corps, and he served in that capacity until 1886. Since the close of the war Brydolf has devoted his time to painting, working with his left hand. An historian, speaking of Col. Brydolf, says: 'He was a brave and gallant officer, always ready to lead

where he expected his men to follow. He has served his
adopted country faithfully in two important wars, and his
empty sleeve bears testimony to his bravery and fidelity to
his duty. His success as an artist in later years of his life is
all the more remarkable when we consider that he is obliged
to do the work with the left hand. His eye is keen, his taste
excellent, and his skill with the brush remarkable, when we
think how late in life the left hand was trained to work.'
In 1850 he was married to Fannie West, an English lady,
who died several years ago. They had seven children, a
few of whom are living yet.

Burnquist, Sam., legislator—Dayton—born 16 Sept.,
1849, in Broddetorp, Vestergötland, Sweden; died 8 Jan.,
1895. He was the youngest of a family of seven children.
Being brought up on the farm, he was accustomed to hard
work; but the poverty of his parents prevented him from
enjoying any better means of education than that afforded
by the parish school. What he lacked in schooling, however, was made up for by a strong will and an upright character. In 1864 he emigrated to America in company with
his brother John, and they soon found profitable employment at Andover, Ill. In the course of one year they saved
nough money to pay for the passage of their parents to this
country, and in 1866 they purchased eighty acres of land
near Dayton and settled on the same. In 1868 their crops
were destroyed by the grasshoppers, and Sam. started for
Ft. Dodge in hopes of obtaining work on the railroad. On
his way he stopped in Dayton, and asked the leading merchant
of the town if he could have a pair of boots on credit. The
merchant eyed him as though he was capable of judging the

character of the poor man before him, and answered, "no."
Burnquist then repeated his request to Geo. Porter, who
kept a small store in the same town; and the reply was a
prompt "yes." This kindness was never forgotten, and the
friendship then formed lasted until Porter's death After
repeated disappointments, Burnquist obtained work and
returned late in the fall with a new suit of clothes on his
back and one hundred dollars in his pocket. He next made
quite a reputation for breaking prairie land, and at the same
time saved enough money to give him the first substantial
start in a financial way. In 1875 he and his brother sold
their farm property and went into business in Dayton.
Year after year their business was enlarged, and some ten
years ago they dissolved the firm, Sam. continuing the business in his own name. To accommodate this, he erected a
new brick block, the most elegant of its kind in the whole
town. It did not take the people of Dayton long to find out
that Burnquist was a public-spirited as well as an absolutely
trustworthy man. Accordingly, they bestowed upon him
the highest honor in the gift of the town by electing him
mayor for a period of eight years. He also served as a
member of the board of township trustees for six years. In
the fall of 1893 he was nominated for representative to the
legislature from Webster county by the Republicans, and
though the county is regarded as strongly Democratic, he
was elected by a handsome majority over his opponent.
During the campaign Burnquist was called "the most popular man in Webster county." In the legislature he was
appointed chairman of the committee to visit the School for
the Deaf, and served as a member of several other com-

mittees. Burnquist's family belonged to the Augustana Synod, and he was a prominent member of the order of Freemasons. At his death he left a wife and two children.

Cassel, Peter, pioneer—New Sweden (post office, Four Corners)—born 1791, in Åsby, Östergötland, Sweden; died 1857. His ancestors had come from Germany and settled in Sweden in the sixteenth or seventeenth century. In his native land he had been a miller as well as a manufacturer of a kind of threshing machine, propelled by the hand, which he had invented and patented. Cassel, no doubt, was a man of energy and mental vigor, although his education had been limited. He could read and write, that was all; but it must be remembered that to be able to do this in those early days was an accomplishment which only a few of the peasants in Sweden had acquired. Captain P. von Schniedau—who was one of the pioneers at Pine Lake, Wis., who have been so admirably described by Rev. G. Unonius in his *Minnen*—had written to his father in Kisa, Östergötland, who was a prominent man, concerning this country. It might in this connection not be out of place to remark, that the most of the Swedish adventurers and fugitives from justice at Pine Lake had received an excellent education in their native land; and although they were unable and unfit to clear the woods in Wisconsin, or directly to be of much account in a new country, yet indirectly they did much in making America known in Sweden. This might serve as a good lesson for that school which looks to the lower strata of society for the originators of great popular movements. The contents of these letters became known among the common people, who at once became interested in America, and a few of the

bolder of them decided to emigrate in order to improve their
economical conditions.   Cassel was then nearly fifty-five
years of age, yet he concluded to take his family with him,
and settle in the American wilderness.   He became, in 1845,
the leader of twenty-five emigrants, mostly farmers, some of
whom had their families with them.   They secured a passage
on a sailing-vessel from Gothenburg to New York for about
$20.00 each, being eight weeks on the ocean.   They seemed
to have had a joyous time, playing and dancing on the deck
during the week days, and attending divine service on the
Sabbaths, the captain of the ship officiating as their religious
instructor.   Besides those people from Kisa, there were on
the vessel about ten other persons from different parts of
Sweden, including some noblemen, and four of the ten had
been several years in America before.   Originally the party
had intended to settle in Wisconsin, probably at Pine Lake,
which place the Swedish adventurers there had, through
correspondences, made known in Sweden, but they decided
to go to Iowa instead.   From New York to Philadelphia
they traveled on railroad, and from the latter place to Pittsburg on canal boats, which part of the time were wheeled
on the railroad tracks.   They sailed, or rather plodded, on
the Ohio river from Pittsburg to the Mississippi, and on that
up towards Burlington, Iowa; where, according to the
assertion of one of Cassel's sons, they met a Dane, who had
a drug store in the village, and who had been in America
some time previously, which goes to prove that the Scandinavians were among the very first pioneers in the Western
states.   Others of the party, however, maintain that no
Dane was met at Burlington, but they remembered having

slept in a museum in Cincinnati which belonged to a Swede or a Dane by the name of *Natt och Dag*. This is probably the same concern which is referred to in the first volume, page 294, in *Minnen*, by Unonius. He claims that an ex.-officer of the Swedish army conducted a kind of museum in Cincinnati, consisting of several curiosities, and among other things exhibited an artificial infernal region, which attracted a great deal of attention, and on which the proprietor became wealthy. At times the owner employed Swedes to manage the thunder and lightning, the falling of brimstone and the movement of evil spirits, as well as to clean the lamps in Gehenna; and in that place he, perhaps, permitted the Swedish immigrants to remain over night. Nearly all immigrants from Kisa settled at New Sweden, Jefferson county, thus becoming the founders of, virtually, the very first Scandinavian settlement in Iowa, and of the first permanent Swedish settlement of any importance in America in the nineteenth century; where also the first Swedish Lutheran church organization was effected by Rev. M. F. Hokanson three years later. Cassel wrote several letters to his native land, and in that way induced many more to cast the die in favor of the "land of the free and the home of the brave." During the religious confusion among the Swedish Americans in the first half of this century, the pious and enthusiastic J. Hedstrom, the learned and ceremonious G. Unonius, the bold and unscrupulous F. O. Nilson, endeavored to convince the Swedes in this country that only by joining the Methodists, Episcopalians, or Baptists, respectively, could they expect to gain salvation in the next world and happiness in this. Cassel, who had, of course, been brought up a Lutheran and had always been a very religious and temperate man, joined the Methodists; and later in life preached occasionally in the interest of that denomination.

Ericson, C. J. A., banker and state senator—Boone—born 8 March, 1840, in Södra Vi, Småland, Sweden. At the age of twelve he came to America with his parents, who were among the early Swedish settlers of Rock Island county, Ill. Young Ericson worked on his brother's farm, besides being engaged in other kinds of common labor until 1855, when he removed to Altona, Knox county, Ill. In 1859 he settled at Ridgeport, Boone county, Iowa, thus becoming one of the Swedish pioneers of that part of the country. In this connection it may be proper to mention that the first white settlers of Boone county located there in 1843, while some Swedes arrived there in 1846 and settled at Swede Point in the same county. Among the latter were four men by the name of Dalander. Ericson was engaged in the merchandise business at Rridgeport for a number of years; served also as postmaster of the village for twelve years; and held various other positions of trust and honor. In 1870 he removed to Boone and began to follow the same line of business as before. Ericson was one of the organizers of the First National Bank of Boone, and for some time its vice-president. In 1878, this bank having voluntarily surrendered its charter, the City Bank was organized by him and others, the capital stock being $50,000, and the surplus accumulated by the bank now amounts to $150,000. Ericson has been the cashier as well as the actual manager of this bank ever since it was started. He is also interested in other business enterprises, and owns a great deal of city and farm property. In 1871 Ericson was elected a representative to the state legislature, and to the state senate in 1895, being the first Swede who occupied a seat in these bodies. Ericson has held various local positions of trust in the city of Boone, such as those of president and treasurer of the school board, city treasurer, and member of the city council. In 1894 Ericson and his daughter made an extensive tour of the Old World, visiting Spain, Italy, Egypt, Palestine, Turkey, Greece, Switzerland, France, Belgium, Germany, England, Denmark, Norway, and Sweden. He had not seen his native country in forty-two years. As to politics, Ericson affiliates with the Republican party. He is a prominent Freemason, and a member of the Presbyterian church. For years he has been a member of the board of trustees as well as treasurer of his home congregation. Ericson is very popular in his own county and in the state. In 1895 Judge Stevens publicly said: "More than forty years ago there came to this county a barefooted Swedish boy with a brave heart, a good brain, and willing hands. He came fully resolved to make a true American, and if ability and willingness to labor intelligently for the best interest of his country makes a good citizen, then he stands a model. Like every true-hearted man, he never forgot the land of his birth. No poor emigrant from his native land ever appealed to him in vain, but his liberality and charity are too broad to be confined to his own nationality." He was extensively and favorably recommended by the leading men in the state, as well as outside of the state, in 1897 for the appointment of minister to Sweden-Norway. In 1873

Ericson was married to Nillie Linderblad, of Princeton, Ill. In 1899 he gave over $12,000 to Augustana College.

Hatlestad, O. J., clergyman and author—Decorah—born 30 Sept., 1823, in Skjold, near Stavanger, Norway; died in 1891. His grandfather, who had been a personal friend of Hans Nilsen Hauge, the great lay preacher and national evangelist of Norway, had charge of the education of the subject of this sketch. The religious instruction thus received made a lasting impression upon the mind of young Hatlestad, and before he was confirmed he resolved to devote his life to the service of his Redeemer. At one time he seriously thought of going to Africa as a missionary; but this plan had to be given up, and for several years he taught the parish school of Nerstrand. In 1846, Hatlestad, in company with his parents, brothers, and a sister, left for America, and after a ten weeks' voyage arrived in New York. They settled at Muskego, Wis., the same year. In 1847 Hatlestad obtained a position as teacher at Jefferson Prairie; but removed in 1850 to Racine, where he, in company with his brother-in-law, Knud Langeland, published *Nordlyset*, the first Norwegian paper published in this country. While here, Hatlestad began to conduct the devotional exercises of a limited circle of friends; but the attendance increased, until a church was organized, O. Andrewson being its first pastor. In the fall of 1853 Hatlestad quite unexpectedly received a call from the Norwegian Lutheran church at Leland, La Salle county, Ill.; and he was licensed to preach by a joint meeting of the Chicago and the Mississippi Evangelical Lutheran Conference at Chicago in January, 1854. A few months later he removed to Leland, and was formally ordained the next

year. The congregation was small, and the salary at first
amounted to about $200 a year. Hatlestad served the
congregation for five years, during which period it enjoyed a
healthy and vigorous growth. In 1859 he removed to Milwaukee, where he spent sixteen and a half years of hard and
almost ceaseless labor. Indeed, so onerous was his position
as a preacher at this flood-gate of Scandinavian immigration, that his health was impaired; and this was the chief
reason why he left his "dear Milwaukee" in 1876. Having
spent the next two years in Forest City Iowa, he accepted a
call from a church near Decorah, where he remained until his
death. For twenty years Hatlestad was the most conspicuous figure in the Norwegian Augustana Synod, which
he served as president from 1870 to 1880, and again from
1888 to 1890, said body being merged into the United Norwegian Lutheran Church at the latter date. He was also
editor of *Luthersk Kirketidende* for a number of years.
In 1887 he published *Historiske Meddelelser om den Norske
Augustana Synode*, which is not only a history of the Norwegian Augustana Synod, but also touches upon the history
of the other Norwegian-American Lutheran churches, as
well as on the settlements. It was the most complete Norwegian-American history that had appeared. In 1848
Hatlestad married Aasa L. Landru. They had eight children, two of whom are James Hatlestad, attorney-at-law,
Canton, S. D., and Joseph Hatlestad, president of Gulf
Coast College, Handsboro, Miss.

Hokanson, Magnus Fredrik, clergyman and pioneer—
Munterville—born 7 Sept., 1811, in Ronneby, Blekinge,
Sweden; died 2 Jan., 1893. His father, whose education

had been very limited, was a shoe-maker in the village, and
he compelled his son to learn the same craft early in life; but
young Hokanson, who evinced an intense religious enthusiasm even as a child, was far more anxious to attend to the
welfare of men's souls than to mend their soles. He desired
to become a clergyman in the state church; his father
objected. The young man consulted a clergyman in the
neighborhood; no encouragement. In this perplexity,
Hokanson left his native town and went to Stockholm,
where he worked in a shoe establishment, owned by an
educated man who sympathized with Hokanson's endeavor
to secure a better education than he had, in order to become
a minister. With this object in view, Hokanson consulted
various leading divines in the Swedish capital, but to no
avail. He had only received a common school education,
and before he could study theology, his mental faculties had
to be trained. After the Foreign Mission Society in London,
England, to which Hokanson had appealed, had refused to
accept his services, he decided to go to the extreme northern
part of Sweden and try to convert the Lapps. But during
his preparation for the Lappish mission, a friend of his, an
influential man in Stockholm, advised him to "stick to his
last" and remain in the capital, and this man promised to
introduce him to a respectable and wealthy young lady; and
thus, his friend argued, his happiness would be secured, and
his anxiety would vanish. This argument was too tempt-
ing even for the would-be clergyman, who had also become
tired of his many adversities. He acted upon this advice;
won the affection of the young lady; but the parents refused
to give their consent to the partnership until he had proved

C. J. A. ERICSON, BOONE.

P. W. CHANTLAND, FORT DODGE.   PROF. A. E. EGGE, IOWA CITY.

E. P. JOHNSON, DECORAH.   B. L. WICK, CEDAR RAPIDS.

to be a successful business man, which he failed to do, and the engagement contract was dissolved. On account of business failure, disappointed hopes, and unsuccessful love, he had become mentally and spiritually depressed. But at this time a friend of his accompanied him, in 1847, to the New World, and paid for his passage. It is proper, however, to remark that Hokanson later settled in full for the expense incurred during the voyage. The same year he reached the colony at New Sweden, Jefferson county, Iowa, which had been founded a couple of years before —— for a more complete description of this early and important settlement, see Peter Cassel's biography in this volume. But Hokanson, who was used to comfortable accommodations in Stockholm, could not and would not endure the hardships of pioneer life. He sold some of his clothes and effects, and intended to return to New York; but during the journey he became sick; lost the trunk which contained his clothes and money, and as a consequence was compelled to stop in St. Louis, Mo. Being unable to speak the English language, he could secure no work; and for seven days he lived on apples, picked up on the streets, and washed in the Mississippi river. During the nights he slept in an open shed. In other words, he was a tramp, but his Northern sense of independence deterred him from begging. By selling his only coat, he secured enough means to return to Burlington, Iowa, and soon recovered all his effects in good condition. His health was broken down, and, being unable to work, he, after a few months' stay in Burlington, decided to return to New Sweden, where board and other necessary expenses were lower than in towns and villages. It was at this place that

45

Hokanson, then about thirty-seven years of age, commenced his life-work. Although he was neither learned nor brilliant, yet, from an historical standpoint, he is an important character. He organized, in 1848, the first Swedish Lutheran congregation in America, in the nineteenth century; and since the Swedish Augustana Synod, with which this congregation is connected, undoubtedly has exercised a greater influence upon the Swedish-American people than all other spiritual and intellectual forces combined, it will be necessary and useful to minutely discuss the attempts of Hokanson to instruct his countrymen in the faith of their fathers. In the first place, Rev. E. Norelius, the historian of the Augustana Synod, says, in *Ev. Lutherska Augustana Synoden i Nord-Amerika*, page 15: "The people of New Sweden united themselves into a Lutheran congregation in 1848, and made use of the privilege of the church of God in selecting one of the multitude to become their instructor and to administer the sacraments"; adding, in a foot-note, that this procedure was a case of necessity, and not recommendable under ordinary circumstances. But the same author in his larger history, published in 1890 (which has been extensively consulted in the preparation of Hokanson's biography), claims that there was no formal church organization in 1848; but that the young people were confirmed, the sacraments administered, the Swedish church ritual used, and the pioneers considered themselves as members of the Lutheran church in Sweden. Secondly, the church reports of the Augustana Synod have annually, for very nearly forty years, asserted that the church organization at New Sweden was effected in 1850. Partly on account of these conflicting statements, the editor of this work made a special visit to New Sweden in the summer of 1894, and with the kind assistance of Rev. C. J. Bengston, the following facts were deduced from the old church books and records, as well as through conversation with several of the men who had been there since the settlement was established in 1845: I. The early pioneers in New Sweden appear to have been extremely moderate in their virtues as well as in their vices. They were not very religious, nor irreligious. But after Hokanson's arrival, he succeeded in arousing a spiritual awakening among them, so that they commenced to feel the need of attending devotional exercises, of partaking of the Lord's Supper, and of having their children brought up under religious influences. It is true, that now and then an American clergyman, or itinerant evangelist, visited the settlement; but most of the Swedish people could not understand English. It was under such circumstances that Hokanson, in 1848, was requested to lead in religious meetings, administer the sacraments, and baptize and confirm the children. At the church parsonage, there are no records of any description that a church was ever organized at New Sweden. But in the church record, compiled by Rev. Håkan Olson in 1859, two persons are registered as having joined in 1848, and five names are entered for 1849. II. Whether this unpretentious organization was formal or not, depends entirely upon the definition of the word *formal*. That the proceedings were not so regular and solemn as the rituals of the Lutheran state church of Sweden, in such cases, prescribe, or that parliamentary rules of order were as closely observed as when the United States Congress con-

venes, could hardly be expected in this instance, when most
of the participants were barely able to read and write. Yet
the organization was unquestionably legal. For according
to the civil law of the land, any set of persons, capable of
making a contract, may engage another to be their religious
instructor, and to perform all the religious ceremonies in
concordance with their belief; and this will be considered a
lawful church organization. But another question arises.
Was the organization of this congregation in conformity
with the discipline of the Lutheran church? Rev. E. Norelius, in *Korsbaneret* for 1894, says: "The manner of calling
Hokanson was simple, natural, and correct." Nor is there
anything in the fundamental doctrines of Lutheranism to
prove that the pioneers at New Sweden did not act in
accordance with the creed of the church in selecting a layman as their clergyman, when no ordained minister could be
secured. In fact, they could by imposition of hands have ordained Hokanson, and no Lutheran church body would have
re-ordained him. Lutheranism, properly interpreted, consists
in unity of faith more than anything else. But it must be
admitted that this is, perhaps, the only instance in the world
where a Lutheran congregation has been organized in such
a democratic manner. III. It has been claimed that Prof.
L. P. Esbjörn re-organized the church when he visited the
settlement in 1851; but this is highly improbable, as neither
Esbjörn himself nor Norelius, in any of their writings, mentions the fact, although both of them speak at length concerning the religious condition at New Sweden. On the contrary,
the former urged Hokanson and his congregation to con-
tinue as they had begun, and to remain true Lutherans, and

Dr. C. M. Esbjorn claims that several Swedish-American Lutheran churches have
had a similar origin as the church at New Sweden. He also maintains that documen-
taly evidence can be produced from his father's writings to prove that his father effected a permanent. or regular, church organisation at New Sweden April 27. 1851.—EDITOR.

he made no attempt to re-confirm any of the five children whom Hokanson had confirmed in 1848. According to Norelius' history, Esbjörn promised to attend to the necessary requirements, that the church might join some Lutheran synod. Esbjörn probably assisted the pioneers in selecting deacons and trustees. It was also then decided to build a church. Norelius, in his large history, page 93, says: "In 1853 Prof. T. N. Hasselquist visited the settlements and further assisted Hokanson in the arrangement of church matters, when also a kind of constitution was adopted"; and five years later a new constitution was adopted.

Hokanson, who had reluctantly consented to lead the pioneers at their devotional exercises, was soon forced to become an unwilling participant in fierce religious strifes and fanatical controversies, in which sectarianism rather than religion seems to have been the main object of some of his opponents. In 1849 the well-known Rev. G. Unonius, Episcopalian, visited the settlement; and, being a strong believer in the Apostolic succession, he, of course could not, nor did he, endorse Hokanson's course. The next year Rev. Jonas Hedstrom, Methodist, arrived upon the scene, and soon succeeded in convincing a large number of the people that they could attain human and divine perfection upon this wicked earth of ours if they joined his denomination. He condemned all the Lutheran forms and practices of worship, and endeavored to convert Hokanson to Methodism, but failed. As, however, more than half of Hokanson's congregation had become Methodists, he was worried and depressed, and in the presence of Hedstrom resigned. After Hedstrom's departure from the settlement, the remaining

Lutherans again requested Hokanson to act as their leader; but he declined, recommending an older member. The people proceeded to vote for the two candidates. Hokanson was elected. But not satisfied with this, he proposed that they cast lots, which they did, proceeding in accordance with the first chapter of the Acts of the Apostles, which describes the manner of choosing a successor to Judas Iscariot. The lot fell upon Hokanson, and he then again consented to take charge of the congregation. In 1854 Revs. G. Palmquist and F. O. Nilson, Baptists, came to New Sweden—Nilson's biogrophy can be found in the first volume. Hokanson had known the former in Sweden as a pietistic Lutheran, and it is claimed that at first Palmquist did not tell any one in the settlement of his change of faith. In the hands of the refined and polished Palmquist, and of the bold and unscrupulous Nilson, the weak and confiding Hokanson became a mere plaything. He wavered, again resigned his charge, and was immersed. Hasselquist, who had heard of Hokanson's vacillation, hastened to the settlement, and met him and others just as they were proceeding towards the river to immerse Hokanson. Hasselquist politely asked them where they were going; they told him; he kindly blessed them, and calmly went into the house and conversed with Mrs. Hokanson. It would be interesting to know the contents of the conversation which occurred between these two men, after Hokanson's return to his house. He was re-converted to Lutheranism in a few hours. The liberal views of Hasselquist were amply illustrated by the fact that he permitted Hokanson to remain as the pastor of the congregation, without any re-ordination whatsoever.

Through the influence of Esbjörn, Hokanson had received a
license to preach from the Joint Synod of Ohio, in 1851, and
$70 in cash; and was ordained by the Lutheran Synod of
Northern Illinois two years later, at Galesburg. Up to 1858
Hokanson was the only Swedish Lutheran clergyman in
Iowa, having charge of five congregations, located in as
many different counties. His churches in Burlington and
Swede Bend, Webster county, were exactly one hundred and
seventy-five miles apart in a straight line. Considering that
there was hardly a bridge, or even a path, in the whole state
at that time, Hokanson's ministerial comforts can be better
imagined than described. In 1856 he left New Sweden and
moved to Munterville; settled at what is now Madrid three
years later; but returned to Munterville in 1862, where he
lived and preached for nearly thirty years. The last two or
three years of his eventful life he spent with his adopted
daughter at Red Oak, where he died. He was buried at
Munterville. Hokanson was married in 1848 to Anna E.
Anderson, from Horn, Östergötland. They had no children.

Jacobsen, Jacob D., educator—Decorah—born 16 July,
1842, near Skien, Norway; died 1 April, 1881. His parents
emigrated to America when he was less than one year old,
and settled at Pine Lake, Wis. Their pastor, N. Brandt, in
the course of time discovered unusual talents in the boy,
who, by the assistance of Brandt and his congregation, was
enabled to enter Concordia College and Seminary, in St.
Louis, Mo., in the fall of 1858. Here he pursued his studies
uninterruptedly until the spring of 1861, his expenses being
largely defrayed by Brandt's congregations. Jacobsen next
studied a few months at Concordia College, Ft. Wayne, Ind.,

but soon returned to St. Louis, where he remained until the spring of 1863. In the fall of 1863, he was employed as assistant professor at Luther College, Decorah; then studied one year at the same place; and again entered Concordia College, Ft. Wayne, finishing his collegiate course and graduating in 1867. Having completed a regular theological course in the Concordia Seminary, in St. Louis, he graduated in 1870. He was ordained for the ministry the same year, and in 1872 accepted a professorship at Luther College, which position he held until his death. Jacobsen was very successful as a teacher. "He was capable of teaching about all the branches comprised in the college course; and the choicest productions of the great authors, he had read either in the original or in translations." He married Guro Ingebrigtsen in 1871; they had four children.

Koren, Ulrik Vilhelm, clergyman and pioneer—Decorah—born 22 Dec., 1826, in Bergen, Norway. He received a college education in his native city, and in 1852 was graduated as a cand. theol. from the University of Norway. Having accepted a call as minister from congregations near Decorah, he emigrated to America in 1853. Although Koren has received numerous calls from other churches, he has remained where he first located. Being the first Norwegian Lutheran minister who permanently settled west of the Mississippi, his charge at first comprised an extensive territory, which since has been divided into a large number of charges. Koren was one of the pioneers of the West, and as such experienced all the hardships characteristic of early settlements. In this connection it is only proper to mention that Koren has been instrumental in drawing a highly desirable class of emigrants from his native country to the northeastern part of Iowa and the southeastern part of Minnesota. Rev. A. Bredesen says of Koren: " The task that confronted him was one before which a weaker, or less devoted, man would have quailed. His parish proper was about fifty by forty miles in extent, and his mission field was all northeastern Iowa and southeastern Minnesota. Passable roads were few, and much of the traveling between the widely scattered settlements must be done on horseback or on foot. There were difficulties, hardships, and privations of every description to overcome or endure. But Koren was the right man for the post. A man of European university education, and accustomed to mingle in the most cultured society of the fatherland, with his equally refined helpmate, he took up his abode in a rude log cabin a few miles from the present city of Decorah, and with an heroism born of a strong faith devoted himself to his life-work, the building-up of the Church of the Reformation among his scattered and destitute countrymen in those western wilds." Since 1861 he has served as a member of the executive committee of the Norwegian Lutheran Synod; from 1876, when the synod was divided into districts, to 1894, as president of the Iowa District; and from the latter date as president of the whole synod. Koren secured the land on which Luther College was established, and, with the exception of President Larsen, no man has done more than he toward making that institution what it is. His culture and solid attainments, his unflagging interest in the institutions of the synod, his enthusiasm and earnestness, his versatility in advocating what he has conceived to be the truth, and his

untiring perseverance, have made him one of the most conspicuous of Norwegian Lutherans in this country. He has
written much for the religious papers of the synod, and is
the author of: *Vore Kirkelige Modstanderes Vaaben*, *Kan
og bör en Kristen vaere vis paa sin Salighed*, *Hvad den
Norske Synode har villet og fremdeles vil*, *De Kirkelige Par-
tier blandt vort Folk i Amerika*, and other pamphlets, which
are contributions to the controversies which have agitated
the Norwegian Lutheran churches in this country, also containing much, especially the last named, of great historical
value. *Det Gamle Hus* is a poem about that schism in the
synod which led to the withdrawal of the Anti-Missourians
during the eighties. His most lasting literary work is his
contribution to the new hymn book of the synod. His gifts
as a preacher, and his conscientious devotion to his duties,
have won for him the lasting esteem and love of his parishioners; his alertness and readiness for any emergency, his
calmness in adversity and prosperity alike, have made him
a tower of strength in the Norwegian Synod. And if any
man, above all others, deserves the title of defender of the
principles and the practices of the Norwegian Synod,
that man is Ulrick Vilhelm Koren. He married Else Elisa-
beth Hysing, of Larvik, Norway, in 1853; they have had
eight children. One of his sons is also a minister in the
Norwegian Synod, and another is a prominent statistician.

Larsen, Laur., educator—Decorah—born 10 Aug., 1833,
in Kristiansand, Norway. "I was born on the same day as
the town organization of Chicago was perfected," said Larsen in a talk to the students of Luther College a few years
ago. "My father was the youngest of twelve brothers and

sisters, and yet I have scarcely any relatives on my father's side." His mother's father, Oftedahl, was a member of the convention of Eidsvold, which framed the constitution of Norway. Larsen further says: "My parents were married 17 Sept., 1832, and I attended their golden wedding in 1882." Larsen's father was an officer in the army, and his income was so small that the family had to practice the strictest economy to make both ends meet. Larsen was exactly nine years old when he entered the Latin school of his native city, and the instruction he received there was certainly of a high grade. "Upon the whole," he says, "I must consider it fortunate that I received a very good school education. Most of my instructors were able men, the classes were small, and we were more isolated from the disturbances of the world than the students of the present day are, or can be." Even as a school-boy, Larsen gave unmistakable evidence of conscientiousness and a strong will. Once, some of his school-mates tempted him to begin to smoke cigars. He soon regretted this, and decided never to touch tobacco again until he became a man, and he kept his promise to the letter. Larsen was enthusiastically devoted to athletic sports, and particularly distinguished himself as an expert swimmer. That these exercises did not interfere with his studies, is demonstrated by the fact that his standing, at the examinations for the degree of A. B., was 1—which virtually equals 100 in this country—for all languages. Upon entering the University of Norway, at Kristiania, in 1850, Larsen rented a room scarcely 8 x 8 feet, for which he paid $2.00 a month; and his expenses were kept correspondingly low in other lines. But a new and rich world was

opened to his mind, and so intensely did the young man
apply himself to his studies that his health began to fail.
He was compelled to leave the university, and spent the first
months of the year 1851 as private tutor at the house of
his uncle, Rev. Bassöe, of Raade. This enabled him to save
some money, and he re-entered the university in the fall.
But his funds were soon completely exhausted, and he had to
earn his living by teaching in schools or private families.
For some time he gave two private lessons every afternoon
for a consideration of $6.00 per month. Larsen received his
degree as cand. theol. in June, 1855, after having devoted
three and one-half years to theological studies. After this
he continued to teach in Kristiania, his favorite branches
being French, German, and Hebrew. But from childhood he
had made up his mind to serve as a minister of the gospel,
and with that aim in view he emigrated to the New World in
1857. He served as pastor of a congregation near Rush
River, Pierce county, Wis., until the Norwegian Synod, on
14. Oct., 1859, called him as its theological professor at Concordia Seminary, St. Louis, Mo. The Norwegian Synod, at
its annual meeting at Rock Prairie, Wis., in the summer of
1861, decided to build a college of its own. Accordingly, a
school was opened the same year in the Halfway Creek parsonage, thirteen miles from La Crosse. Larsen was
appointed principal of the school, which was removed to
Decorah, Iowa, the next year, and has since been known as
Luther College. As Larsen has been at the head of this college from its beginning until now, his subsequent biography
and the history of the school are intimately interwoven.
The accommodations at Halfway Creek were so limited that

the office of the president had to be utilized as sick-chamber for the students, and another room served both as sitting-room and bed-chamber for him and his family. The professors and their families dined with the students, and all the inmates of the building became accustomed to look upon themselves as members of the same family. And they all agree that those days were some of the happiest and most beautiful in their lives. After the removal to Decorah, larger quarters were secured; but the reputation of the school was such that in a year or two many applicants for admission had to be turned away for lack of room. Hence a magnificent brick structure was erected during the years 1864–65, and the formal dedication of it occurred on 14 Oct., 1865. Great numbers, even from distant congregations, came to attend the dedication exercises. With surprise they witnessed the grandeur and beauty of the new building. About six thousand people attended the ceremonies, and the occasion marked an epoch in the history of the Norwegian Lutheran churches in America. The building cost $75,000. In view of the comparative poverty of the congregations which had to raise the funds, this amount was large, and no one knows better than the president of the college how difficult it was at times to save the whole plan from temporary collapse, to say the least. "It often happened," he says, "that on a Saturday we did not know whence the $1,000 were to come wherewith the numerous laborers were to be paid on the following Monday." The attendance at the college steadily increased, and in a couple of years the whole building was occupied. Nine years later an addition was built. In 1889 the main college building was destroyed

by fire, but at the meetings of the three districts of the synod
the same year, it was resolved immediately to rebuild it.
The next year it was again completed at a cost of $56,000.
Larsen has always enjoyed the utmost confidence of the
synod, and the devotion of many of its members to the college was once expressed by an aged clergyman in these
words: "I am sure I have offered up as many prayers for
Luther College as there are bricks in the building." In the
fall of 1884 Larsen had served the synod as a professo
uninterruptedly for a quarter of a century, and the event
was fittingly commemorated at Luther College. On 22 Oct.
some three hundred students and other friends of Larsen,
including many of the ministers of the synod, gave vent to
their feelings of gratitude and devotion by demonstrations
of various kinds, and in the evening Larsen was the recipient
of several valuable presents. As to Larsen's work at Luther
College, *The Midland Monthly*, June, 1894, says: "The
amount of work he has performed, and to a great extent is
still performing, will be better appreciated when it is stated
that his duties as president alone have comprised what in
many colleges is distributed among the offices of president,
registrar, and dean, and, inasmuch as Luther College is a
boarding school, also a general supervision of the students'
conduct." And yet Larsen finds time to do all his work
thoroughly. Not only is his private work performed with
the minutest care; but every public duty assigned to him is
discharged with the same conscientious painstaking, the
same scrupulous exactness. This characteristic undoubtedly
furnishes the main key to the reputation of Luther College
as an institution of learning. It is at least certain that

Luther College has a far better standing among our great institutions of learning than has any other of the advanced Norwegian schools in this country. Larsen has also performed a large amount of work not connected with the college. While the college was located at Halfway Creek, he served as pastor of five congregations in and around La Crosse, besides preaching at Trempealeau and Beaver Creek, during the Christmas and Easter vacations. After having removed to Decorah, Larsen at first preached regularly every other Sunday, and afterwards was called as regular pastor of a new congregation in Decorah. In 1865 he was relieved of this duty, but still for many years continued to preach on two Sundays out of every three. In 1882 the Decorah congregation called Larsen as its pastor, which position he held for some time. Since 1890 he has not been connected with any church as pastor, though he still continues to preach occasionally. In 1868 Larsen was appointed editor-in-chief of *Kirkelig Maanedstidende*, the official organ of the synod, and held the position until January, 1889. As a member of the most important boards and committees in the synod, he has directly exerted a powerful influence upon the history of that body, and from 1876 to 1893 was its vice-president. Most of the clergymen serving in the Norwegian Synod today, as well as several other Norwegian-American Lutheran ministers, have completed their literary studies at Luther College; and since Larsen became president of the institution up to 1897, about three hundred persons—including clergymen, lawyers, physicians, authors, journalists, etc.—have graduated from the college. Besides, there has been many times that number who have attended the school without completing any regular course of study; and Larsen has, unquestionably, been able to stamp his individuality upon the educated Norwegian-Americans to a greater extent than any other person, living or dead. In 1855 Larsen was married to Karen Neuberg. She died in 1871, leaving him with four children. The next year he was married to Ingeborg Astrup, by whom he has had ten children. In 1895 he lost his oldest son, who, a year before, had entered upon a promising practice as physician in Texas.

Linn, John, clergyman and pioneer—Dayton—born 29 May, 1826, in Dödringhult, Småland, Sweden. He emigrated in 1849 and, after much suffering, settled at Swede Bend, Webster county, Iowa, which was then a wilderness. While log huts were being put up for the winter, Linn and his wife took up temporary quarters under the trunk of a basswood tree which had been felled so that its butt end rested on the stump! They were among the earliest settlers of Webster county, and it is claimed that their daughter Julia was the first white child born in that county, her birthday being 8 Jan., 1851. Meat was plenty in those days. Professional hunters were in the habit of taking only the hind quarters of the deer, leaving the rest of the carcasses; wild turkeys were so abundant that Linn one winter caught dozens of them by a peculiar trap; and he was engaged by a Boone county farmer to catch a lot of hogs which had been running at large until they were practically wild, Linn receiving one-half of the hogs for his trouble. The distance to the nearest reliable grist-mill was so great that Linn constructed a hand-mill on which a strong man could grind two bushels of corn in a day, and this for some time was a great

REV. M. F. HOKANSON, MUNTERVILLE.

REV. L. HOLMES, BURLINGTON.

REV. U. V. KOREN, DECORAH.

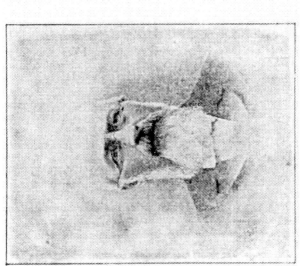

PROF. LAUR. LARSEN, DECORAH.

boon to the neighborhood. These mill-stones may still be seen in the foundation of William Linn's house, at Pilot Mound, Boone county. Salt cost ten cents a pound; but, on the other hand, maple sugar was abundant, and Linn, in company with another man, gathered three barrels of wild honey in one week! In 1853 a man tried to sell eighty acres of land, where the city of Des Moises now stands, to Linn for $320; but the latter declined the offer, looking upon the price as excessive. Linn for years tended to his work as a common farmer, without paying any extraordinary attention to religious matters. But in the spring of 1854 he was aroused to an unusual degree by Gustaf Smith, a Methodist preacher; a church was organized, and Linn became its first member and exhorter the following year, though no licence to preach was given him until 1857. He now divided his time between the cares of his home church and the management of his farm. As road supervisor Linn acquired the title of "Swede King," by requiring the farmers of his district to work so long on the road that they received vouchers for the payment of their poll tax for the next ten years! In 1868 he accepted a call as pastor from a church in Moline, Ill., where he remained three years. He next served churches successively at Rockford and Galesburg, Ill.; and in 1874 was appointed presiding elder of the Iowa district, and removed to Des Moines. In 1877 he settled at Sheldahl, as presiding elder of the new Burlington district, and in the course of the next few years served charges at Sheldahl and Des Moines. His work in the capacity of presiding elder was most satisfactory, and in 1884 he raised $700 for the Swedish theological seminary at Evanston, Ill. In the fall of 1888 he removed to Dayton, in order to spend the eve of his life with his brothers. The native powers of Linn were of a high order; yet it seems strange that he could accomplish so much, considering that he never enjoyed a day's schooling, nor could even write his name until he was a grown man. In 1848 Linn was married to Mary Somberg, who died in 1853; and again to Mrs. Jacobsen in 1854. Linn had children in both wedlocks.

Lysnes David, clergyman and educator—Beloit—born 31 July, 1832, near Larvik, Norway; died 11 Aug., 1890. He lived and worked among the peasants of his neighborhood until he was nineteen years old, at which time he began to teach parochial school, and he continued uninterruptedly for seven years, his salary being $20.00 a year and room and board. In 1859–61 he completed a course at Asker Seminary, and afterwards taught three years at *Hans Kappelens Minde*, an orphans' home. at Skien; and four years at Kristiania. In 1868 he emigrated to America, and settled as pastor of a Norwegian congregation at Pontiac, Ill.; in 1870 removed to Decorah, Iowa, where he labored for eight years; and four years later was called as theological professor, by the Norwegian Augustana Synod, whose theological seminary was located successively near Decorah, at Marshall, Wis., and finally at Beloit. Lysnes worked in this capacity until the Augustana Synod was merged into the United Church, at Minneapolis, in 1890, when he was appointed one of the theological professors of that body. For some time he also served a church at Elk Point, S. D. Though Lysnes never had enjoyed the advantages of a classical training, his intellect was keen and powerful, and his personal influence upon his pupils and parishioners was marked. He was married in 1867 to Maren Andrea Heiret, of Eidsvold, Norway, who died in 1868; and in 1871 to Maren Jonetta Nas, of Asker, Norway. He had four children by his second wife.

Olsen, Johan, clergyman—St. Ansgar—born 3 July, 1834, in Bindalen, Tromsö stift, Norway. His parents had come under the influence of the great revival inaugurated by Hans Nilsen Hauge in the early part of this century, and the boy was brought up in a religious atmosphere. At an early age he evinced a keen taste for books, and more than once he would give vent to his religious feelings by preaching while herding cattle in the woods and mountains, his audience consisting of cows and sheep. But the boy was bound to rise. Though his opportunities for learning were meager indeed, he had learned enough to become a public school teacher at the age of fifteen. Three years later he entered the Tromsö normal school, and was graduated with honors in 1854. He next served as teacher and precentor at his home. In 1857 he was appointed principal of a higher school in Kaafjorden, where he remained two years. For some time he had cherished the desire of studying theology, and this desire at last became irresistible. In spite of the lack of means, he went to Kristiania for the purpose of fitting himself for the ministry. His life in the capital meant ceaseless work and privation. His patience and perseverance, however, overcame every obstacle, and he received the degrees of A. B. and Cand. Phil. in 1863 and 1864, respectively. The next two years were spent in studying theology. By this time his health was seriously impaired by over-work in studying and supporting his family.

now consisting of five persons. In 1866 Olsen emigrated to America, and was appointed adjunct professor of Hebrew and some other branches at Agustana College, Paxton, Ill. In 1867 he was ordained for the ministry by the well-known Prof. T. N. Hasselquist, and settled as pastor of a congregation at Neenah, Wis. Later he removed to Ft. Howard, and while here he organized many new congregations in the northeastern part of Wisconsin. Olsen was a prominent figure among those who organized the Norwegian-Danish Lutheran Conference at St. Ansgar, Ia., 16 Aug., 1870. He served this body as vice-president from 1870 to 1872, and as president from the latter date to 1881. Since 1873 he has resided at St. Ansgar, where he enjoys the esteem and love of his parisioners to an unusual degree. St. Ansgar Seminary and Institute was started in 1878, chiefly through the efforts of Olsen, and for years he has given lectures at that school. He was married in 1858, and has had eleven children, six of whom are still living. One of his sons, Sigurd Olsen, is a professor in St. Ansgar Seminary and Institute.

Ottesen, Jacob Aall, clergyman and pioneer—Decorah—born 1 June, 1825, in Fet, Kristiania stift, Norway. His father and grandfather were clergymen at his birthplace for fifty years previous, and more than forty of his relatives are, or have been, clergymen. Ottesen completed his theological studies at the University of Norway, and graduated with honors in 1849. Having spent three years as instructor in Kristiania, he emigrated to America in 1852. Upon the request of Ole Bull, the famous violinist, who had started a Norwegian colony at Oleana, Pa., Ottesen stopped at that

place and preached to his countrymen before going west.
He settled as pastor at Manitowoc, Wis., the same year, his
charge consisting of three organized congregations in and
about Manitowoc, and ten missionary stations located
along the lake shore from Green Bay to Milwaukee. He was
an exceedingly busy man in those days. His time was spent
in unceasing travel, mostly on horseback, and he would
cover from thirty to fifty miles a day. His exposure to all
kinds of weather resulted in a chronic rheumatism, which
ever since has reminded him of the hardships of those early
pioneer days. He was one of the seven clergymen who
organized the Norwegian Evangelical Lutheran Synod at
Koshkonong, Wis., in 1853, and for a number of years served
as secretary of that body. In 1857 Ottesen, together with
Rev. N. Brandt, was appointed a delegate of the synod to
visit the theological seminaries at St. Louis, Mo., Columbus,
O., and Buffalo, N. Y., with the view of finding a suitable
institution for the education of young Norwegians for the
ministry. The seminary at St. Louis was chosen, and Prof.
Laur. Larsen was appointed to represent the Norwegian
Synod in the theological faculty of that institution. In 1860
Ottesen moved to Koshkonong. Here he served as pastor
of the oldest church of the Norwegian Synod until his removal to Decorah in 1891. For a number of years Ottesen
was associate editor of *Kirkelig Maanedstidende*, the official organ of the synod. When the synod established Luther
Seminary at Madison, Wis., in 1878, he was requested to
serve as its first president, but declined. Later he served as
a member of the board of visitors of his district for a number of years. In 1893 Ottesen wrote *Kort Uddrag af den*

Norske Synodes Historie, which was exhibited at the World's Fair in Chicago the same year. As is indicated by the title, this work is brief; but it is one of the most correct and impartial histories of the Norwegian Synod written up to date. Since 1891, Ottesen has had no regular charge, but officiated from Nov., 1894, to Aug., 1896, as temporary pastor during a vacancy in the Norwegian church in Decorah. Rev. J. C. Jensson in his great work, *American Lutheran Biographies*, says of Ottesen: 'His classical training, keen reasoning powers, ability as writer and counsellor, and, above all, his ardent devotion to the truths embodied in the confession of the Lutheran church, has made him a representative man among his brethren—honored and revered as one of the fathers of the Norwegian Lutheran churches in America. Though the life and work of Ottesen have not attracted the attention of the world—his work having been carried out in that obscurity which necessarily surrounds one, no matter how gifted, who devotes himself to the welfare of any small community of foreigners in this country—his life has none the less been one of heroism and selfdenial, which deserves an honored mention. To men who, like him, have made it their aim and purpose of life to carry the truths of eternity to their fellow beings, our country owes its noblest achievements of true progress and civilization, and they deserve a lasting gratitude.' Ottesen married Catherine Döderlein, of Kristiania, in 1852. They have had six children, four of whom are dead. His only living son, Otto Christian, is also a clergyman in the Norwegian Synod.

Torgerson, Torger Andreas, clergyman—Somber—born 26 Jan., 1838, near Tvedestrand, Kristiansand stift, Nor-

way. He emigrated in 1852 with his parents, who settled in
Scandinavia,Waupaca county, Wis. After his arrival in this
country, Torgerson's boyhood was spent mostly in attending school, working on his father's farm, and preparing for
college. At the age of twenty he entered Concordia College,
St. Louis, Mo. Three years later this institution was moved
to Fort Wayne, Ind., where he graduated in 1862; and,
having completed a course at the Concordia Theological
Seminary, St. Louis, Mo., was ordained for the ministry in
the Norwegian Lutheran Synod by Rev. H. A. Preus in 1865.
The staying qualities of Torgerson may be inferred from the
fact that he has served as a minister at his present home for
thirty years. Rev. A. Bredesen says of him : "With the exception of Rev. Koren, no man in the Iowa District has done
longer, harder, and more faithful and effective service than
Torgerson." His field of labor has extended one hundred
and fifty miles from east to west, and one hundred and
twenty-five miles in the opposite direction, comprising in all
thirty-four different churches, and for some time his charge
consisted of eighteen congregations, scattered over this
large territory. At present no less than thirteen ministers of
the Norwegian Synod are laboring in that territory, besides
a fair number of Norwegian Lutheran ministers not connected with the synod. Torgerson has been in danger of
losing his life on no less than eight different occasions, his
escape in several cases having been very narrow, not to say
miraculous. His position in the synod has always been
prominent, and he has officiated as secretary of the pastoral
conference of the synod and of the Iowa District for twenty
years. He has been president of the Albert Lea special pas-

toral conference since its organization in 1873; president of
the general ministerial conference for six years; and is at
present president of the Iowa District, and a member of the
church council of the synod.   In 1870 Torgerson published *Märkelige Tildragelser*, a pamphlet of fifty-eight
pages on local church disputes. He has also contributed
much to different papers, and many of his sermons have
been printed by request in *Evangelisk Luthersk Kirketidende*. He married Dina Anderson, a sister of Prof. R. B.
Anderson, in 1866. They have had seven children, all boys,
one of whom is a successful attorney-at-law at Lake Mills,
Iowa, and another a clergyman in the synod.

Biographies of Scandinavians in Wisconsin.

Anderson, Mons, manufacturer and wholesale merchant —La Crosse—born 8 June, 1830, in Valders, Norway. He attended the parish school of his native valley; and, being compelled to shift for himself by the death of his father, departed of his own accord for the New World at the early age of sixteen. During the first year after his arrival in this country he was employed at a hotel in Milwaukee, kept by the Hon. Daniel Wells, and afterwards attended school for two years. Having spent another year in the same city as salesman in a grocery store, he pushed further west, settling at La Crosse in 1851. He first engaged as clerk in the store of S. T. Smith; was soon admitted as partner in the firm; and afterwards formed partnerships successively with W. W. Ustick and S. E. Olson, the latter now having a large dry goods store in Minneapolis. He finally bought out his partners and continued the business, in which he proved so successful that the volume of his trade was the second largest of its kind in the state. In 1885 he admitted both of his sons into the company, the firm assuming the name of Mons Anderson & Sons. In the same year he closed out his retail establishment, and since that time the firm has

been doing a wholesale dry goods and manufacturing business. The firm employs several traveling salesmen and hundreds of hands in the factory and the store. It is generally
admitted that this establishment is the largest of its kind in
America in proportion to the population of the locality in
which it is situated. He owns a great deal of real property,
besides being interested in various financial enterprises.
The reasons for Mons Anderson's success may be summarized
as follows: From the very start he kept strictly one price,
treated everyone alike, and endeavored to represent his
goods just as they were. The main key to his success, however, is undoubtedly to be found in his great energy, and the
systematic order in which his affairs are managed. He is at
his store at seven o'clock every morning. While he endeav-
ors to do his duty as a Christian and a citizen, he permits
neither politics, religion, nor anything else to interfere with
his business. Anderson has had in his employ three hundred
clerks who have since gone into business on their own
account, and who received their first training under Anderson's guidance. Some of these have since almost equalled
him in business success. An authority says: "Anderson, as
a man, does his own thinking, is original, has positive convictions, and shows his character and ability more by what
he does than by what he professes. In his pursuit of wealth
he has not been unmindful of the comfort of his employes,
nor has he been wanting in public spirit." Although he is a
member of the American Baptist church, yet he has given
large sums to Luther College and other Scandinavian institutions. Anderson has traveled very extensively both in
this country and in Europe. His large collection of sculp-

ture, statues, paintings, and curiosities has been gathered from nearly every country in Europe. Few Scandinavian-American business men have such a large and well selected library as Anderson has. His books are counted by the thousand, including some rare productions, and several works on art. Anderson was married in 1853 to Jane Halvorson, who came with her parents from Norway to Wisconsin in 1846. They have two sons; Alfred H., the oldest, owns and manages a large property in the state of Washington; and Samuel W., the youngest, is a member of his father's firm, which in 1891 was formally organized into a stock company; his oldest daughter is married to a prominent attorney, C. W. Bunn, located in St. Paul, Minn.; and his youngest daughter is Mrs. W. L. Crosby, of La Crosse. Anderson has in all ten grand-children, of whom he is very proud.

Anderson, Rasmus B., author and United States minister to Denmark—Madison—born 12 Jan., 1846, in Albion, Dane county, Wis. His father was the son of a peasant near Stavanger, Norway, and his mother a member of the von Krogh family, the name of which for two hundred and fifty years past has figured very prominently in the military records of Norway and Denmark. Her relatives were greatly displeased with the union because of Anderson's humble rank in society. This difficulty was further aggravated by the fact that he was a Quaker, and in order to evade what virtually amounted to a mild type of persecution, they left for America in 1836. They lived successively at Rochester, N. Y., and in La Salle county, Ill.; but in 1841 removed to Wisconsin, being the first couple of white settlers in the township of Albion, Dane county. Here Rasmus B. Anderson was born. During his early boyhood he worked on the farm in summer, and attended the district school in winter. At the age of fourteen he left home for the purpose of acquiring an education, and in the fall of 1861 entered the school established by the Norwegian Lutheran Synod at the Halfway Creek parsonage, near La Crosse, Wis., afterwards located at Decorah, Iowa, and known as Luther College. Being impatient of the restraint imposed upon him by the faculty, Anderson rebelled to such an extent that he was expelled from the school when he had almost completed a classical course. In 1890, however, after Anderson had made a reputation, Luther College conferred the degree of A. B. upon him. In 1866 he was appointed professor of Greek and modern languages in Albion Academy, near his home. This was the signal for a genuine stampede of Norwegian students to that institution, and three years later, when he withdrew, there was a similar stampede in the opposite direction. Having entered the State University of Wisconsin, at Madison, as a post-graduate student, he was appointed instructor in languages in that institution in 1869. In this capacity he served until the summer of 1875, when he was appointed to the chair of Scandinavian languages, which had just been established in the university, being the first native of Wisconsin to be honored with a full professorship in this institution. In this connection it must be mentioned that he was instrumental in establishing a Scandinavian library, which at present contains 1,500 volumes of choice Scandinavian literature. In founding this library he was generously assisted by Ole Bull, the world-famed violinist, who, on 17 May, 1872, gave a concert in Madison for the benefit of the enterprise. In 1883 Anderson severed his connection with the university, and for nearly two years was connected with the New York Equitable Life Insurance Company. Up to this time he had generally supported the Republican party. But in the campaign of 1884 he gave his support to Cleveland, thus drawing upon himself the opprobrious title of "mugwump," a term introduced by the Republicans during that compaign to stigmatize those who left their ranks and joined those of the Democrats. In 1894 he again joined the Republican party, for which he stumped the state two years later, though not exactly "sound" on the fundamental principles of Republicanism. In 1885 President Cleveland appointed Anderson United States minister to Denmark, and he served in this capacity for the next four years. During his stay in Copenhagen, most of his time was devoted to literary pursuits. After his return to America in 1889 he became connected with a New York firm which controls the sale of Moeller's cod liver oil in America, a position which he resigned in 1894. In 1895 he assisted in the organization of a new life insurance company in Madison, Wis., and was elected its president. For nearly thirty years past Anderson has been a speaker at 17th of May celebrations and other public demonstrations arranged by Norwegian-Americans, and in 1890 he began to agitate for the establishment of a "grape festival" in the fall of the year, in commemoration of the discovery of America by the Norsemen. This movement met with vigorous opposition on the part of those who wish to maintain the habit of celebrating the 17th of May;

but in the fall of 1894 the originator of the idea was pleased to receive accounts of "grape festivals" from different localities in the Northwest. Anderson shares the honor with Ole Bull of having raised the funds for the erection of a monument to Leif Erikson in Boston. Perhaps no American of Scandinavian birth or blood has produced anything in the English language which has created such a wide-spread stir as have some of Anderson's works. There are two productions in particular which deserve special consideration. By his *Norse Mythology* he has made the religion of the old Norsemen more accessible to the world at large, and the select translations from the Eddas incorporated into this work give English readers fascinating glimpses of the old Norse literature. Next to this ranks *America Not Discovered by Columbus*, his first literary production. It is true that this is chiefly a compilation, and even its author no longer maintains all assertions originally made in it. But the extensive and favorable reviews which it received gave such a prominence to the discovery of America by the Norsemen that thenceforth nearly every American historian took it into account, and treated the matter as a legitimate historical fact. Some of his books have been translated into French, German, Italian, Norwegian, and Russian. A complete list of the books either written or translated by Anderson would fill at least one page in this volume; hence, only some of the most important ones are given below. *Den Norske Maalsag, Julegave, Where Was Vineland?* and *The First Chapter of Norwegian Immigration* are among his leading original works. Of the translations may be mentioned: *Heimskringla; Viking Tales of the North; The Younger*

Edda; seven volumes of Björnstjerne Björnson's novels; *History of Scandinavian Literature,* by F. W. Horn; *The Spellbound Fiddler,* by Kristofer Janson; *Eminent Authors of the Nineteenth Century,* by Georg Brandes; *Teutonic Mythology,* by Viktor Rydberg; and *Among Cannibals,* by Carl Lumholtz. As to bulk, Anderson's original books aggregate about 1,500 pages, and the books translated by him about 5,000 pages. Besides the books he has also written contributions to the American supplement to the *Encyclopædia Britannica,* to five other cyclopædias, and to a few magazines. Anderson is a fighter, and a great number of articles, mostly in Norwegian-American papers, amply testify to his combativeness. In 1868 he was married to Bertha Karina Olson, of Cambridge, Wis., a sister to Prof. Julius E. Olson. They have four children living, some of them grown and married

Dundas, Johan Christian, physician and poet—Cambridge—born 1815, in Helgeland, Norway ; died in Madison, in 1883. He was a lineal descendant of Peter Dundas, or Don Dass, a Scotchman, who in about the year 1630 settled in Norway, having left his native land on account of religious persecution. This man married a Norwegian woman, Maren Falch, and was the father of Peter Dass, the famous poet of northern Norway, who was the first real poet in Norway after the Reformation, and whose poems are still widely read, for they contain sparks of nature's fire. Dass was a minister, and such an impression did he leave upon those to whom he sang and preached two centuries ago, that many strange traditions of his supernatural powers are still current among the people of Norway and their kinsmen in

Since 1898 Prof. Anderson has been the editor and proprietor of "Amerika," the semi-official organ of the Norwegian Synod, which organization he joined at about the same time.—EDITOR.

this country. Tradition has it that he could pray so fer-
vently that the air was suddenly filled with birds which
devoured the worms and insects that were destroying the
crops; subdue the thunder with his preaching; control the
malicious magic of the hostile Finns and Lapps by a word;
and even force the devil into his service. These traditions
indicate that Peter Dass was a man of marked personality,
to whom the people in their adoration ascribed supernatural powers, and are interesting in this connection, as they
serve to explain an inherited trait of J. C. Dundas's character. His personality, too, was so marked, that any one
who met him, even once, would scarcely forget him; and
many of his countrymen about Cambridge verily believed
that he could cure any disease, if he simply wished to do so.
Björnstjerne Björnson, who made his acquaintance in this
country, considered him the most original person that he
had ever met. Ole Bull was very fond of him, and visited him
twice in his Cambridge home. His father, Isaac Georg Dundas, was a man of means, and liberally educated. He had
eleven children, and sought to give them a good education.
Johan, the youngest, was early sent to Bergen to attend
school, and later went to the University of Norway, where
he studied during the years 1837–39. Here he began the
study of medicine, which he continued at Copenhagen, Vien-
na, Helsingfors, and Berne. After a voyage to the East Indies in the service of the Dutch East India Company as a
surgeon, he spent the year 1849 in the larger English hospitals. The next year he came to America, and proceeded to
the Koshkonong settlement in Wisconsin, where his countrymen were suffering from the cholera. After having made a

N. P. HAUGEN, RIVER FALLS.

REV. T. H. DAHL, STOUGHTON.   REV. H. HALVORSEN, WESTBY.

REV. L. LUND, ELROY.   II. STEENSLAND, MADISON.

tour of the country he returned to Holland, whence he sailed as physician on board a ship bound for China. In the course of about two years he returned to Cambridge to take up his permanent abode, and here he remained as a practicing physician until his death. Dundas was a remarkable character, a skilful surgeon, and a clever poet, being well versed in literature, history, and politics. In his younger days he had familiarly known the poets Henrik Wergeland and Johan Ludvig Runeberg. In his later years he wrote a great deal of verse, much of which was printed in the Norwegian and Danish papers in this country. In 1856 he married an American lady, Malina E. Tracy. They had two daughters.

Gjertsen, J. P., clergyman—Stoughton—born 25 Oct., 1803, in Askvold, Bergen stift, Norway; died in 1892. While a young man he served as school teacher, and later on held a couple of local offices. He was also engaged as temperance lecturer for five years, and was deeply interested in the spiritual and moral welfare of his countrymen. In 1864 he emigrated to this country, and for a series of years served as pastor of churches at Racine, Bostwick Valley, Winneconne, and Oshkosh, Wis. The last nineteen years of his life were spent with his children in Stoughton, Wis. Mainly through his tireless efforts, the Zion Mission Society for Israel was organized in 1877, Gjertsen himself serving as its first president. He devoted much time and labor to this society, which during its history has been the means of converting a number of Jews to Christianity. Gjertsen also edited a hymn-book, *Missionssange for Israel*, especially adapted for use at services devoted to the cause of the Jewish mission. He was married in 1841 to Berthe

Johanne Gaasevor. Among their children may be mentioned Rev. M. F. Gjertsen, of Minneapolis, and Mrs. Rev. T. H. Dahl, of Stoughton. Wis.

Haugen, Nils P., congressman—River Falls—born 9 March, 1849, in Modum, Kristiania stift, Norway. In 1854 he emigrated with his parents, who located in Rock county, Wis. In the spring of 1855 they moved to Martell, Pierce county, where his father purchased government land, and where he made his permanent home until his death in 1896. His father was a school teacher in Norway, and had some experience in blacksmithing, which was the trade of young Haugen's grandfather. Young Haugen spent most of his boyhood working on his father's farm; but also tried his hand at other kinds of hard work, such as logging in the pineries, working in a saw mill in Menomonie, and rafting on the St. Croix river. He attended the common school until fourteen years of age; entered Luther College, Decorah, Iowa, in 1868, where he remained over two years, finishing the studies up to the sophomore class. After returning from college he taught one term of Norwegian parochial school, and common school for two years, in his county. In 1872 he entered the law department of the State University of Michigan, at Ann Arbor, graduating two years later; then located at River Falls, and began to practice law. But in 1874 he was appointed court reporter of the eighth judicial circuit, including several counties, in which capacity he served for a period of seven years, besides devoting some time to his practice. In 1881 he resigned this position, and formed a law partnership with Frank L. Gilson. In 1879 and 1880 Haugen served two terms in the state assembly. While in this position he was one of the main supporters of Mat. H. Carpenter, who was elected U. S. senator in 1879; and was a member of several important committees. In 1881 he was elected railroad commissioner, to which position he was re-elected, serving five years in all. Upon the death of the congressman-elect of his district, in 1887, Haugen was made his successor at a special election, and was re-elected three times successively, serving as a member of congress for a longer period, excepting M. N. Johnson of N. D., than any other Scandinavian. Both Haugen and Lind, of Minnesota, were firm opponents of the proposition which aimed at placing the three Scandinavian kingdoms under a common legation, and this proposition was defeated. The bill by which Oklahoma was organized as a territory originally provided that persons who were not citizens of the United States should be debarred from entering government lands. Haugen proposed an amendment to the bill, placing all who have declared their intention to become citizens, on an equal footing with actual citizens in regard to government lands, and the amendment was carried. He strongly advocated the commercial interests of the Great Lakes; made several strong and consistent speeches in favor of a protective tariff; deprecated experimentation, and recommended conservatism in regard to the money question. Haugen was a very strong candidate for governor of Wisconsin in 1894; but Upham proved a trifle stronger than Haugen at the state convention, and the latter failed to receive the nomination. Haugen has always been a Republican. He has devoted much time to the German language, and has made French a special study, being better versed in modern literature than is usually the case with our public men, and may be said to have made a special study of the humorous and witty literature of the Scandinavian countries. In 1875 he was married to Ingeborg A. Rasmussen, of Pierce county, Wis. They have one grown daughter, who has been attending the normal school, River Falls, for years.

Heg, Hans Christian, pioneer and soldier—Waterford—born 21 Dec., 1829, near Drammen, Norway; died 20 Sept., 1863, at Chicamauga, Tenn. In 1840 he came to America with his father, who settled in town of Norway, Racine county, Wis.; and was one of the early settlers of the noted Muskego settlement. Young Heg was a wideawake boy, and although he enjoyed no means of a higher education, he managed to keep himself well informed on all questions of the day, and took pains to familiarize himself with the English language. In short, he became withal the brightest young man of the neighborhood, and was noted as an enthusiastic and active anti-slavery man long before he became of age. In 1849 he went to California, where he was fairly successful as a gold digger, but upon the death of his father, in 1851, was forced to return and take care of his younger brothers and sisters. Having settled down on his father's homestead, he was elected to some local office at every election, and invariably discharged his duties to the entire satisfaction of his constituents. In 1859 he removed to Waterford where he, in company with two Americans, opened up a general merchandise business. In the fall of the same year he was elected state prison commissioner on the Republican ticket, being perhaps the first Norwegian elected to any state office in America. Many of his countrymen were somewhat apprehensive lest he should fail to give satisfaction in such a trying position. But, to use the language of K. Langeland, "he was praised by his colleagues as well as other leading men in the state. He introduced many important reforms and improvements, and never has there been such order, activity, and economy within the walls of the penitentiary as during his administration. The expenses were smaller and the receipts larger in proportion to the number of convicts than ever before or since; but to crown his work: His accounts were perfectly clean, which had never been the case with those of his predecessors. Said a leading Milwaukee man to the writer shortly after the funeral of Heg: 'He is the only man who has left a clean record at the state prison.' " He was renominated for the same office in 1861, but declined the nomination because he had already decided to enter the war. He was appointed colonel of the Fifteenth Wisconsin, or Scandinavian, Regiment, which was organized under his supervision—a full account of the regiment is given in the first volume of this work. At the battle of Chickamauga, in which he was killed, he commanded a brigade, having been brevetted brigadier general. Heg left an enviable record in the war. He displayed true bravery on several occasions, and if his life had been spared a little longer he would have been advanced to a higher rank. His participation in the battle which cost him his life is described as follows by K. Langeland: " His conduct in the battle at Chickamauga won the admiration of all who saw him. When his brigade was overwhelmed and beaten back on

that terrible Saturday afternoon, he was present everywhere, encouraging his soldiers to check the victorious
march of the rebel legions. The Twenty-first Illinois was
sent as re-enforcement to Col. Heg. They marched bravely
on, but their lines were broken, and they were repulsed.
Then Col. Heg rode up, swung his hat, and shouted they
should follow him. It seemed as though they were almost
electrified, with a shout they charged the rebels and drove
them back almost six hundred feet, but were again overwhelmed and forced to retreat. An officer has told me that
Heg continually remained in the thickest of the fray
unscathed." As he was riding to another part of the line,
however, he was mortally wounded by a stray shot, and
died the same night. Heg was a man of more than ordinary courage and ability, and his sincerity was beyond all
doubt. This accounts for his great popularity, which was
most conspicuously demonstrated when his remains were
laid to rest in the Norway church cemetery, near his home.
Heg is one of the few Norwegians who prominently distinguished themselves in the Civil War. He was a Freemason, but was not connected with any church organization.
He was married in 1851 to Gunhild Einung. They had
four children. One of them is James E. Heg, who has held
the office of vice-president of the state board of control of
Wisconsin, and who has held numerous minor offices. He
was president of the Wisconsin press association for several
terms, and also president of the Republican editorial association for a number of years. Another son, Dr. Elmer E.
Heg, has been president of the state board of health of the
state of Washington. A daughter, Hilda S. Heg, married

Congressman C. N. Fowler, of the state of New Jersey.

Hoyme, Gjermund, clergyman—Eau Claire—born 8 Oct., 1848, in Valders, Norway. He came to America in 1851 with his parents, who settled at Port Washington, Wis. Four years later they removed to Winneshiek county, Iowa, where young Hoyme soon had to earn his living as a wage-worker on the farm. Having an insatiable craving for knowledge, he borrowed books and devoted every spare moment to reading. For twelve successive winters he attended English schools, and in 1869 entered the theological seminary at Marshall, Wis., where he remained two years. He next took up a course in languages, especially English, German, Latin, and Greek, in the State University of Wisconsin, at Madison. Hoyme still remembers with gratitude how Hon. J. A. Johnson met him at the depot, took him to his home, and kindly assisted him in many ways. Prof. R. B. Anderson, who at that time was instructor in the university, also took pains to encourage and assist him. Having finished his course at the university, he resumed his theological studies at Augsburg Seminary, Minneapolis, Minn. Lacking pecuniary means, and receiving urgent calls to enter the ministry, he discontinued his studies earlier than he originally had intended, and began his life-work as pastor at Duluth in 1873. While there he taught a Norwegian parochial school in the day, devoted the evenings to English instruction, and preached twice every Sunday. But Jay Cook's failure all but ruined the young city, and the congregation was so crippled financially that Hoyme had to leave it. He next served three congregations at Menomonie, Dunn county, Wis., and finally settled at Eau Claire in 1876. This

date marks a turning point in his external life. Earlier in
life he and grim poverty had been on most familiar terms.
According to *Am. Luth. Biographies*, by J.C.Jensson, Hoyme
himself once wrote to a friend about his trials at college
as follows : " The money I earned at hard labor during the summer vacation, was not sufficient to carry me
through to the next vacation. It frequently happened that
I did not have enough money to pay the postage on letters
to my old mother. My apparel was often too plainly an index to the condition of my purse. When a change of clothes
seemed indispensable, my method of renovation generally
consisted in giving the old and threadbare ones a thorough
brushing." His success since his arrival at Eau Claire forms
a pleasant contrast to this picture. Gradually his power for
good has increased, and in many respects he is now absolutely the strongest man in the city of Eau Claire.   His influence in the church union to which he belongs, is thoroughly in keeping with his local standing.   From 1881 to 1886
he was the secretary, and from the latter date to 1890, the
president of the conference; and since the organization of
the United Church in 1890, he has served that body as president. As a parliamentarian and presiding officer he has no
superior and, perhaps, no equal among the Scandinavian
clergy in the United States.   His preaching is very earnest;
his language lofty and dramatic; in fact the man is so serious that it would be difficult to find a single humorous sal-
ly in all his public utterances.   Hoyme, unlike most of the
leading men in the Norwegian American churches, has written very little for publication.   *Harpen*, a hymn-book published by him and L. Lund, has had a large sale, seventeen

editions having been exhausted.   In 1893 Hoyme published
Saloonen, a strong invective against the saloon, and fifteen
thousand copies of the book were disposed of in a few weeks.
In 1874 he was married to Mrs. Ida Othelia Olsen, of Duluth.

Johnson, John A., state senator and manufacturer—
Madison—born 15 Apr., 1832, near Skien, Norway. He
came to America in 1844 with his parents, who settled in
Walworth county, Wis., but a few years later removed to
Pleasant Spring, Dane county. Young Johnson began the
battle of life at the early age of twelve. His educational advantages were rather meager; but by dint of untiring efforts,
guided by a decidedly practical turn of mind, he not only
made steady progress in his purely practical work, but also
acquired a considerable amonut of theoretical knowledge.
In 1861 he settled at Madison, and was dealing in farming machinery for the next few years; and in 1881 began to
manufacture the same kind of goods as he had been trading
in, by organizing the manufacturing firm of Fuller & Johnson. A little later he was also the chief organizer of the
Groutholdt machine company, and has always been president of these two enterprises, which now give employment
to about three hundred men the year around. The farming
machinery turned out by the former company is sold chiefly
in the Northwest, while the turret lathes manufactured by
the latter are largely shipped to the East. Johnson is one of
the very few Norwegian Americans who are engaged in manufacturing enterprises on a large scale. Though the business
enterprises over whose destinies Johnson presides are so extensive as to actually furnish employment to the bulk of the
laboring people of his city, he has also found time for prac-

tical politics and literary pursuits. Thus, from 1861 to 1869 he served as county clerk of Dane county; in 1857 as member of the state Assembly; and in 1873 and 1874 as state senator. He was also a member of the board of trustees of the State Hospital for the Insane, near Madison, from 1878 to 1882. Johnson is a Republican on general principles. In 1884, however, he supported Cleveland for president, and in 1886 received 117,909 votes for state treasurer on the Democratic ticket. This was a couple of thousand more than the average number of votes cast for the other candidates on the ticket, but he was defeated by the Republican candidate, who received a majority of 11,649. Johnson's most noted literary work is *Det Skandinaviske Regiments Historie*, which was published in 1869. This is the earliest systematized account of the famous Fifteenth Wisconsin Regiment. In 1888 he published *Fingerpeg for Farmere og Andre*, a book containing about 200 pages. The newspaper articles written by Johnson cover a considerable number of different topics, and these as well as his books are characterized by a systematic arrangement of the subject matter, coupled with an easy and lucid style, and an unmistakable tendency to arrive at practical results. Johnson has contributed liberally to some of the Norwegian-Lutheran institutions of learning, but is himself a member of the Unitarian Church. He was married in 1861, and has five children, four of whom have graduated from the University of Wisconsin.

Kumlien, Thure L. T., scientist—Milwaukee—born 9 Nov., 1819, in Härlunda, Vestergötland, Sweden; died 5 Aug., 1888. His father, who was a quartermaster in the Swedish army, owned several large estates in that part of

the country. Kumlien, having received his first instruction
from a private tutor, entered the college at Skara, and subsequently attended the University of Upsala, graduating in
1843. During his stay at the university, he devoted himself
especially to the study of botany, and was the favorite
pupil of the celebrated Swedish botanist, Elias Fries, the
most-renowned Swedish botanist since the days of Linne,
under whose guidance he laid the foundations for his thorough knowledge of that branch of science, and acquired such
a familiarity with the lower types of plant life, as, for
example, ferns, mosses, lichens, fungi, etc., that he equalled,
if not surpassed, his more renowned instructor in these
departments. What makes his familiarity with so many
branches of botany the more remarkable, is the fact that
from boyhood his special study seems to have been ornithology, and even in later years he devoted a great deal of time
to this study. In 1843, shortly after having completed his
studies at Upsala, Kumlien, then but twenty-four years of
age, emigrated to America, accompanied by his young wife.
They came at once to Lake Koshkonong, Jefferson county,
Wis., having decided upon this locality without any previous knowledge of the place, but merely from the study of the
map, for a locality affording facilities for the pursuit of his
favorite studies. It is, however, probable that he had
received some information in regard to Wisconsin from a
former acquaintance during his stay at Upsala, Gustaf
Unonius, a Swedish Episcopal clergyman, who came to this
country in 1841. Unonius, who visited Koshkonong in
1843, says in his *Minnen* in regard to Kumlien: "It was
really curious to see how he divided his time between agri-

culture and scientific researches. Necessity tied his hands to
the plow and hoe, while mind and disposition were fastened
upon flowers, birds, and insects. A fine herbarium, and a
not inconsiderable, though on account of limited space,
somewhat confused, ornithological cabinet testified to
greater activity as a naturalist than as a farmer." Ulti-
mately, he found it more profitable to rent out his farm and
to devote himself exclusively to the care of his garden and to
his favorite studies. In addition to a thorough scientific
education, he possessed also an unusual skill in taxidermy,
which enabled him to procure some additional income. At
last, several scientific associations in the Eastern states had
their attention drawn to the young naturalist, who had
concealed himself from the eyes of the world in an insignificant cottage in the western wilderness. During the first
twenty years after his arrival at Koshkonong, he was
engaged in making collections in many branches of natural
history for several large museums, both in Europe and in
this country. Among the institutions whose collections he
thus enriched, are the celebrated museums in Stockholm and
Leyden, the British Museum in London, and the Smith-
sonian Institute, in Washington, D. C. In 1867 he was
called to a position as instructor in botany and zoology in
Albion Academy, Albion, Wis., remaining for a few years.
Later he was employed in forming and arranging collections
for the state normal schools and the State University. From
1883 to the time of his death he held the position of conser-
vator at the Public Museum in Milwaukee. Kumlien
received several honorary degrees from institutions of learning, and was corresponding member of various scientific

societies in Europe and America. On account of his modest
and reserved disposition, he was averse to parading his own
superior attainments before the public. Consequently, very
few of his valuable observations have been published, and
he himself has remained almost unknown to the world,
while others have succeeded in acquiring both fame and
honors, though not so well equipped either intellectually or
morally. A friend and colleague, writing shortly after the
death of Kumlien, gives the following estimate of his character: " Mr. Kumlien was no narrow man. He was passion-
ately fond of painting, music, and poetry. I have heard
him repeat, with a glow of delight, verses from Runeberg
and from Tegner's *Frithiofs Saga*, rendering the wonderful
rhythm of the latter with exquisite grace and precision. He
was a man of most refined tastes, without any of the extra-
vagant desires which such tastes often engender. He was
satisfied to live most simply a life which philosophers might
envy. Higher than his intellectual accomplishments rose his
moral qualities. The leading features of his character were
harmlessness and truthfulness." Two of his children sur-
vived him, one of whom, Ludwig Kumlien, is professor in
Milton College, Milton, Wis.

Langeland, Knud, pioneer and journalist—Milwaukee—
born 27 Oct., 1813, in Samnanger, Bergen stift, Norway;
died 8 Feb., 1888. At the age of thirteen he lost his father,
and a little later was forced to begin to make a living on his
own account. His school facilities were of a very inferior
grade; but by availing himself of every means within reach,
he acquired more knowledge than his comrades. For generations past Langeland's ancestors had been of an inde-

pendent turn of mind, and he himself was a chip of the old block in that respect. Thus, according to his autobiography, when the sons of the pastor and the government officials of his neighborhood made fun of the ragged clothes he was compelled to wear in his early teens, he wept and swore and was offended. In comparing his fate with that of the upper classes, he says: "This painful question, like the sharp steel, forced its way to my young heart. What have I done, and what have these people done, to create such a difference between us?" At the age of fourteen he learned German, his only means of instruction being a German Bible which he compared with the Norwegian Bible; and in spite of the protestations of the other members of the family, he began to extend his field of knowledge, without, however, having any distinct purpose in view. He was impelled by a natural inclination, and proceeded to Bergen, where he continued his studies under the guidance of a young student. Having taken a six months' course, he was appointed public school teacher and precentor in a settlement near his birthplace. Here Langeland worked very faithfully and with signal success, and he always looked back upon this time as one of the happiest of his life. "In a life so full of vicissitudes, of joys and sorrows, of happiness and misfortune," he says, "there is nothing else in my past life which affords me so much joy and comfort as the memories from this time." His income the first year was about $11.00; but his position as precentor and sexton gave the people of the parish an opportunity to testify to their great satisfaction with his services by giving him larger collections on Sundays and holidays, and his annual income more than doubled in a couple of years.

At the early age of twenty he was also appointed public vaccinator, and for several years his time was spent in teaching in winter and vaccinating children in summer. As important incidents from this time may be mentioned that he spent several months in England, in 1835, on which occasion he made a return trip by rail from Newcastle to Shields; and that later he was awarded a prize as the best teacher in the fifteen school districts of the parish. One of the most discouraging experiences of Langeland as an educator was his attempt to establish a parish library. Having raised about $100 for that purpose, he was authorized to make a selection of books. The list of the books shows that they were all of an educational, scientific, or practical character. But a few bigots succeeded in making the people believe that the books were detrimental to religion and morality, and no end of abuse was heaped upon the head of Langeland, the soul of the undertaking. *Almanakmanden* was the most offensive book in the lot because it was supposed to contradict Joshua, X, 13: "And the sun stood still." The library was continued, but the stir which it had created henceforth hampered Langeland somewhat in his work, and after a seven years' service as a public educator in general, and an official teacher in particular, he resigned and became interested in a fishing smack. As to his success in this business, suffice it to say that whatever profits he made in one year, were generally lost the next year, and in 1843 he gave it up as a failure and emigrated to America, following in the wake of a brother, Mons A. Adland, who had left Norway in 1837, with the first emigrant vessel that sailed from Bergen, and on which was also the well-known Ole Rynning.

Langeland made his first home at Yorkville Prairie, Wis.; but in 1845 he settled in the southern part of Columbia county, and was one of the founders of the prosperous Norwegian settlement of that locality. He sold out his claim and returned to Racine county in 1846, and in the course of the next few years made himself conspicuous by supporting everything that would tend to promote the prosperity of the Yorkville settlement. In 1849 he bought the outfit of *Nordlyset*, the first Norwegian paper in America, and, in company with Rev. O. J. Hatlestad, began to publish it at Racine. The name of the paper was changed to *Demokraten*, because the Democrats had poked fun at it and called it 'a will-o-the-wisp that led the Norwegians into the morasses of the Free Soil party.' The paper at one time had about 300 subscribers, but its publication had to be suspended the next year for lack of funds. Shortly afterwards Langeland began to print *Maanedstidende*, and in 1852 removed to Janesville, Wis., but shortly afterwards sold out his printing outfit. He now spent some time on his farm at Yorkville. In 1856 he was engaged as editor of *Den Norske Amerikaner*, at Madison, Wis. The owner of the paper, Elias Stangeland, however, wanted to support Buchanan for president, while Langeland was an implacable anti-slavery man, and Langeland resigned, thus proving himself more of a man than the average American editor. The paper met with little or no sympathy among the readers, and soon died for lack of support. In 1860 Langeland was elected to a seat in the state assembly, and his most noteworthy effort as a legislator was the introduction and successful engineering of a bill by which 2,500 acres of state swamp land located

REV. GJERMUND HOYME, EAU CLAIRE.

REV. A. BREDESEN, STOUGHTON.   PROF. JULIUS E. OLSON, MADISON.

P. O. STROMME, MADISON.   T. E. TORRISON, MANITOWOC.

in the township of Norway, was granted to said township. Having spent a number of years on his farm, Langeland was again induced to enter the field of journalism, this time as editor of *Skandinaven*, which was started in Chicago in the summer of 1866, by John Anderson and Iver Lawson. This paper was an out-and-out advocate of Republican principles, and the rapid increase of its circulation soon made its editor known among his countrymen from one end of the country to the other. During the sixties and seventies, a considerable number of Norwegians, chiefly ministers of the gospel, defended the doctrine of slavery as a mere theory—"slavery in itself" was the exact term used—and, on the other hand, they sometimes criticized the American common school system as "godless." For a long series of years Langeland kept up a systematic warfare against these parties, and his advocacy of the cause of our common school system was subsequently recognized by the board of education of Chicago, which named one of the public schools after him. It must be recorded as an historical fact that Langeland did more than any other man to attach his countrymen to the Republican party as well as to our common school system. In 1872 he severed his connection with *Skandinaven*, and for a time edited *Amerika*, of Chicago. The latter was soon sold to the former, and Langeland again contributed to *Skandinaven* until the eighties, when he withdrew to Milwaukee to spend the closing days of his life. In 1880 the Republicans recognized his services by nominating him for presidential elector, and, being elected, he cast his vote for James A. Garfield. From this time on, however, he gradually became displeased with the practical politics of our

48

country. "The large Republican majorities have brought
unscrupulous politicians to the front," he says, "and a little
independence on the part of the voters is in its place—nay, it
is the very essence of voting." Langeland's spirit of independence remained unimpaired to the very last, ample proof
of which may be found in the fact that a few months before
his death he publicly defended the much-abused Prohibition
party. The year after his death *Skandinaven* published his
book *Nordmaendene i Amerika*. This work contains some
valuable information in regard to the Norwegian immigration, the first settlements, and the early Norwegian-American press; but, on the whole, it is more of an autobiography
of Knud Langeland than a history of the Norwegians; and
it would, perhaps, never have appeared in its present form, if
Langeland had lived to edit it. Langeland was married to
Anna Hatlestad, who is a native of Skjold, Kristiansand
stift, Norway, and is now living at Milwaukee. They had
nine children, five of whom are still living. Among these
may be mentioned Peter Langland, who is practicing medicine in Milwaukee, and James, who is on the editorial staff
of the *Chicago Record*.

Nattestad, Ole K., pioneer—Clinton—born 24 Dec., 1807,
in Veggli, Kristiania stift, Norway; died 28 May, 1886.
While a young man he tried his hand at farming and blacksmithing; but, upon seeing that even his best-efforts did not
enable him to save anything for the future, he decided to
emigrate; and in 1837, in company with his brother Ansten,
went to America by way of Gothenburg, Sweden. Nattestad, or Natesta, as he spelt his name in this country, had
first heard of America while on a visit to Stavanger. He

spent the first winter at Beaver Creek, Ill.; but settled at Clinton, Wis., 1 July, 1838, being, as far as is known, the first Norwegian settler in the state of Wisconsin. Here he spent the rest of his life as a quiet and unassuming, but very prosperous farmer. His children received a good education, and several of them are prominent and respected members of the communities in which they reside.

Nielsen, Andreas Sixtus, clergyman — Withee — born 6 Apr., 1832, in Aalborg, Denmark. His school advantages in his boyhood appear to have been very limited. In his younger days he spent a couple of years in Norway, where he became interested in a religious movement; returned to his native land; bought a small farm and engaged in agricultural pursuits; and began as a layman in 1866 to lead religious meetings in Vendsyssel, where he lived. During his travel as an itinerant missionary, he came in contact with several clergymen who called his attention to the fact that a committee, called *Udvalget*, had been formed for the purpose of promoting the preaching of the gospel among the Danes in America, and the pastors advised Nielsen to go to the Western world and become a minister. After having, at the age of thirty-nine, attended a high school for one winter, he, in company with a clergyman, Grove Rasmussen, set sail for America in 1871 with the intention of taking a view of the field of his future labor. He landed in Cedar Falls, Iowa, where he became pastor of a Danish Lutheran congregation, which had been organized by Rev. C. L. Clausen a short time previously. Before accepting the pastorage, however, Nielsen returned to Denmark for the purpose of bringing his family with him, and in order to be ordained. As a matter of historical curiosity it may be mentioned that Nielsen had the Danish consul in Chicago indorse the letter written by five members of the congrega tion in Cedar Falls to *Udvalget* in Denmark, in which letter they requested *Udvalget* to ordain Nielsen as their pastor. The incident is an excellent illustration of the futile attempts, often indulged in, of bringing the western pioneers under the control, or at least under the influence, of the state church machinery of some European country. Nielsen, however, was not ordained in his native land, his time and education being too limited. But *Udvalget* did recommend that he should be ordained by Rev. Clausen in accordance with the Danish rituals, which was done. He remained in Cedar Falls for eight years, going through the usual hard-ships of pioneer life, his salary being only three or four hundred dollars a year. He was pastor in Chicago for four-teen years, and has since resided at his present place, where he organized a new congregation. His influence upon the Danish Evangelical Lutheran Church in America has been great, most of its pastors having been ordained by him. His services have been recognized not only by his friends, but also by his opponents, and even on the other side of the water, for in 1896 the king of Denmark made him a knight of the order of Daneborg as a recognition of the meritorious work he had done among the Danes in this country. In 1858 he was married, and he has eight children.

Preus, **Herman Amberg**, clergyman and pioneer—Mor-risonville—born 16 June, 1825, in Kristiansand, Norway died 2 July, 1894, at Lee, Ill. His ancestors were Germans, the earliest known being Hans Preus, a rich estate owner,

living at Eisfeldt, Sachsen-Meinigen; and this man's son
settled in Norway about the year 1700. Preus's grandfather was a Lutheran clergyman; his father, a college
president; and his mother, a member of the illustrious
Keyser family. He received a fine preparatory education at
home, and spent the years 1843–48 at the University of
Norway, receiving the degree of A. B. in 1843, and that of
can. theol. in 1848. The next three years were devoted to
teaching in the capital. In 1851 he accepted a call as pastor
from three churches in the vicinity of Spring Prairie, Dane
and Columbia counties, Wis., and was ordained before leaving for the New World. Upon his arrival at Spring Prairie
there were no church buildings, and he had to enter upon his
work as a minister by preaching in small log cabins which
often were literally packed, while occasionally a large number of people had to stand outside the open doors and
windows during the services. Being a hard worker, Preus
soon extended his field of activity far beyond the original
charge. He thus preached in numerous places within a
radius of fifty miles, and often he would preach at places
located over one hundred miles from his home. It has been
estimated that his travels averaged 3,500 miles a year for
several years before there were any railroads in that part of
the country. During this pioneer period Preus preached
once or twice every day, or at least once every other day.
His qualifications soon assigned to him a prominent position in the Lutheran church of America. On 4 January,
1851, a few ministers and lay delegates had organized a
union of Norwegian Lutheran churches. But the constitution agreed upon contained a few words referring to bap-

tism in such a way as to favor *Grundtvigianism,* and Preus
became very active in endeavoring to persuade the contract-
ing parties to dissolve the organization, in order to get
wholly rid of this "leaven of *Grundtvigianism*" which
already had caused some trouble. Accordingly, the organization was dissolved in 1852, and Preus was one of the
seven ministers who participated in the organization of the
Norwegian Lutheran Synod of America on 5 Feb., 1853. At
the annual meeting of the synod in 1854, he was elected a
member of the executive committee, and since that date till
his death forty years later, he was one of the most prominent and influential men in the synod. Preus, Laur. Larsen,
V. U. Koren, and J. A. Ottesen have justly been called the
"venerable fathers" of the Norwegian Synod; and Rev. A.
Bredesen says, "If any one man, before all others, deserves
to be designated as the Patriarch of our church in America,
that man is Herman Amberg Preus." But Preus was not
such a successful organizer and leader among the Norwegian-American Lutherans, as, for instance, Muhlenberg was
among the Germans, or Hasselquist among the Swedes.
Preus was too inflexible and conservative to adapt himself
to the new conditions in the New World, even in cases when
it is difficult to understand how the doctrine and practice of
pure Lutheranism would have suffered by yielding a little.
He was too frank to practice what may be called diplomacy
or policy. His unrelenting conservatism has always to a
great extent characterized the Norwegian Synod up to the
present time; and that organization has largely on this
account been forced to participate in many religious controversies. which have resulted in schisms and direct loss to the

REV. H. A. PREUS, MORRISONVILLE.

KNUD LANGELAND, MILWAUKEE.

synod. Yet this very conservatism has not been without its
bright sides. It has counterbalanced the anarchistic ten-
ency, often misnamed freedom, which a new country is
always subject to, not only religiously, but also socially,
politically, and financially. The original loose organization
of Elling Eielsen's *Samfund* has, for example, in later years
developed into the more stable Hauge's Synod, as a direct
result of the conservative influence which the Norwegian
Synod has exercised upon that body. Among all the prominent Scandinavian-American pioneers, it is quite difficult to
find a man that was more conservative than Preus; and
this characteristic to hold on to what is old and stable,
constitutes a double virtue in an age when change, for either
good, bad, or indifferent, is the ruling passion of mankind.
Realizing the power of the press, he devoted much time to
the publication of *Kirkelig Maanedstidende*, the organ of
the synod, and was appointed editor-in-chief of it in 1859,
discharging his duty as such during the next nine years. In
1862 he was elected president of the synod, and so satisfactory were his services in this capacity that he was
re-elected at every subsequent meeting as long as he lived.
He was a strong man; but his endurance was often severely
tested. Says a personal friend of his: "When he had to
travel day after day he would sit up and work half of the
night, and yet the next day be as vivacious as ever in
preaching or debating, or presiding at some large meeting."
In the early seventies he traveled several thousand miles a
year, and in one year he covered no less than eight thousand
miles. The division of the synod into three districts, in
1876, relieved him of a part of the burdens which had

become too onorous for almost any one man. His fine physique and his frankness won the sympathy of the people, and his earnestness and sincerity inspired thinking men and women with confidence. Hence, it is no wonder that so many people yet speak in a strain of touching tenderness about " Old Preus." His character was a rare combination of gentleness and firmness. Even his physiognomy was striking, and it is claimed that Prof. Walther, of St. Louis, upon first seeing him, exclaimed: "A determined man; he will make his mark." He was rather slow in making up his mind, but did not often recede from a position he had once taken. On the other hand, his heart was highly responsive to the sufferings of his fellow-men, and his generosity was more than ordinary. Experience had taught him the difficulty of building up churches in new settlements, and throughout his career as president of the synod he was particularly solicitous about the needs of the frontier missions. Another marked feature of his great life-work was his untiring efforts to give the people of the synod a thorough and Christian education, by means of parochial schools. In 1866 he expressed himself on that subject as follows: "It is our endeavor to arrange our parochial schools so that the English common schools may become superfluous to our church members. This, of course, can only be accomplished by taking up such branches in the parochial schools as are taught in the English schools. It involves many difficulties, but we must work with this purpose in view." And again in 1893: "Strive with all your might to build up good parochial schools! Try earnestly to give your children a Christian education! The growth of the Lutheran church, nay its very existence, largely depends upon this; for the future belongs to the rising generation." His personal contributions to the schools of the synod were comparatively large, and the example thus afforded undoubtedly has had something to do with the fact that the synod has done more for the cause of education than all the other Norwegian church organizations in the country combined. Preus was a Lutheran of the old school. Indeed, the following expressions from his report to the synod in 1893, remind one strikingly of the very language of Martin Luther himself: "At this moment an exceedingly dangerous tendency pervades nearly all Christian denominations in the world. It may not be the aim of the leaders and their followers, but it is the aim of the originator of this tendency, Satan, the deceiver, to get rid of the absolute, divine authority, by rejecting the biblical doctrine of the inspiration of the Scriptures." Having reviewed this tendency in the great Protestant churches in America and Europe, he continues: "We see the error threatening our very lives, and the spiritual atmosphere surrounding our church people is full of its poisonous microbes. The Scriptures are subjected to the judgment of the reason, and doctrines of men take the place of the divine articles of faith. The foundation of Christianity and of Holy Writ, which is the Prophets and the Apostles, with Christ as the chief corner-stone, is thus undermined, justification by faith alone becomes a problem, divine certainty of faith yields to uncertainty and doubt, and the sinner is deprived of his consolation and peace." The Catholics also received some attention in the same report: "The Catholic church stretches forth its arms for prey. Its efforts to get the common schools into its clutches are well known; in direct violation of the constitution it appropriates the money of the state for its church schools, and struggles for the acquisition of political power, in order to utilize it in the service of the Papal church. Woe to the Protestant churches if it succeeds! For still the Papal church thirsts for the blood of 'heretics!' " The materialism of this age is sized up thus: "Last but not least, the synod will faithfully testify against the increasing worldiness, pursuit of riches, and love of pleasure. Our age is materialistic, it wants something for the eyes, something tangible. Here is the greatest danger that the church may become secularized." These expressions were not dictated by any policy whatsoever. They sprung from the intense conviction of a cultured, intelligent, and singularly sincere man. Hence they give us, brief as they are, a reliable insight into the working of his mind. Such a man as Preus naturally found himself surrounded by true and trusty followers, whose devotion made life's arduous task less irksome. The great bulk of his parishioners looked up to him as a respect-inspiring, yet loving and tender father. His family relations were the most beautiful and happy. On the other hand, his life was not without streaks of shadow. During the eighties the synod was rent in twain by doctrainal controversies. This was brought home to him in a particularly painful manner. On Good Friday, in the spring of 1883, a majority of the Norway Grove congregation which he had served as pastor for thirty years, deposed him because he refused to subscribe unconditionally to resolutions adopted by said majority. Upon receiving the news he said: "Father, forgive them, for they know not what they do." According to Prof. L. Larsen, however, something worried Preus still more than these reverses. Said Larsen at the dedication of the East Kosh-konong Pioneer Monument 10 Oct., 1894: "The man who by right ought to have dedicated this monument, the man who for thirty-two years was the president of our synod, but who last summer entered the rest of his Lord, throughout his whole life-work complained of nothing so much as of the negligence which we have manifested in regard to the Chris-tian schooling of our children." Preus has written a large number of contributions to the organ of the synod. *Syv Foredrag over de kirkelige Forholde blandt de Norske i Amerika*, 144 pages, published in 1867; and *Oftedal's og Weenaas's Wisconsinisme*, 146 pages, published in 1876, are valuable contributions to the history of the Norwegian-American Lutheran churches. He made visits to Norway in 1866-67 and in 1888-89. On the former occasion he deliv-ered the seven lectures mentioned above, thereby arousing renewed interest in American church affairs among the Nor-wegians. He also officiated at the funeral of his youngest sister and that of his father, the latter having reached the age of eighty-eight years. In the spring of 1876 his silver wedding was remembered by a few old friends who gathered at his house; in the fall of the same year the twenty-fifth anniversary of his entering upon the service as a minister of the gospel, was fittingly celebrated by a large concourse of people in a grove near his home; and in June, 1887, at the annual meeting of the synod, at Stoughton, Wis., a great number of his friends devoted one evening to a commemora-

tion of the work accomplished by him during the twenty-five
years he had served as president of the synod. On this occasion he was the recipient of a valuable present from his
brethren in the ministry. He was married in 1851 to Caroline Dorthea Margrethe Keyser, of Kristiania, Norway, who
died in 1880. She was an accomplished lady, and equally
shares the honor with her husband of having brought up
children who are an ornament to the Norwegian-Americans:
Rev. C. K. Preus, Rev. J. W. Preus, Mrs. Rev. I. Nordby, and
Mrs. Rev. Dan. Kvaase. The remains of Rev. H. A. Preus and
his wife rest in the Spring Prairie cemetery, at Keyser, Wis.

Steensland, Halle, vice-consul of Sweden and Norway—
Madison—born 4 June, 1832, in Sandeid, near Stavanger,
Norway. His father, who was a farmer, for more than a
quarter of a century held the position of non-commissioned
officer in the Norwegian army. At the early age of twelve,
young Steensland gave indication of that spirit of self-
reliance which has characterized his later life, by leaving his
parental homestead and entering the battle of life on his own
account. He first hired out as a farm hand; this occupation, however, being neither pleasant nor remunerative, he
obtained a position as clerk in a store in Stavanger. But in
the long run this position did not suit the ambitious young
man, and in 1854 he left for America, arriving in Chicago
with less than ten dollars in his pocket. He proceeded to
Wisconsin the same year, and since the spring of 1855 has
been a resident of Madison. The record of Steensland as a
business man for nearly half a century past is bright, indeed.
Beginning at the foot of the scale, as clerk in a store, he
soon embarked in business for himself, first as member of a

mercantile firm, and afterwards as sole owner of the business. In 1871 he entered upon an entirely new branch of business by taking an active part in organizing the Hekla Fire Insurance Company, perhaps the first enterprise of its kind undertaken by Scandinavian-Americans. Steensland was the first secretary and treasurer of the company, acting in the capacity of the former about ten years, and in that of the latter for the whole period of eighteen years during which he was connected with the enterprise; and served also as its president for the last few years of its existence. The company was started with a nominal paid-up capital of $25,000, and its affairs were so well managed that in 1889 the company's assets amounted to nearly half a million dollars; but next year the Hekla was transferred to other parties and moved out of the state. Immediately after the consummation of this deal Steensland organized the Savings Loan and Trust Company of Madison, the paid-up capital being $100,000. In less than six years the assets of this company increased to over $530,000. Halle Steensland is its president and treasurer, and his son, Edward B. Steensland, its secretary. From the above it will be seen that Steensland, notwithstanding the limited advantages he had in his early life as to education and opportunities for advancement, has succeeded not only in acquiring a competency, but has built up for himself a reputation as a business man of high rank. In 1872 Steensland was appointed to the office of vice-consul of Sweden and Norway, and has filled that position with signal tact and ability, and to the entire satisfaction of his fellow-citizens, as well as to the governments of Sweden and Norway. In this connection it may be mentioned that he takes pardonable pleasure in an interview which he had with King Oscar II, in Norway, in 1889, on which occasion the king gave him a very cordial reception and, as a special mark of esteem, created him a knight of the Order of Vasa in 1898. Politically, Steensland has always been identified with the Republican party, and has taken active part in some of the campaigns, especially that of 1884, when James G. Blaine was the Republican candidate for president. Steensland and family belong to the United Church, and he has served as member of the board of trustees of said body since 1890. In the summer of 1895 he, in company with a son, made an extensive trip through the Mediterranean countries and the Orient, and an account of his travels, which he sent to the papers, was eagerly read by thousands of people in this country and Norway. In 1857 he was married to Sophia Halvorson, of Madison, and their home is widely noted for its attractiveness and the hospitality of its occupants. Their children are also making their mark: Morten M. is a graduate of Luther College, Decorah, Iowa, and of the Lutheran theological seminary at Philadelphia, Pa.; Edward B., mentioned above as secretary of the Savings Loan and Trust Company, and Helen A. are both graduates of the University of Wisconsin; Halbert S. is studying medicine at Johns Hopkins University. They have also two other sons, Henry H. and Adolph E.

Thorsen, John, pioneer and manufacturer—Milwaukee— born 20 March, 1820, in Stavanger, Norway. He received a common school education, and at the age of fourteen left his native city. Having made several voyages on the Baltic and Mediterranean seas, and visited the East and

West Indies, he spent two years on the coast of Norway. He came to America as early as 1838, and took up his home in Milwaukee in 1844, where he has resided ever since. In 1895 he returned to Norway to visit his native land after an absence of sixty years. On settling in Milwaukee he commenced as a ship chandler, and continued in that business until 1868, when he entered the lumber business in Manistee, Mich., but continued to reside in Milwaukee. He was one of the first to discover and develop the large salt resources of eastern Michigan, and had one of the first salt blocks in Manistee. In 1895 he sold out his salt and lumber business and retired. In his younger days he was a great oarsman, and on the Fourth of July, 1856, won the boat race in Milwaukee against all comers. Early in the sixties a large ship with a number of people on board was wrecked in a terrible storm off Milwaukee. He organized a life saving crew and brought one boat-load safely ashore, but the second load was not so fortunate, the boat being overturned in the surf, but with the heroic exertion of those on shore, all were saved. Thorsen, however, was taken home in an insensible condition, and for some time his life was despaired of. He has been one of the most public spirited citizens of Milwaukee, having held many offices of trust and responsibility; for instance, in the Chamber of Commerce, the Milwaukee Club, and the North-western National Insurance Company. He has always been an enthusiastic Republican, but would never accept any political office. In 1849 he was married in Milwaukee to Sarah Kildahl, of Kristiansand, Norway. They have five children, three daughters and two sons, each of whom received a liberal education. Their son, William R., is a

large manufacturer at Manistee, Mich.; their daughter
Emma is married to an English merchant in Rio de Janeiro;
and the others are residing in Milwaukee.

Thrane, Markus, radical agitator and writer—aEu
Claire—born 14 Oct., 1817, near Kristiania, Norway; died
30 April, 1890. He received a college education, and graduated from the University of Norway, and he afterwards
carried on a private school at Lillehammer. During a short
stay in France, the liberal movement agitating the masses
of that country made a powerful impression upon his
liberty-loving mind, and upon his return to Norway he
became the champion of a similar movement there. The
movement culminated in the Revolution of 1848, which
swept western Europe in the course of a few months. His
paper, *Arbeiderforeningernes Blad,* soon reached a circulation of 40,000, and for a time no name was more frequently
mentioned throughout Norway than that of Markus Thrane.
His demands seem eminently reasonable and moderate at
the present time; but they were so far ahead of the age that
Thrane was made to suffer for his labors in the interest of
human progress. He was finally arrested, and though his
followers seemed both willing and able to liberate their
leader, he dissuaded them from doing so, believing that the
authorities would dismiss him in a few days. In this he
was mistaken, however, and he had to remain four years in
jail, and afterwards three years in the penitentiary.
Thoroughly disgusted with a government that was capable
of perpetrating such an outrage against an honest man, he
emigrated to America in 1864, remaining one year in New
York, and afterwards settling in Chicago. In the latter

OSULD TORRISON, MANITOWOC.

REV. J. A. BERGH, ORFORDVILLE.

O. GRANBERG, BLAIR.

A. JENSON, EDGERTON.

F. L. TRONSDAL, EAU CLAIRE.

city he published *Den Norske Amerikaner*, *Dagslyset*, and *Den Nye Tid*, which papers were not only radical on social and political questions, but also very bitter against many of the practices of the Christian church. His *Wisconsin-bibelen* is a sarcastic attack on leading Norwegian Lutheran clergymen, and the biblical form in which the language of the book was cast made it exceedingly obnoxious to those against whom it was directed. Upon the whole, Markus Thrane was not in touch with the bulk of the Norwegian-Americans, on account of his pronounced hostility to the church. The closing days of his life were spent with his son, Dr. Thrane, of Eau Claire. Consistent to the last, he insisted that no clergyman should be allowed to speak at his funeral. He was married in 1840 to Josefine Buch, who died in 1863. They had five children.

Torrison, Osuld, merchant—Manitowoc—born 6 March, 1828, near Grimstad, Kristiansand stift, Norway; died 3 Nov., 1892. His ancestors for many generations back had been highly respected tillers of the soil. Torrison received a common school education in his native land, at the same time learning to make himself useful as a farm laborer; emigrated to America at the age of nineteen, making his first home at Port Washington, Wis., where he began to attend school; removed to Manitowoc Rapids, where he clerked for about two years; and in 1851 settled at Manitowoc, where he resided during the remainder of his life. Here he began to clerk in a store; but two years later he, in company with another man, bought out his former employer, and success-fully conducted a general merchandise business for five years. In 1858 Torrison purchased his partner's interest, and

19

under his able management the business became one of the
most extensive enterprises conducted by Scandinavian-
Americans. In 1882 he built a very large brick building,
where his heirs, under the management of his son, Thomas
E. Torrison, still conduct the business. But his activity
was not confined to his general store; he also dealt in real
estate, lumber, etc., on an extensive scale; he owned several
saw-mills and ware-houses; his vessels plowed the great
lakes; and his annual transactions aggregated about half a
million dollars. Torrison was a patriotic American, took
some interest in politics, but had no political ambition, and
on one occasion he made his Republican friends understand
that their wishes to have him accept a nomination as candidate for Congress could not be complied with. He was a
member of the Norwegian Synod and a generous supporter
and patron of Luther College, Decorah, Iowa. Being a
generous man, Torrison brought his mother, brother, and
sisters to this country as soon as he had saved enough
money to do so. One of the traits of Torrison's character
was his love for his native land, which he visited four times,
and he took active interest in the welfare of his countrymen everywhere. He was married in 1854 to Martha
Hansen Findal, who was born near Langesund, Kristiansand
stift, Norway. They had ten children. Six of their sons
are graduates of Luther College, the other two attended
several years, and some of them have taken post-graduate
courses in the best universities of this country and Europe.
Thomas E., the oldest son, succeeded his father in the business; Inanda A. is the wife of Rev. A. Bredesen, of Stoughton, Wis.; Isac B. is a clergyman in the Norwegian Synod.

Oscar M. and George A. are practicing law and medicine, respectively, in Chicago, Ill.   Gusta H., Norman G., Aaron J., and William S. are connected with the business at Manitowoc, and Agnes M., the youngest child, is attending college at Wellesley, Mass.   Every member of this family is developed to an unusual degree, physically as well as mentally, and it has been stated that in point of bodily development and intellectual vigor and equipoise, these ten brothers and sisters constitute a family which have no peers among the two hundred and odd thousand Norwegian-American families.

Warner, Hans B., secretary of state—Ellsworth—born 12 July, 1844, in Gudbrandsdalen, Norway; died in 1896. In 1849 he emigrated with his parents, who first settled in Dodge county, Wis.   In the summer of 1855 they moved to Pierce county, where Warner resided ever since.   During his boyhood, young Warner received such education as the common schools afforded, the greater part of his time being spent on the farm.   In 1864 he enlisted as a private in company G, 37th Wisconsin regiment, but after a few months' service was wounded and captured by the Confederates during the campaign in front of Petersburg, Va., and was held as prisoner of war in Danville and Libby prisons until paroled.   In July, 1865, he received his discharge from the service on account of wounds received in battle.   He returned to his home, and at the election in 1868 was elected county clerk, and held that office until he resigned, in 1877, to assume the duties of secretary of state, to which position he had been elected.   Warner has the distinguished honor of being the first Scandinavian in Wisconsin elected to one of

the more important state offices, though in a few cases
others had succeeded in reaching elective offices of minor
importance and rank. He was re-elected in 1879, holding
office until 1881. In 1883 he was elected state senator, and
held that office for four years, being among the few Scandinavians ever elected to the upper branch of the state legislature. At the close of his legislative career he was elected
to the position of supervisor for the village for seven years,
and was chairman of the county board of supervisors for
the same length of time. In 1895 Warner was appointed a
member of the state board of control for a term of five
years, and at the organization of that body was elected
president of the board. Warner was a life long Republican.
In 1866 he was married to Julia E. Hudson; they had no
children.

Biographies of Scandinavians in Wisconsin and Iowa.

Ager, Wm., author—Eau Claire, Wis.,—born 23 March, 1869, in Fredrikstad, Norway. His ancestors for generations had been soldiers, and his father served in the Norwegian army a long series of years. Young Ager received a good common school education, and has always been an ardent student of modern literature. In 1885 he emigrated to America, locating in Chicago, where he learnt the printer's trade. Much of his time has been devoted to the temperance movement, and in 1891 he took a very active part in the organization of a Norwegian Grand Temple of the Templars of Temperance. From 1891 to 1894 he edited *Templar-Bladet*, the official organ of the Scandinavian templars, and has organized a number of local temples. Since 1892 he has been connected with *Reform,* of which he has been manager since 1896. In 1894 he published *Pan Drikkeondets Konto*, a collection of short stories and poems bearing on the drink problem, which work met with a very flattering reception. In 1896 he was elected treasurer of the total abstinence congress. He married in 1899.

Åkermark, Gudmund E., poet and journalist—Wood Lake, Wis.,—born 1863, in Gothenburg, Sweden. For some time he attended college in his native city, completing three classes; emigrated in 1887; was editor of a couple of Swedish papers in Omaha for some time; for one year held the same position on *Svenska Amerikanska Posten,* Minneapolis. Since 1893 he has edited *Skördemannen,* a Swedish semi-monthly agricultural paper published in Minneapolis, and is also connected with *Svenska Folkets Tidning,* although he and his family reside on his farm at Wood Lake. The great Swedish-American literary critic, Ernst Skarstedt, in his *Svenska Amerikanska Poeter,* speaks highly of Åkermark as journalist and poet. In 1891 he was married to Constance Nelson; they have children.

Anderson, Abel, banker—Sioux City, Ia.,—born 17 June, 1855, at Jernskog, Vermland, Sweden. He received a common school education in his native country; emigrated to this country in 1874, coming directly to Sioux City, where at first he worked in brick yards, as well as on a farm in Union county, S. D. In 1877 he started a small grocery store of his own in Sioux City, which he kept for nine years; then traveled as a commercial traveler a couple of years in the Northwest, and in 1890 he, in company with others, organized the Northwestern National Bank, capital stock $100,000, of which he was vice-president one year, having since been president, and is now the principal owner of this bank. In 1892 he was elected, by the Republicans, city treasurer, being re-elected in 1894 by a very large majority. He is respected, not only by the Scandinavians, but is looked upon by other nationalities as being one of the most successful and prosperous financiers among the Scandinavians in the Northwest. He is a member of the Swedish Lutheran church, having been one of the trustees of his home congregation nearly ever since the church was organized in 1875. In 1882 he was married to Henrietta L. Carlstrom, of Sioux City. They have children.

Anderson, Joseph Alfred, clergyman—Creston, Ia.,—born 10 July, 1868, in Lommaryd, Småland, Sweden. His father was a farmer, who emigrated in 1868, and settled in Des Moines, Iowa. Young Anderson, whose mother died when he was an infant, came to this country at eight years of age, joining his father at Des Moines, where he attended the public schools during the winters, and parochial school during the summer time. In 1882 he entered Augustana College, from which institution he graduated six years later; took the degree of A. M. at his alma mater in 1891, being the first graduate of Augustana College to complete the regular course of study leading to the master of arts degree; completed his theological course the following year. During his school days, he clerked in grocery stores a couple of years; taught parochial school at Iron Mountain, Mich., during the summer of 1887-88; was professor at Hope Academy, Moorhead, Minn., the first year of its existence, in 1888–89. At the end of that time he went to Washington, where he had charge of the Swedish Lutheran churches in Seattle and Tacoma. During his vacation in 1890 he had charge of the Swedish Lutheran church in Keokuk, Iowa, and was stationed at Dalsborg and Newman Grove, Neb., the following year. Since his ordination in 1892 he has been pastor of the Swedish Lutheran church in Creston, served as secretary of the Iowa Conference of the Augustana Synod in 1893-8. He has been a member of the executive committee of the Alumni Association of Augustana College and of the Iowa Conference. Anderson married Ellen S. Carlson in 1896. They have children.

Anderson, J. E., state legislator and journalist—Forest City, Ia.,—born 29 March, 1846, in Småland, Sweden. In 1852 his parents came to America, and settled on a farm in Winnebago county, Ia., in 1860. Young Anderson attended the Upper Iowa University in 1866–69; took a full course of scientific and classical studies at the State University, graduating in 1872; and completed his law studies at that institution four years later. Anderson is the author of a work on business calculations, and in 1872-75 visited about three hundred colleges, lecturing on his specialty. In 1881 he was elected state legislator on the Republican ticket. Up to about 1890, he was a Republican; since he has joined the People's party, and was president of the first state convention of that party in 1891. Anderson is a member of the American Methodist Church. He is married, and has children.

Bengston, Carl J., clergyman—New Sweden (Postoffice Four Corners), Iowa,—born 22 July, 1862, in Slafsinge, Halland, Sweden. He emigrated to this country at the age of thirteen; graduated from Augustana College in 1888; and completed his theological studies at that institution two years later. Bengston served for three years in Hartford, Conn., and in the summer of 1893 accepted a call to his present charge, which is the first Swedish Lutheran congregation in America organized in the nineteenth century. He has since 1898 been secretary of the Iowa Conference, and is a member of the constitutional committee. In 1899 he was elected to the state legislature on the Republican ticket. In 1891 he married E. Otilia Swanson, of Jamestown, N. Y.

Bergh, J. A., clergyman and author—Orfordville, Wis., —born 12 Jan., 1847, in Kristiania stift, Norway. His father was a clergyman, and he received a good education at a private school in Kristiania. He emigrated to America in 1860; studied at Paxton, Ill., and graduated from the theological department of the seminary at Marshall, Wis., in 1871. He accepted a call from Tordenskjold and other congregations in Otter Tail county, Minn. In 1877 he removed to Iowa; and in 1882 settled at his present home. Bergh, in addition to his labors as pastor of a large congregation, has also extended his work into the fields of journalism and literature. Some of his ablest newspaper articles are contributions to the controversies in the Norwegian Lutheran church, and his book, *Den Gamle og Nye Retning,* is an exposition of a controversy which was started in 1882. Among the books compiled by Bergh may be mentioned *Underfuld Bönhörelse, I Sidste Öieblik, Livsbilleder,* and *I Ledige Stunder.* He was married in 1873 to Birgitta Meland, who died in 1897. They had six children.

Bergh, Martin, lawyer—La Crosse, Wis.,—born 16 Sept., 1862, in Kristiania, Norway. His father was of Norwegian, and his mother of Swedish parentage. In 1870 he emigrated with his parents to this country, going directly to La Crosse, Wis. Bergh graduated from the high school of La Crosse in 1882. After devoting three years to the study of law, he was admitted to the bar in 1885. Besides an extensive practice in Wisconsin, he has conducted important cases in the adjoining states. After a partnership with J. H. A. Ginder from 1885 to 1887, he practiced alone until 1894, when the firm of Bleekman, Bloomingdale & Bergh was formed, with which firm he has since been connected. In 1895 and 1897 he was elected city attorney of La Crosse. Bergh has taken a prominent part in the affairs and campaigns of his party, and has several times represented his city in Republican state conventions. He ranks high in the Masonic order. In 1880 he was married to Hanna C. Fleischer, a daughter of the well-known journalist, Frederick Fleischer. They have children.

Borchsenius, Hans, soldier and public officer—Baldwin, Wis.,—born 19 Sept., 1832, in Nestved, Själland, Denmark. Borchsenius emigrated to America in 1856, settling at Madison, Wis. In 1858 he became proprietor and editor of *Nordstjernen,* which position he occupied for the next two years. At the breaking out of the Civil War he enlisted in the army, being appointed adjutant in the famous Fifteenth Wisconsin, and served as major on the march to Louisville, Ky. In 1864 he was appointed clerk of the state school land department, which position he occupied until 1869. In the fall of 1868 he was elected clerk of the board of supervisors of Dane county, on the Republican ticket, and was re-elected two years later. During this period he also studied law at the State University of Wisconsin, and was admitted to the bar in 1872; removed to Baldwin in 1877; served five years as state agent for the government timber land along the Chippewa and Menomonie rivers; was chief of a division of the internal revenue department at Washington for two years; and in 1896 was elected to the state assembly.

Bothne, Gisle, educator—Decorah, Ia.,—born in Fredrikshald, Norway, 7 Sept., 1860. He is a son of Th. Bothne. He attended the Latin school in his native city until fifteen years of age, emigrated with his parents to this country two years before he had completed his course, and graduated from Luther College in 1878, receiving the degree of A. M. from his alma mater in 1883. After he had completed his studies in Luther College, he graduated from the Northwestern University in 1879, and spent one year at Johns Hopkins University. Bothne was called to the professorship of Greek and Norwegian literature in his alma mater, Luther College, in 1881, where he has since remained, excepting the year 1883–84, when he again attended Johns Hopkins University. He has written a history of Luther College.

Bredesen, Adolph, clergyman—Stoughton, Wis.,—born 25 Oct., 1850, in Solör, Hamar stift, Norway. His ancestors for many generations back were farmers, smiths, or lumbermen. He came to America in 1852 with his parents, who settled in Adams county, Wis. Bredesen entered Luther College at the age of fifteen, and was graduated in 1870.

Having completed a theological course at the Concordia Theological Seminary, he entered the ministry in 1873, and for the next three years served a number of churches in Columbia county, Wis., as the assistant of Rev. H. A. Preus. During the school years of 1876–78 he was an instructor at Luther College; then accepted a call from three churches in the western part of Dane county, Wis., where he remained until the fall of 1881; and since the latter date has served a church at Stoughton, and another at McFarland, near the same city. For many years past Bredesen has been chairman of the board of directors of Stoughton Academy and Business Institute, and also of the board of directors of Martin Luther Orphans' Home, at Stoughton, and is a member of the Wisconsin Historical Society. Bredesen generally prepares his public utterances with great care, and some of his lectures in favor of total abstinence and prohibition have been published in pamphlet form. He was chosen to deliver the English address at the dedication of the pioneer monument at East Koshkonong, Wis., 10 Oct., 1894. This address, published in a book called *Koshkonong*, contains, besides other important historical matter, an excellent summing up of the peculiar social conditions prevalent among the early Norwegian pioneers, and it has been liberally quoted by other authors. In 1878 he was married to Inanda A. Torrison, a daughter of Osuld Torrison, of Manitowoc—an account of this remarkable man and his family is given in this work. Bredesen has children.

Bull, Storm, educator—Madison, Wis.,—born 20 Oct., 1856, in Bergen, Norway. He is a nephew of Ole Bull, the world-famed violinist. He attended school in his native city, and completed a course at the celebrated polytechnic institute of Zuerich, Switzerland, graduating with the highest honors in 1877. In 1879 he emigrated to America, and at once accepted a position as instructor in mechanical engineering in the University of Wisconsin; five years later was appointed assistant professor in the same branch; from 1887-91 occupied a regular chair of mechanical engineering; and at the latter date took charge of the department of steam engineering. He is familiar with several languages, and speaks Norwegian, English, German, and French with fluency; belongs to several societies; and is a Unitarian.

Burg, P. N., merchant—Shell Lake, Wis.,—born 15 Apr., 1860, in Sallerup, Skåne, Sweden. His parents were farmers, and young Burg commenced to earn his own living at the early age of fourteen. He worked as a farm hand until twenty years of age, when he emigrated to America, coming to Grove City, Minn. For a couple of years he worked on the railroad during the summer, and attended school in the winter. He then moved to Princeton, Minn., where he remained for five years, being employed as clerk in a store. In 1887 he settled at Shell Lake, Wis., and after having clerked for three years, started a general merchandise store, having at that time a capital of only $200. In this undertaking Burg has been very successful; has built up a large business; has an annual trade of about $50,000; and has one of the largest establishments of its kind owned by any Swedish merchant in the state. In 1885 he was married to Lizzie Hillman, of Falun, Dalarne, Sweden, whose ancestors were prominent in the public affairs of that place.

Carlson, Anton, journalist—Des Moines, Ia.,—born 17 Oct., 1859, in Misterhult, Småland, Sweden. After completing a course of study at a preparatory school in Oscarshamn, Carlson entered Frans Schartau's commercial school at Stockholm, from which he graduated. In 1881 he emigrated to this country. After working as clerk in clothing stores in Chicago, Ottumwa, Ia., and Holdrege, Neb., he moved in 1889 to Des Moines, where he became connected with the Swedish Publishing Company. In the latter part of the same year he became editor of *Svithiod*, a newspaper published by said company, continuing in the same capacity until May, 1898, when he, during the Spanish-American War, accepted a position in the office of the Assistant Quartermaster General at New Orleans, La. Carlson is a Republican, and ably advocated the principles of that party as an editor. He is a Freemason.

Carlson, Oscar W., physician and surgeon—Milwaukee, Wis.,—born 1 Aug., 1843, in Stockholm, Sweden. At the age of ten he emigrated to America; resided at Columbus, Ohio, for one year; moved to Waukesha, Wis., where he attended the public schools; worked for some time in a lumber camp. At the outbreak of the Civil War he enlisted in the 28th Wisconsin Infantry, serving for three years. He took active part in the siege of Mobile and other places. After having returned from the army, Carlson commenced to study medicine in Milwaukee, and completed his studies in Chicago, in 1872. He then practiced his profession in Milwaukee for seven years; visited his native land as well as other European countries, studying at some of the larger hospitals in England and elsewhere. After his return he has practiced in Milwaukee, being the only Swedish physician in the city. His large practice, however, is mostly among the Americans, as he is hardly able to speak the Swedish language fluently. Carlson is a member of several societies, in which he has held high offices.

Chantland, P. W., sheriff—Fort Dodge, Ia.,—born 11 Oct., 1840, in Aardal, Stavanger amt, Norway. His father was a sea captain, sailing along the coast, and most of his mother's ancestry had been in military service. At the age of thirteen he came from his native country to Primrose,

Wis., where he remained until 1861, when he enlisted in the famous Fifteenth Wisconsin Regiment, serving over two years. In 1864 he moved to Fort Dodge, where he purchased land, being one of the earliest Norwegians in Webster county; but soon returned to Wisconsin, where he attended Albion Academy for a couple of years, as well as teaching some; then settled permanently in Webster county, and farmed from 1867-75. Chantland was sheriff for eight years; has since dealt in real estate and insurance, and was elected justice of peace in 1892 and 1894. He is a member of the order of Freemasons, of the I. O. O. F., and of the A. O. U. W., having held the highest offices in some of these organizations. He is also an active member of the G. A. R.; was for a number of years captain of Company F, Sixth Regiment, Iowa National Guards, and afterwards promoted to lieutenant-colonel on the governor's staff. Chantland is a very prominent public man in Webster county, and has done a great deal for the welfare of the Scandinavians in the vicinity. He is a Republican. In 1869 he was married to Julia Skavlem; she died in 1872, and three years later he was married to Anna Natesta, or Natestad, whose father was the earliest Norwegian settler in Wisconsin, coming there in 1839. Chantland has had children by both wives. His eldest son, Wm. T. Chantland, was born 22 June, 1870; is a graduate of the collegiate and law departments of the University of Iowa; was captain of company G, 52nd Iowa Infantry Volunteers, during the Spanish War in 1898; has been county attorney of Webster county for some time; and is also interested in the beet sugar industry.

   Dahl, J. M., clergyman — Ratna, Ia., — born 14 Dec., 1836, in Karlsö, Tromsö stift, Norway. He left his native land and studied from 1860 to 1866 at the missionary school at Hermannsburg, Germany, and passed the theological examinations required by the royal consistory of Hanover. Shortly afterwards he was ordained, and departed for India as a missionary in the Telugu country. Dahl became a personal friend of the rajah of Venkatagiri, and the progress of his work was gratifying. But he was sunstruck at two different times, and was compelled to return to Europe. In 1873 he accepted a call from a congregation in Winnebago county, Iowa, arriving at his present home in the fall of that year. Dahl is a highly influential member of the United Church. He has been married twice, and has children.

Dahl, T. H., clergyman—Stoughton, Wis.,—born 2 Apr., 1845, in Baadstad, Kristiania stift, Norway. He attended a Latin school in Kristiania for a while; emigrated to America in 1865; completed his theological studies at Paxton, Ill.; and in 1868 accepted a call from congregations in Meeker county, Minn., being the first Norwegian Lutheran pastor who settled west of "the Big Woods." In 1873 he removed to Ft. Howard, Wis., and settled at his present home in 1881. He joined the Norwegian-Danish Lutheran Conference in 1871, and served that body as secretary from 1876 to 1881, and as president from the latter date to 1886. His words and works alike are characterized by Christian charity, and even in the heat of controversy he generally remains calm and impartial. His preaching is universally popular. In 1894 he published *Fred og Strid*, treating of the controversy raging in the United Church at that time. The same year he was elected vice-president of the United Church. In 1867 he married Lina Gjertsen, a daughter of Rev. J. P. Gjertsen. They have several children.

Dahle, Onon B., merchant—Mt. Horeb, Wis.,—born 4 Oct., 1823, in Nissedal, Kristiansand stift, Norway. He graduated from Hvideseid normal school in 1842, and emigrated six years later. He settled in Dane county, Wis., after having been in California for some time; and for over forty years had a country store in Perry, being one of the leading men in that vicinity, as well as one of the most successful and wealthy Norwegian business men in the state of Wisconsin. He is a member of the United Norwegian Church. In 1854 he was married to Betsey Nelson, of North Cape, Racine county; they have three sons, and their daughter is married to the able ex-county attorney of Hennepin county, Minn., James A. Peterson. His son, H. B. Dahle, was born 30 Mar., 1855; attended the University of Wisconsin for a few years; has for many years been in the mercantile business at Mt. Horeb; and was elected on the Republican ticket to the U. S. Congress in 1898.

Dan, Adam, clergyman and author—Fredsville, Ia.,— born 8 Feb., 1848, in Odense, Island of Fyen, Denmark. Dan's father was an officer in the Danish army; his mother was of French descent. He studied for some time at the University of Denmark and at Basel, Switzerland. After extensive travels in Europe he proceeded to Egypt, then to the Holy Land, where he was missionary for nearly a year, when he accepted a call from the Danish Lutheran church in Racine, Wis., arriving there in 1871. After a period of nine years' successful labor in this field, Dan went to San Francisco, where he remained for four years. He now visited Denmark, and while there was called as pastor of the Danish Lutheran Church in Minneapolis, Minn., where he resided from 1884 to 1893, being also pastor of the Danish churches in St. Paul and Hutchinson. From 1893 to 1896 he filled the pulpit of one of the Danish churches in Chicago, and while there celebrated the 25th anniversary of his ordination, receiving expressions of esteem from Danes all over the country. Since 1896 Dan has been pastor at Fredsville. Dan was the first clergy-

A. PETERSON, SOLDIERS GROVE.

M. BERGH, LA CROSSE.   P. N. BURG, SHELL LAKE.

A. T. LINDHOLM, STILLWATER.   PROF. E. G. LUND, MINNEAPOLIS.

man of the Danish Lutheran Church in America. He was once president of the denomination, once vice-president, twice editor of the church paper, *Kirkelig Samler*, which he founded, once editor of the children's paper, and has also been president of the board of trustees of the theological seminary. He is the author of numerous poems, essays, novels, and books of travel. His largest work, *Kanaan*, has gone through several editions, and gives an excellent description of his travels in the Holy Land. Dan is an able speaker, and his writings are polished and sympathetic. In 1871 he was married to Signe Sörensen, who died in 1895. His daughter Thyra is a good singer.

Davidson, James O., state treasurer—Soldiers Grove, Wis.,—born 10 Feb., 1854, in Norway. He received a common school education in his native land, and emigrated to America in 1872, settling in Madison, Wis. Since 1877 he has resided at Soldiers Grove, where he has been engaged in mercantile business. He was elected to represent his district in the state assembly in 1892, in 1894, and in 1896; and was elected state treasurer as a Republican in 1898.

Egge, Albert E., educator—Iowa City, Ia.,—born 12 Feb., 1857, in Winneshiek county, Ia. His parents were born in Östre Slidre, Valders, Norway. They emigrated to this country in 1850, residing until 1853 in Dane county, Wis., and afterwards in Winneshiek county. When a boy he attended the district school near his father's farm. In 1873 he entered Luther College, from which he graduated in 1879. After teaching for three years he went to Johns Hopkins University, where he spent five years (1882-87). Here he devoted himself specially to Teutonic philology and history, but gave much attention also to the Romance languages, comparative philology, and pedagogy. In 1884 he was appointed, by the trustees of Johns Hopkins Uni-

versity, graduate scholar in English, and shortly afterwards
also assistant in English, holding the latter position for
three years. In 1885 he was appointed fellow in Teutonic
languages, and in 1887 received the degree of Ph. D. From
1887 to 1892 he was professor of English, German, and
history in St. Olaf College. Then for four years he was
instructor in English in the State University of Iowa, Iowa
City. In 1896 he accepted the chair of English literature in
the Washington Agricultural College and School of Science,
Pullman, Wash. Egge has acquired an enviable reputation
as a philologist, and as an authority on the English language. In 1891 he married Sina Berge, of Decorah.

Erdall, John L., assistant attorney general—Madison,
Wis.,—born 5 June, 1863, in Deerfield, Dane county, Wis. His
grandfather and father came from Hardanger, Norway, in
1847, and settled in Deerfield. Young Erdall graduated from
the classical department of the State University in 1885,
from the law department in 1887. In 1888 he was elected
district attorney of Dane county, holding that office for
two years. In 1895 he was appointed assistant attorney
general for the state, being, perhaps, the first Scandinavian
in the United States who has been appointed to a position
which requires such high legal attainments, and involves
such great responsibility. He is a member of the United
Church. He was married in 1885, and has children.

Erickson, Halford, commissioner of statistics—Superior,
Wis.,—born 7 July, 1862, in Fogelvik, Vermland, Sweden.
He received a common school education in his native land;
emigrated in 1882; attended Minneapolis Academy for some
time; worked for the Northwestern railroad company until
1889, when he removed to Superior, Wis. In 1890 Erickson
was elected register of deeds of Douglas county, and was
re-elected in 1892, being the first Swede in Douglas county

to be elected to that office. Erickson is a Republican, and in 1895 was appointed by the governor commissioner of the bureau of statistics, and re-appointed two years later, being the first person of Swedish parentage who has received an appointment to any important office in Wisconsin, in fact the only Swede in the state who at present is in any manner prominent in public life. Erickson has paid special attention to the study of political economy, and possesses one of the largest private collections of books treating of that subject in the Northwest. As a statistician and political economist Erickson has, probably, no superior or equal among the Scandinavians in America. In 1889 he was married to Annie Carlson.

Estrem, Andrew, educator—Clinton, Ia.,—born 6 Mar., 1864, near Cresco, Iowa. His parents came from the vicinity of Haugesund, Norway, in 1855, and settled in Howard county, Iowa. He graduated from Luther College in 1886; studied for a short time at the State University of Iowa; then went to Cornell University, receiving the master's degree at that famous institution in 1889. He was instructor in Latin and history at Luther College the following year, after which he returned to Cornell to pursue a more extended course in American history and in political science. He received the Ph. D. degree at Cornell University in 1892, and has since 1894 taught the English language and literature in Wartburg College, Clinton, Iowa. His ability as a writer and teacher is generally recognized.

Fleischer, Frederick, ournalist — La Crosse, Wis.,— born 18 June, 1821, in Vaaler, Kristiania stift, Norway; died 12 Nov., 1878. Being the son of a minister, young Fleischer received a liberal education, and received from the University of Norway the degree of A. B., and of LL. B., in 1840 and 1844, respectively. He emigrated to America in

1853, and spent eight years in California, his chief occupation being gold-digging and farming. In 1863 Fleischer settled at La Crosse, and began the publication of *Fädre-landet*, but changed the name of the paper in 1868 to *Fädrelandet og Emigranten*, which he published during the remaining ten years of his life, and accumulated a small fortune. In 1871 he was elected county treasurer of La Crosse county, and one year later presidential elector at large from his state. In 1875 he was appointed register at the U. S. land office at La Crosse. His generosity and nobility of character made him popular among his acquaintances, and at his death he had won the hearts of thousands of his countrymen in the New World. Fleischer was an active Republican, and a member of the Lutheran church. He was married in 1866 to Josephine Johnson, of Rushford, Minn., and one of his daughters is the wife of Martin Bergh, a prominent attorney in La Crosse.

Granberg, Ole, grain dealer—Blair, Wis.,—born 11 Sept., 1856, in Grue, Hamar stift, Norway. He received a common school education, and emigrated to America in 1868, coming with his parents directly to Trempealeau county, Wis., being among the early Norwegian settlers of that part of the country. He worked on farms at first, but has dealt in grain most of the time, doing an annual business of about $50,000. He has been chairman of the board of supervisors for one year, but has since refused to accept any kind of office, although several nominations have been offered him. He affiliates with the Democratic party. In 1882-84 he resided in Yellowstone Park, engaged as a carpenter. Granberg is a radical free thinker, and has written newspaper articles on that subject, both in American and Norwegian papers, and has also performed other literary work. He takes interest in scientific topics and political economy.

In 1895 he married Kate Blottenberger, of Philadelphia.

Grundtvig, F. L., clergyman and author—Clinton, Ia.,—born 15 May, 1854, in Copenhagen, Denmark. He is a son of the renowned Danish bishop and poet, N. F. S. Grundtvig. F. L. Grundtvig graduated from the University of Denmark in 1880, having made a special study of the natural sciences. The next year he emigrated to this country, and settled in Outagamie county, Wis., where he resided a couple of years. During his stay here he made a special study of ornithology, on which subject he published a small pamphlet, which has been very favorably received by eminent naturalists. He has also written several other books and pamphlets on various subjects, both prose and poetry. He was ordained as a minister in 1883, having ever since had charge of a Danish Lutheran church in Clinton. Grundtvig was the chief organizer of *Dansk Folkesamfund i Amerika*, in 1887, of which he was president until 1894. In 1881 he was married to Kristina Nelson, a Swedish lady.

Halland, B. M., clergyman—Stanton, Ia.,—born 15 Oct., 1837, in Drängsered, Halland, Sweden. He emigrated to this country in 1855; attended the theological department of Augustana College, Paxton, Ill., for a while; and was ordained in 1864. He served the congregation in Burlington, Ia., until 1870, when he founded the large Swedish settlement in the vicinity of Stanton, generally known as the Halland settlement. He remained in Stanton for nearly thirteen years, then accepted a position as business manager of Augustana College, which position he held for two years. He was a missionary in Wisconsin and Michigan for a couple of years, and served the Iowa Conference as secretary and also as president in its earlier days. During President Harrison's administration he was postmaster at Stanton. He was married in 1865, and has several children.

Halvorsen, Halvor, clergyman—Westby, Wis.,—born 15 Sept., 1845, in Stavanger, Norway. During the years 1859–65 he was a sailor, serving one year as first mate; graduated from a Latin school in Kristiania in 1867; attended the theological department of the University of Norway, receiving the degree of candidate of theology in 1871. For one year Halvorsen served as principal of a private school in Stavanger; emigrated to America in 1872, coming directly to Coon Prairie, Vernon county, Wis. In the early days of his work in this charge, Halvorsen traveled 5,000 miles in one year, in order to attend to his ministerial duties. For several years he served as secretary of the Eastern District of the Norwegian Synod; in 1887 he was elected secretary of the synod, and re-elected at the meetings held in 1890 and 1893; from 1888–93 served as vice-president of the Eastern District; and since the latter date has been president of that district. He has written several articles for *Evangelisk Luthersk Kirketidende,* as well as for several other papers. He has published one book; besides, a few of his sermons have been published. He was married in 1871, and has several children.

Haugen, G. N., congressman—Northwood, Ia.,—born 21 April, 1859, in Rock county, Wis. His parents came from Hallingdal, Norway, in 1846, and settled at his birthplace. He received a common school education, attended school in Decorah for some time, and a business college in Janesville, Wis. In 1880 he started a hardware store at Kensett, and in 1887 was elected, by the Republicans, county treasurer, which position he retained for six years. In 1890 he was one of the organizers of the Northwood Banking Company, of which concern he became president in 1894. In 1893 and 1895 he was elected to represent his constituency in the state legislature, and was elected to Congress in 1898.

Hendrickson, Peter, educator and journalist—Albion, Wis.,—born 6 June, 1842, near Skien, Norway. In 1845 he came to America with his parents, who settled in Racine county, Wis.; entered Beloit College in 1859, graduating with honors in 1867; spent one year at the University of Norway, devoting his time to the study of literature, philology, and philosophy; proceeded to Germany and studied about one year at the University of Erlangen; traveled through Switzerland, Italy, France, Scotland, and England; and, having returned to America in the fall of 1869, concluded his studies by attending the Chicago Theological Seminary for one year. In 1870 he began to teach Greek at Beloit College, and at the end of the year was elected professor of modern languages in the same institution, which position he held for over fourteen years. In 1885 he severed his connection with the college, and for the next eight years served as editor-in-chief of *Skandinaven*. After two years of partial rest he purchased the Albion Academy. Hendrickson served with the 40th Regiment of Wisconsin Volunteers during the Civil War. He was married in 1873, and has several children.

Holmes, Ludvig, clergyman and poet—Burlington, Ia., —born 7 Sept., 1858, in Ströfvelstorp, Skåne, Sweden. Young Holmes was forced to begin to shift for himself early in life, entering the struggle for existence as office boy and typesetter, in Helsingborg, at the age of fifteen. He next spent some time in Stockholm, and in 1879 emigrated to America; entered Augustana College the following year, where he spent three years; but on account of ill-health was unable to complete his literary studies, although he graduated from the theological department of that institution in 1886. Both before his ordination and afterwards, he preached in Connecticut, and settled in Jamestown, N. Y., in

1888; but moved to Burlington, Iowa, the next year, where he has since served as pastor of a Swedish Lutheran congregation. Holmes was a member of the committee which edited *Nya Hemlandssångboken*—the authorized hymn-book of the Augustana Synod—and has also served as secretary of the executive committee of the Augustana Synod, and of the Iowa Conference. He is a fluent and happy speaker, and very popular as a preacher. He is widely known as a writer of religious and semi-religious poems. His poetry, according to Ernst Skarstedt, in *Svensk-Amerikanska Poeter*, "is generally characterized by a beautiful form and by warmth of feeling." Bishop Von Scheele in his *Hemlandstoner* says: "Ludvig's *Jubel Poem* is remarkable for its deep thoughts, and the brilliant expression of these thoughts." In 1896 he published a large volume, being a collection of his poems, under the name of *Dikter*. For some years he has been president of the Swedish Lutheran Mutual Fire Association. In 1891 he received the degree of A. M. of Bethany College, and 1897 the same institution conferred the degree of doctor of literature upon him. King Oscar II. of Sweden honored him with a silver medal in 1898. Holmes was married in 1887 to Sophia Johnson, of Altona, Ill. They have one child.

Holst, Martin, journalist—Cedar Falls, Ia.,—born 13 Apr., 1856, in Rödding, Slesvig. Young Holst received a common school education and attended a college in Askov for three years. He taught Danish private schools in Denmark and Slesvig for seven years; but he concluded to emigrate, and came to Elk Horn, Iowa, in 1881. In 1882 he began to work in the office of *Dannevirke*, Cedar Falls, which paper he, in company with N. U. Christianson, bought the following year, and which Holst has ever since continued to edit. He is one of the most prominent lay members of the Danish

Evangelical Lutheran Church in America. He is married and has children.

Homme, Even Johnson, clergyman—Wittenberg, Wis.,—born 17 Oct., 1843, in Moland, Kristiansand stift, Norway. He attended the common school of his native parish until emigrating with his parents to America in 1854. At the age of nineteen he entered Luther College, where he remained for two years, and in 1864 began to study theology at Concordia Theological Seminary, graduating in 1867. Shortly afterwards he accepted a call from the Norwegian Synod congregation at Winchester, Wis., where he resided for fifteen years. In 1880 Homme founded the village of Wittenberg. For years the Norwegian Synod had been discussing the need of an orphan asylum, and Homme decided to start such an institution on his own account at Wittenberg. Accordingly, a building was put up in 1882. The institution has experienced a healthy growth, and some 250 children and aged people have been cared for under its roof. In 1886 Homme superintended the erection of a building for an Indian mission school at Wittenberg, and through his efforts said school received large appropriations from the national treasury. In 1885 Homme established a printing office in connection with the orphans' home, and has since published three weekly papers. For several years he served as secretary of the Norwegian Synod, but since 1890 has been a member of the United Church. In 1893 he was nominated for state senator by the Republicans, but accepted the nomination with reluctancy. He was defeated at the polls. Homme was married in 1869, and has several children.

Hougen, J. O., clergyman—Decorah, Ia.,—born 6 Mar., 1857, in Kvinnherred, Bergen stift, Norway. His parents emigrated when he was only two months old. He received a common school education, entered Luther College at the age of fifteen, graduating in 1879, and completed his theological studies at Madison, Wis., three years later. He served churches successively at Fargo, N. D.; Canton, S. D.; and Manitowoc, Wis. In 1898 he accepted a call from a church in Decorah. Hougen originally was a member of the Norwegian Synod, but joined the United Church in 1890. He was one of the founders of Concordia College, at Moorhead, Minn.; has been a member of the board of missions of the United Church; and has held other positions of trust and honor in the religious circles in which he has moved. Hougen is an active and energetic man, a fair speaker, a great reader, an extensive traveler, and a voluminous newspaper writer. He has been married twice, and has children.

Jeanson, R. E., emigration agent—Des Moines, Ia.,— born 4 July, 1832, in Karlskrona, Sweden. His great-grandfather came from England in the sixteenth century, and established a factory to color leather near Karlskrona. Young Jeanson received a common school education; went to sea at the age of eleven; for about ten years was captain of a vessel sailing on the coast of Sweden; emigrated to America in 1865, settling in New York City; and was engaged as agent for the American Emigration Company. Jeanson remained with said company until 1893, having had the controlling interest of the concern till 1889. Through mismanagement the company failed in 1893. He moved to Swea, Kossuth county, Iowa, in 1879, where he organized a large Swedish settlement. In 1894 he removed to Des Moines. Jeanson has always taken great interest in religious matters, having been ordained as a Baptist clergyman two years after his arrival to this country, and organized the first Swedish Baptist church in New York in 1867. He is married, and has children.

Jenson, Andrew, merchant—Edgerton, Wis.,—born 4

June, 1843, in Sandsvär, near Kongsberg, Norway. At the age of twenty-six he emigrated to America, coming directly to Edgerton, Wis., where he worked in the vicinity as a farm hand the first summer, and attended school during the first winter, and one year after his arrival started to grow tobacco by working land on shares. He settled in Edgerton, and commenced to deal in leaf tobacco on a small scale; but in a short time Jenson became one of the leading dealers in his line in the state, besides being interested in other financial undertakings in the city, for example, in a brick yard and a pottery plant. He is one of the five proprietors of *Amerika*. He is a member of the Norwegian Synod, and the main supporter of his home congregation, having also been one of the trustees of Luther College, and a member of the church council of the synod. Jenson has affiliated with the Democratic party since 1884; was presidential elector in 1892; has been mayor of Edgerton for several terms; and was one of the judges on leaf tobacco at the World's Fair in Chicago, in 1893. In 1877 he married Hannah P. Johanson, of Edgerton; they have children.

Johnson. E. P., county attorney—Decorah, Ia.,—born 25 June, 1846, in Sogn, Bergen stift, Norway. When he was five years old his parents emigrated to this country, settling at Norway Grove, Wis. Young Johnson worked on his father's farm and attended the public schools during his boyhood; graduated from a business college in Madison, Wis., in 1872; received his literary education at the University of Wisconsin; and graduated from the law department of the State University of Iowa in 1874. For one year he was assistant principal of Marshall Academy, Marshall, Wis. After having completed his legal education he settled in Decorah, where he successfully has practiced his profession ever since, and has now a very lucrative practice. Johnson has been secretary of the Decorah board of education for ten years, member of the city council for two terms, city attorney for a couple of terms, and was elected county attorney on the Republican ticket in 1892, being re-elected twice. He is a member of the Norwegian Lutheran Synod. In 1875 he was married to Carrie Grinde, of Norway Grove, Wis. They have five children, their two sons are graduates of Luther College, and one of their daughters is a graduate of the University of Wisconsin.

Johnson, Ole C., soldier—Beloit, Wis.,—born 1838, in Hollen, Telemarken, Norway; died in 1886. His father was an inn keeper at a place called Skibsnäs, from which Ole took the name by which he was generally known. He came to America in 1844. He had attended Beloit College two years when the Civil War broke out, and he immediately enlisted in the service, recruited a company of volunteers, and received his commission as captain of the same, which became a part of the Fifteenth Wisconsin Regiment. Later he was promoted to the rank of major; then to that of lieutenant-colonel, and at the battle of Chickamauga commanded the regiment. During the second day of this battle he was captured by the Confederates, and was sent to Libby Prison, where he remained for eight months. While being transported to another prison, he succeeded in making his escape, and made his way to the Union lines, rejoining his regiment a couple of months later. At the expiration of his term of enlistment, Johnson was appointed colonel of the Fifty-third Wisconsin Regiment. Most of the time after the war he resided at Beloit, where he was engaged in business and held various offices.

Larsen, Iver, merchant—Decorah, Ia.,—born 1 Nov., 1837, in Hardanger, Norway. He came to America in 1850, and settled in Winneshiek county, Iowa., in 1851. In

1860–61 he studied at Concordia College, and in the fall of 1861 entered the new school of the Norwegian Lutheran Synod at Halfway Creek, Wis. He soon left his school, however, because he could not agree with his professor who held that "slavery in itself is not sinful." From 1866 to 1878 he was engaged in business on his own account at Brownsville, Minn.; but at the latter date removed to Decorah, where he has since built up the largest dry goods establishment in the city. Besides making his own business an unqualified success, Larsen, during the past fifteen years, has managed to perform a large amount of work connected with his church. The following are some of the positions filled by Larsen: Treasurer of the Lutheran aid fund of St. Olaf College 1886–90; treasurer of the Anti-Missourian Brotherhood endowment fund, in which capacity he raised $90,000 by subscription; and president of the board of trustees of the United Church since 1890. In the last-mentioned capacity he had to conduct the famous lawsuit of the United Church against Augsburg Seminary, involving the title to the Augsburg Publishing House.

Larson, Ole, county judge—Osceola, Wis.,—born 2 Apr., 1841, in Nordre Aurdal, Hamar stift, Norway. He received a high school education, and visited various places in Norway, before leaving for America in 1868. In 1872 he settled at Osceola, and five years later was elected county judge of Polk county, to which position he has been re-elected several times, having served over twenty years. Larson has been engaged in the real estate, loan, and insurance business during his entire stay at Osceola. In 1890 he bought Bethania Mineral Springs. Larson is one of the most influential Scandinavian Republicans in the state, and in 1895 Governor Upham appointed him a member of the board of immigration of Wisconsin. In 1870 he married Ingeborg Johnson; they have two sons well educated.

Lund, Lars, clergyman—Elroy, Wis.,—born 13 March, 1845, in Vefsen, Tromsö stift, Norway. He graduated from the normal school at Tromsö in 1864; taught in the public schools for five years; and emigrated in 1868, coming directly to Racine, Wis., but shortly afterwards entered Augustana College, Paxton, Ill., where he remained one year. He completed his theological course in 1870 at the school of the Norwegian branch of the Augustana Synod, located at Marshall, Wis. For six years Lund had charge of Conference congregations in southwestern Minnesota. From 1876-97 he was located at Menomonie, Wis. Since the latter date he has been located at his present place. Lund was cashier for the mission during eight years of his connection with the Conference, and since that organization became a part of the United Norwegian Lutheran Church of America, he has held the same position, being an influential member of this organization. Lund, in connection with Rev. G. Hoyme, published a hymn book called *Harpen*, in 1888. He was married in 1872.

Naeseth, Christen A., educator—Decorah, Ia.,—born 1 March, 1849, in Koshkonong, Dane county, Wis. His father came from Nedre Telemarken, Norway, in 1844. In 1869 Naeseth entered Luther College, graduating five years later. He completed his theological studies at Concordia Seminary in 1877; spent one year, traveling and studying, in Norway; from 1878-82 he served Norwegian Synod congregations in Rock county, Minn.; then accepted a call as professor at his alma mater, where he has since remained, having charge of English history, English literature, and other branches, besides being the college librarian. Having been granted a year's leave of absence, he spent 1884-85 at Cornell and Johns Hopkins universities. In 1886 he married Caroline M. Koren, a daughter of Rev. V. Koren.

Nelsenius, John D., clergyman—Ashland, Wis.,—born 12 Oct., 1850, in Mistelås, Småland, Sweden. He received a common school education in his native land, and worked on his father's farm until eighteen years of age when he emigrated to America. In 1875 he entered Augustana College, pursuing studies in the collegiate and theological departments of this institution for seven years, and graduating from the latter department in 1882. He had charge of congregations at Anoka and St. Cloud, Minn., and other places in the vicinity until 1886, when he moved to Ashland, being the first Swedish Lutheran clergyman to permanently locate in the northern part of Wisconsin. Nelsenius has been a member of the board of education of Ashland for three years, and has also taken a great deal of interest in local affairs, especially whatever concerns the welfare of the Swedish people. In 1896 he was one of the presidential electors at large, on the Republican ticket, and he received the largest number of votes cast for any person during the whole history of the state. He was married in 1882.

Nelson, Oley, state legislator—Slater, Ia.,—born 10 Aug., 1845, in Rock county, Wis. His parents came from Rollag, Numedal, Norway, to Jefferson Prairie, Wis., in 1844. Young Nelson received a common school education, and worked on his father's farm. His father served in the army during the Civil War, and after his death, through disease, young Nelson took his place in the army, and participated in the battles of Memphis, Holy Spring, Jackson, etc. In 1867 he settled in Polk county, Ia., close to his present place of business, and has resided in the vicinity ever since, except for about eight years, when he lived in Des Moines. He has been in the general merchandise business ever since he came to Iowa, and now does an annual business of about $100,000, being also engaged in banking. In 1885 he was elected to the state legislature, and was re-elected two years later. During his legislative career he secured the passage of several important bills, for example, one in regard to general tile drainage, and another for the purpose of securing cheaper text-books—these two laws were very important, and Nelson deserves the credit of having done some of the best work in the legislature that has ever been performed by any of the Scandinavians in the Iowa legislature. He is a member of the United Church, taking active part in the secular affairs of that body; was one of the trustees of the Norwegian-Danish Conference for several years; and has held the same position since that organization became a part of the United Church. He has also been one of the trustees of Jewell Lutheran College. Nelson was the chief organizer, in 1896, of the Norwegian-American old settlers' association, of which society he became president. In 1869 he was married to Lizzie Ersland, of Story county. They have several children.

Nelson, Otto, publisher and state binder — Des Moines, Ia.,—born 14 Nov., 1843, in Ulrika, Östergötland, Sweden. He received his education mostly through private instruction; enlisted in the army at the age of eighteen, and passed a non-commissioned examination, after having served for three years. For three years he was sergeant, but after having been in the army for six years, he emigrated to America in 1867. In 1870 he settled in Des Moines; worked for thirteen years for one book-binding firm, being the foreman of the establishment the last seven years; and commenced, in 1883, to publish *Svithiod.* Several other Swedish newspapers have been started before and since, yet *Svithiod* has been, and is, the most influential and widely circulated Swedish paper in Iowa. In 1895 Nelson severed

O. C. PETERSON, DES MOINES.

O. NELSON, SLATER.

C. H. TOLLEFSRUDE, ROLFE.

REV. J. OLSEN, ST. ANSGAR.

REV. J. A. OTTESEN, DECORAH.

all connections with the paper, and engaged in the business of real estate and insurance until 1899, when he secured a position in the government printing office at Washington, D. C. In 1888 Nelson was elected state binder of Iowa by the legislature, being the first Scandinavian that has ever been elected to any state office in the state. In 1890-92 he was re-elected to the same position. Nelson has taken active part in everything which pertains to the welfare of the Swedes in the city. Few Swedes are more widely known in the state, or out of the state, than he is. In 1874 he was married to Alfrida Jonson, who died in 1881, leaving two grown daughters, who have received a good education.

Nordberg, Bruno V., mechanical engineer—Milwaukee, Wis.,—born 11 Apr., 1858, in Helsingfors, Finland. He is a direct descendant of Nordberg, the chaplain and historian of Charles XII., king of Sweden. Young Nordberg received a college education in his native place, and graduated from the Polytechnic College of Helsingfors in 1879, and shortly after emigrated, coming to Buffalo, N. Y., where he remained for about one year; then came to Milwaukee. In 1890 he started to manufacture steam engines of his own, is considered one of the best engineers in the Northwest, and has about thirty patents of his own. He was married in 1884, and has children.

Norrbom, August, clergyman—Swedesburg, Ia.,— born 19 June, 1860, in Sjögestad, Östergötland, Sweden. He received a common school education in Sweden; emigrated in 1876; studied during the winter for four years; attended Augustana College from 1881 to 1887, and graduated from the theological department of that institution the latter year; served Swedish Lutheran congregations at Peoria and Knoxville, Ill., for over three years, and in Topeka, Kan., from 1890 to 1896, settling at his present place at the latter

date. Norrbom has been secretary of the Kansas Conference for two years, and treasurer of the conference for the
same length of time, having also been a member of the
board of directors of the orphans' home at Mariadahl,
Kan., for six years, besides having held other offices in connection with church work. During 1891–6 he published, in
Topeka, Kan., a small religious monthly called *Tempel-
klockan*. In 1887 he was married to Emma A. Ahlgren, of
Kossuth, Iowa. They have children.

 Oden, Martin P., clergyman—Alta, Ia.,—born 13 Nov.,
1852, in Onsala, Halland, Sweden. He almost completed a
course at the Latin school in Gothenburg; emigrated to
America in 1876, for the purpose of entering the ministry;
spent one year at the college department of Augustana College; graduated from the seminary in 1879; accepted a call
to Big Rapids, Mich., where he remained for about two
years; had charge of a congregation in Ottumwa, Ia., for
eight years; returned to Michigan in 1889, and for a couple
of years was pastor of the church at Tustin; then moved to
his present place. In 1877–78 he was vice-president of the
Iowa Conference of the Augustana Synod, and was re-elected
to the same position in 1893; in 1895 was elected president
of that organization. Being one of the oldest and best
educated ministers in the Iowa Conference, he has naturally
taken a conspicuous part in the affairs of that organization.
He was married in 1870, and has children.

 Oleson, Ole, sea captain and soldier—Oshkosh, Wis.,—
born 30 Dec., 1839, in Tönsberg, near Skien, Norway. He
emigrated to America in 1843; received a common school
education, and settled in Oshkosh in 1859, where he was
engaged in the steam boat business until the outbreak of
the Civil War. In 1861 he enlisted in Company E., of the
Second Wisconsin Volunteers, serving until the next year.

Then at the call of the navy department for volunteers to man the gun boats on the Mississippi river, he volunteered for the gun boat service, and took an active part in all naval battles until the river was opened a couple of years later. In 1864 he returned to Oshkosh, where he resumed the boating, which he continued until he was appointed postmaster by President Harrison in 1890, which position he held for four years. Oleson has taken an active part in the welfare of the Republican party, and is one of the influential public men in the state, especially in that part of the country. He was married in 1871, and has one daughter.

Olson, Julius E., educator—Madison, Wis.,—born 9 Nov., 1858, in Cambridge, Dane county, Wis. His parents, who were born in southeastern Norway, emigrated to America in 1852, and have resided at Cambridge since that date. He graduated with honors from the University of Wisconsin in 1884, and was immediately appointed instructor in the Scandinavian languages and German, and was elected professor of Scandinavian languages and literatures in 1892. Professor Olson is peculiarly well fitted for his work as an educator, his eloquence and enthusiasm arousing the interest of his students, and the accuracy and scope of his knowledge making him an authority upon which they cheerfully rely. He has made a special study of the early history of the peoples of northern Europe, and the conclusions arrived at by his researches in this line may be summarized as follows: Scandinavia was the original home of the Aryan ancestors of all the fair-haired, blue-eyed peoples now scattered over Europe. According to this theory, the different Teutonic races did not enter western Europe from the east, as hitherto supposed, but came from the Scandinavian peninsulas. Olson is a fine lecturer and an inspiring orator. His Seventeenth of May and Fourth of July ora-

tions are polished, patriotic, and scholarly. Besides making
contributions to various periodicals, Olson in 1889 published an English translation of *Titus Bering, the Discov-
erer of Bering Strait*, a work originally written in Danish
by Peter Lauridsen. In 1898 he published *A Norwegian
Grammar and Reader, with Notes and Vocabulary*,
and a high authority on the subject with which it deals. In
1897 he was married to Helen O. Ericksen.

Olson, Ole Br., journalist and temperance lecturer—Eau
Claire, Wis.,—born 19 May, 1857, in Kristiania, Norway.
When a yonng man he started *Fakkelen*, a humorous
paper, which after a few years gave up the ghost. In 1879
he emigrated to America, settled in Chicago, and in 1882
started *Afholdsbladet*, a small monthly devoted exclusively to the cause of temperance. In 1887 Olson removed
to his present home, where he began to publish *Reform*, a
weekly which for years past has been the most influential
temperance and prohibition paper published in the Norwegian language in this country. Besides editing and manag-
ing this paper, Olson has also lectured more or less on temperance, having delivered more than one thousand lectures
on that subject in the course of the past twenty years. The
Prohibitionists of Wisconsin have nominated him for member of Congress and lieutenant governor, and in the latter
case he ran ahead of the state ticket of his party. In 1888
he issued, in two volumes, *Haandbog for Afholdsvenner*,
which, however, as the author says himself, is mainly a
compilation. Olson has unquestionably done more for the
cause of temperance than any other Scandinavian-American.
In 1895 he visited Norway and made a successful lecturing
tour of the country, partly at the expense of the Norwegian-
American temperance people. He was married in 1878.

Paulson, Ole, soldier and clergyman—Blanchardville,

Wis.,—born 26 April, 1832, in Solör, Hamar stift, Norway. He came to America in 1850; entered the theological seminary of the Augustana Synod in 1861; but soon discontinued his studies in order to defend the cause of the Union on the battle field. He served two years in the war, holding the rank of second lieutenant in company H, Ninth Regiment Minnesota Volunteers; and resumed his studies at the same seminary in 1866. In 1868 he received a call as pastor in Minneapolis, and for two years was the only Scandinavian Lutheran minister in that city. In 1870 Paulson participated in the organization of the Norwegian-Danish Lutheran Conference, which body he repeatedly served as vice-president. He did more than any other man towards locating Augsburg Seminary in Minneapolis, and the supporters of this institution have honored him with the title "Augsburg's Father." From 1874 to 1885 he lived at Willmar, Minn., serving a number of congregations in and around that city; and since the latter date has resided at his present home. Paulson is an ardent advocate of total abstinence; for fifteen years past has been a frequent contributor to *Folkebladet*; and has written a few hymns, the most popular of which is *Jeg er en Vandringsmand*. He was married in 1857, and has several children.

Peterson, Atley, banker and legislator—Soldiers Grove, Wis.,—born 21 Feb., 1847, in Lärdal, Bergen stift, Norway. At the age of five he emigrated to America with his parrents, and they settled near Soldiers Grove in 1854. He opened a general store here in 1866, remaining in this business for eight years, when he started a saw mill. He is proprietor of the Bank of Soldiers Grove, and was the leading spirit in bringing about the building of the Kikapoo Valley and Northern railroad. Peterson has held many local offices, in 1878 was elected to the state legislature, and

was re-elected three times.   In 1886 he was elected railroad
commissioner, and was re-elected in 1888.   Peterson has
been very active and influential in state politics.   His success
in the political arena is certainly to his great credit, when
we take into consideration the fact that he resides in a
county where only a small proportion of the population is
of Norwegian extraction, thus having nothing of that
nationality pull which often promotes persons in this
country.   In 1892 he was candidate for state treasurer on
the Republican ticket, but was defeated with the rest of the
ticket.   He is a member of the I. O. O. F. and of the Free
Masons, having taken many of the higher degrees in the
latter order.   He was married in 1869, and has children.

   Peterson, O. C., lawyer and lecturer—Des Moines, Ia.,—
born 15 Dec., 1857, in Misterhult, Småland, Sweden.   He
attended the common school of his parish, and left for
America with his parents in 1868.   They located in Webster
county, Ia., and young Peterson graduated from the Iowa
Agricultural College in 1882.   He next took a post graduate course at the same institution, devoting himself especially to the study of philosophy, and received the degree of
M. Ph. in 1883.   The same year he entered the Iowa College of Law, at Des Moines, and was admitted to the bar
the following year.   Peterson practiced law in Des Moines
for twelve years, then settled in Chicago, where he is now
engaged in an extensive practice, besides being president
of the Swedish National Association and secretary of the
Swedish-American Central Republican Clubs.   But he manages to snatch enough time from his law practice to lecture
on historical and popular themes.   As a Republican campaign speaker he has built up quite a reputation in the
West, and has been engaged as such by the national and
state committees during the past twenty years.   *The*

North says: "As a speaker he is strong and convincing; magnetic rather than eloquent. He is pleasant in his manner and voice, and a good thinker with an exhaustless fund of historical information." Peterson speaks English and Swedish with equal fluency. His literary taste is strongly developed, his favorite subjects being history and political science. Peterson was married, in 1886, to Florence E. Felts, of Indiana, an American lady. They have two children.

Peterson, Sewell A., state treasurer—Rice Lake, Wis.,— born 28 Feb., 1850, in Solör, Hamar stift, Norway. He emigrated in 1864; in 1883 entered the mercantile business at Menomonie; and since 1887 has been running a general store at Rice Lake. He has held various local offices; was register of deeds of Dunn county for six years; has been a member of the state assembly; and was elected state treasurer in 1894 and 1896, being the first Scandinavian ever elected to that position in Wisconsin.

Qvale, Sigvald A., capitalist—Eau Claire, Wis.,—born 18 July, 1852, in Haugesund, Norway; died 1890. He attended the high school of his native town; emigrated to America in 1868. He clerked in a dry goods store in Minneapolis, and in the land office of the Omaha railway company at Hudson, Wis. At Eau Claire he was so successful in his business that he was worth several hundred thousand dollars at his death. His memory was so rententive that for many years in his extensive dealings with men he hardly kept a memorandum. He intended to establish a hospital; but he died before he realized his philanthropic plan.

Reque, L. S., educator—Decorah, Ia.,—born 12 Aug., 1848, in Dane county, Wis. His father came from Voss, Norway in 1845. Young Reque graduated from Luther College in 1868, then studied law at the Iowa State University. He taught one year at St. Olaf College, but accepted a call as regular professor at Luther College in 1875. This position he has since held, his principal branches being English and Latin. He is a Democrat and in 1893 President Cleveland appointed him United States consul to Holland. Reque married Margarita Brandt in 1882. They have children.

Roe, O. O., deputy auditor of state—Des Moines, Ia.,—born 4 June, 1854, near Bergen, Norway. When he was eight years old his parents came to this country, and settled in Story county in 1868. Young Roe graduated from the law department of Simpson College, Indianola, Iowa, in 1878. Soon after he opened a law office in Story City, but was elected principal of the city schools at the same time. After having been principal for three years, he was elected county superintendent of schools; was re-elected four times, and served in that capacity for ten years. In 1892 he was appointed deputy auditor of state, and was re-appointed twice. Roe is a Republican, and a member of the English Lutheran church. He has been married twice.

Sagen, Aandreas K., clergyman—La Crosse, Wis.,—born 11 Feb., 1851, near Rockdale, Wis. His parents came from Bö, Telemaken, Norway, in 1845. In 1869 he entered Luther College, graduating five years later, and completed his theological studies in 1879 at Concordia Seminary. He entered the ministry as pastor of a congregation at Wild Rice, Norman county, Minn.; in 1884 removed to Calmar, Ia., where he acted as assistant pastor to Rev. V. Koren; and since 1888 has had charge of a synod congregation in La Crosse. Sagen has published a lecture on the question, *Hviler Kristendommen paa Historisk Grund?* and a pamphlet, *Om Kiliasmen*. Sagen has been chairman of the committee having charge of the church extension fund; member of the committee on missions for the Eastern District; and vice-president of the Eastern District

G. N. SWAN, SIOUX CITY.

REV. T. A. TORGERSON, SOMBER.   REV. O. P. VANGSNES, STORY CITY.

PROF. A. A. VEBLEN, IOWA CITY.   REV. N. P. XAVIER, RIDGEWAY.

of the Norwegian Synod. He was married in 1875.

Stromme, Peer O., journalist and author—Madison— Wis., born 15 Sept., 1856, in Winchester, Winnebago county, Wis. His father came from Vraadal, Telemarken, Norway, to America in 1844, and his mother arrived four years later. Stromme graduated from Luther College in 1876; completed his theological studies at Concordia Seminary three years later; had charge of a Norwegian Synod congregation at Ada, Minn., for seven years; was pastor in Buffalo county, Wis., during 1886–87; taught in St. Olaf College, Northfield, Minn., for some time; and was principal of Mt. Horeb Academy in 1893–94. From 1888–92 he had charge of the editorial department of *Norden*, Chicago; was proprietor and editor of *Posten*, West Superior, in 1892–93; in 1895 became part owner and editor of *Amerika*; but severed his connection with this paper in 1898; and has since been on the editorial staff of the *Minneapolis Times*. He served as county superintendent of schools of Norman county, Minn., for three terms; stumped the country, under the auspices of the Democratic national committee, during all the campaigns from 1888 to 1896; organized tariff reform clubs in Wisconsin in 1892; visited and wrote up Norway, Sweden, Finland, and Russia in 1890; and was the Democratic candidate for secretary of state in Wisconsin in 1898. Stromme is well versed in American and European literature; speaks English, Norwegian, and German with equal fluency; but his reputation rests mainly on the merit of his historical fiction, *Hvorledes Halvor blev Prest,* published in 1893. This work contains many fine gems of wit and humor, and is written in a brilliant, but simple literary style. Throughout it bears the stamp of originality, and on the whole it is true to life, dealing principally with the trials and triumphs of a Norwegian-American pioneer, and the education of his son,

Halvor, at Luther College. He has also written *Paa Vest-ens Vidder* and other works, both prose and poetry, and, of course, numerous newspaper articles—all of which evince the individuality of Stromme, being bright and pointed rather than deep or learned. In fact, the personality of the man himself is erratical rather than systematical, being more a man of genius than a man of talent. In 1879 he was married to Laura Ericksen; they have several children.

Swan, Gustavus N., banker and vice-consul of Sweden-Norway—Sioux City, Ia.,—born 16 May, 1856, in Tjärstad, Östergötland, Sweden. After having completed the regular course of instruction in the public schools, he emigrated with his parents at the age of fourteen; they settled in Belinda, Lucas county, Ia., where he attended the public school in the winter, and assisted on his father's farm the balance of the year. From 1877–79 he studied at Augustana College, and in 1880 removed to Sioux City, and accepted a position as secretary of the Sioux City Plow Co., which position he filled until 1887. Since 1889 he has been connected with the Merchants National Bank, of which he is one of the directors and assistant cashier. In 1882 he was elected vice-president and secretary of the Scandia Printing and Publishing Company, the publishers of *Nordvestern*. From 1882–87 he served as secretary, and, from 1889 to 1896, as treasurer and member of the board of trustees of his home church, which he also has frequently represented at conference and synodical meetings. From 1892–99 he served as treasurer of the Iowa Conference, and in 1894–96 was treasurer of the board of home missions of the synod. In 1893 he was elected member of the board of directors of Augustana College. In 1892 Swan was instrumental in organizing the Swedish Publishing Company of Sioux City, publishers of *Skandia*, serving also as editor of that paper for a few months. In 1899 he was appointed by the Swedish government vice-consul of Sweden–Norway, having previously been acting vice-consul in 1896 and 1898. For many years he has been a frequent contributor to many of the leading Swedish-American, some English-American, and some Swedish newspapers and magazines; is also the anonymous translator of *Fjettrad*, a work of fiction of 356 pages, published in 1885; and contributed a list of pseudonyms and initials used by Swedish authors, for Cushing's *Initials and Pseudonyms*, second series, published in 1888. He served as leader of the choir of his home church for more than fifteen years, and spends all his leisure moments in his well stocked library, which contains, perhaps, the choicest collection of rare and standard books, in various languages, owned by any Scandinavian-American, and which Swan has spent a life-time in gathering. In 1891 he visited Europe and traveled extensively in England, France, Belgium, Holland, Germany, Switzerland, Denmark, and Sweden. Swan was married in 1884 to Carrie S. Samuelson, who died in 1888. A boy survives her.

Thorvilson, T. K., clergyman and lecturer—Eau Claire, Wis.,—born 16 July, 1852, near Stoughton, Wis. His parents had emigrated from Nissedal, Norway. Thorvilson entered Luther College, graduating in 1878. For eight years he had charge of Norwegian Synod congregations at Orfordville, Wis.; then moved to Menomonie in 1889, where he served as pastor of congregations in that place for four years. Since 1893 he has lectured in the Northwest in the interest of the temperance cause, and is considered to be the most thorough and scholarly Norwegian-American temperance lecturer. In 1889 he married, and has children.

Tollefsrude, C. H., banker—Rolfe, Ia.,—born 1 May, 1845, in Rock Prairie, Wisconsin. His parents emigrated from

Torpen, Land, Hamar stift, Norway, in 1844, and settled in Rock county, Wis. Young Tollefsrude attended Beloit college for three years, taught in the public schools of Wisconsin for some time, and in 1870 removed to Pocahontas county, Ia. The following eleven years were occupied in farming and teaching. In the fall of 1881 he was elected county auditor of Pocahontas county, and re-elected two years later, serving till 1886. That year he became assistant cashier of the Farmers' Bank of Pocahontas; later on assisted in the organization of the Pocahontas Savings Bank, and became its cashier. Since 1888 he has been connected with the Pocahontas Land and Loan Company, and removed to Rolfe in 1893, connecting himself with the State Savings Bank of that city. He has been an active and successful business man, and is a Republican. He married Maria G. Shirley, of Avon, Wis., in 1869. They have one daughter.

Torrison, Thomas E., merchant—Manitowoc, Wis.,—born 10 Oct., 1855, in Manitowoc. He is the son of Osuld Torrison. Thomas Torrison graduated from Luther College in 1876. After his graduation he assisted his father in the business, and since 1890 has had full charge of the same, which includes, besides a general merchandise business, various other financial enterprises, the annual trade of which amounts to over half a million dollars. Besides having been a member of the board of aldermen and county board, he served as mayor of his city in 1887-89, and again in 1895-97, at the latter date receiving the unanimous support of the two leading parties. Torrison has been a member ot the school board for six years; is a member of the Norwegian Synod; and has been a member of the board of trustees of Luther College. In 1884 he was married to Jorgine Tostensen, of Manitowoc. They have one son.

Trönsdal, F. L., subscription manager of publishing

houses—Eau Claire, Wis.,—born 13 July, 1859, in Rindalen, Trondhjem stift, Norway. He received a good common school education and attended a high school in Opdal. In 1880 he emigrated to America; worked on farms a couple of years; and spent two years at Augsburg Seminary, three years at Minneapolis Academy, and two years at the Northern Indiana Normal School, Valparaiso, Ind. He graduated from the rhetorical and law departments of the latter institution. In 1889 Trönsdal settled in Eau Claire; where he has built up a prosperous business as subscription manager of some of the largest publishing houses in the country. Much of his time has been devoted to temperance work, and he has been one of the leading members of the executive committee of the Scandinavian Total Abstinence Association of Wisconsin; and for four years did very creditable work as secretary of said association, and was elected its president in 1897. He has also been secretary of the Total Abstinence Congress. He has been the backbone of the former association, as well as of the local temperance society of his city. Since 1893 he has been president of the company which publishes *Reform*. Trönsdal is a member of the United Church, having been one of the leading lay delegates at the annual meetings of said organization ever since he joined his home congregation. In 1889 he was married, and has children.

Vangsnes, O. P., clergyman—Story City, Ia.,—born 11 Jan., 1855, in Sogn, Norway. At the age of eleven he came with his parents to America. Having finished his studies at Luther College, he entered, in 1875, Concordia Seminary, where he studied for three years. He was pastor in Minneapolis from 1878 until he moved to Story City in 1899. In 1888 he was elected vice-president of the Minnesota District of the Norwegian Synod. When Luther Seminary was moved from Madison to Minneapolis, in 1888, he became connected with the institution as English professor in homiletics for two years, when he resigned. In 1878 he married Oliva Brecke, by whom he has several children.

Veblen, Andrew A., educator—Iowa City, Ia.,—born 24 Sept., 1848, in Port Ulao, Ozaukee county, Wis. His parents came from Valders, Norway, to Wisconsin, in 1847; moved to Sheboygan county the next year; settled in Manitowoc county in 1855; and ten years later removed to Rice county, Minn. He taught school for about one year; entered Carleton College at the age of twenty-three, graduating in 1877, receiving the degree of A. B. For four years he taught English at Luther College; went to Johns Hopkins University in 1881, where he remained two years, studying principally mathematics and physics. In 1883 he became instructor in mathematics in the State University of Iowa, and assistant professor two years later; was appointed assistant professor of physics in 1886, of which subject he was elected professor two years later. Veblen earned his own way in school, and has been very successful in building up his own department in the State University. He is a charter member of the Baconian Club, which was organized for discussing scientific topics, and of which he has been secretary for a number of years, and president one year. Before numerous gatherings of scientific men, he has read papers and delivered lectures on various subjects in connection with his specialty. Veblen was married to Kirsti Hougen in 1877. They have several children.

Vig, Peter S., educator—Elk Horn, Ia.,—born 7 Nov., 1854, in Egtved, Denmark. He received a common school education; studied theology for three years at Askov; emigrated in 1879; but returned in 1882 and completed his theological studies at Askov and Copenhagen. Since he has been pastor of Danish Lutheran congregations in Shelby county, Ia., and Polk county, Wis., and professor of theology at a seminary in West Denmark, Wis., for four years. In 1894, when a theological chair was established at Elk Horn College, Vig was elected to occupy the same, being a leading Anti-Grundtvigian. When the United Danish Lutheran Church was organized in 1896, he was elected president of the theological seminary of that body, and moved from Elk Horn to Blair, Neb., to assume his new duties. Vig has published four treatises on practical theological questions, and was elected chairman of the board of directors of the Danish Lutheran Publishing House, Blair, Neb., in 1898. He was married in 1884, and has several children.

Vinje, Aad John, circuit judge—Superior, Wis.,—born 10 Nov., 1857, in Voss, near Bergen, Norway. He came to America in 1869; entered the University of Wisconsin in 1878; and graduated from the literary department of that institution six years later. From 1884 to 1888 he was assistant state librarian at Madison, and at the same time pursued the study of law at the university, graduating in 1887; was appointed assistant reporter of the supreme court in 1888, which position he held till the spring of 1891, when he settled in West Superior. In 1895 he was unanimously endorsed by the bar of Douglas county for the office of judge of the eleventh judicial circuit of Wisconsin, and was appointed by the governor; and the following year he was re-elected, without opposition, to the same office for the term ending the first of January, 1901, being, perhaps, the only Scandinavian in the United States who has ever been elected to a judgeship of such importance and requiring such high legal proficiency. He was married in 1886, and has children.

Wick, Barthinius L., lawyer and author—Cedar Rapids, Ia.,—born 1864, near Stavanger, Norway. His father was a cousin of Asbjörn Kloster, the great temperance apostle of

Norway.   Young Wick came to America in 1876, settling on a farm in Benton county, Iowa.   He graduated from the Iowa City Academy in 1887; from the State University of Iowa in 1891, receiving the degree of B. Ph. from the latter institution, which also conferred M. A. and LL. B. on him in 1893.   For two years he was fellow in history and instructor at the University, of Iowa, and has since practiced law. Wick is a frequent contributor to magazines and newspapers, and is the author of *A History of the Amana Society* and of *Amish Mennonites in Iowa*.   Both works indicate a most thorough research concerning the subject matter dealt with, besides proving that the author is exceedingly well versed in church history in general.   He has traveled extensively in this country and in western Europe. He is a Republican, a member of the Society of Friends, and of the Y. M. C. A.

Xavier, Nils Paul, clergyman—Ridgeway, Ia.,—born 26 Sept., 1839, in Kautokeino, Tromsö stift, Norway.   He graduated from Tromsö seminary in 1860; came to America in 1873; completed a theological course at the German Lutheran Seminary at Springfield, Ill., in 1876; and has since served as pastor in the Norwegian Synod, having resided in Renville county, Minn., from 1876 to 1891, and at Ridgeway since the latter date.   Xavier has been a member of the executive committee of the Lutheran Publishing House, and of the mission committee of the Iowa District of the synod.   He married Amanda Magdalena Norum in 1868.   They have several children.

Printed in the United States
30018LVS00001B/71

9 781410 216816